Masculinities, Crime and Criminology

Masculinities, Crime and Criminology

Men, Heterosexuality and the Criminal(ised) Other

Richard Collier

SAGE Publications
London • Thousand Oaks • New Delhi

© Richard Collier 1998

First published 1998

SAGE Publications Ltd
6 Bonhill Street
London EC2A 4PU

SAGE Publications Inc
2455 Teller Road
Thousand Oaks, California 91320

SAGE Publications India Pvt Ltd
32, M-Block Market
Greater Kailash – I
New Delhi 110 048

British Library Cataloguing in Publication data

A catalogue record for this book is available from the British Library

ISBN: 978-0-8039-7997-0

Library of Congress catalog card number 98–60954

Typeset by Photoprint, Torquay, Devon

Contents

Preface

This book is about a subject which has, in recent years, assumed an increasing visibility, prominence and political significance: the relationship between men, masculinities and crime. Within both the academic discipline of criminology and in relation to a series of public and high-profile debates around crime, criminality and social (dis)order, the subject of masculinity and crime has begun to emerge as one of the most contested, talked about and pressing issues of the day. Different strands of feminist thought have, of course, for some time recognised the association between the 'problem of crime' and the more general 'problem of men'. The deleterious consequences of what is taken to be men's 'normal' behaviour, and in particular a concern to challenge the scale and diversity of men's violences, has been historically central to feminist theoretical and political engagements with the concept of masculinity. Over the past twenty years this idea of the 'masculinity' or 'masculinism' of crime can itself be seen as having become something of an organising concept within a body of feminist scholarship which traverses the fields of criminology, law and related disciplines. In more recent years, however, both in Britain and elsewhere, some rather different conversations have begun to take place about this relationship between men, masculinity and crime. In relation to debates around such topics as dangerous male youth and an emerging urban 'underclass', in concerns about family breakdown, 'absent' fathers and youth crime, and in debates around violence against women and children, an understanding of the crimes of men has been sought through reference to a rather different conceptualisation of masculinity; not just that the crimes of *individual* men might be explained through reference to their masculinity, but rather the idea that *society* itself is presently experiencing what has been termed a 'crisis' of masculinity, a crisis made manifest in both the changing nature and extent of men's criminality. Many of these debates could hardly be described as being 'pro-feminist' in content. Yet, like contemporary feminism, they seek to address the apparently pervasive and intractable problem of crime in contemporary society through reference to the seemingly ubiquitous concept of 'masculinity'.

Themes and issues: what is this book about?

> ... one very important new topic is already on the agenda: masculinity.
> ... If emphasis on gender is a key aspect of feminist work, then the

further study of masculinity must be vital. *Without it there will be no progress.* . . .

(Heidensohn, 1995: 80–1; my emphasis;
see also Walklate, 1995: 160–84)

This book is an attempt to make sense of what is happening in these debates about the 'masculinity' of crime. In one sense this growing, explicit concern with masculinity can be seen as indicative of, and reflecting, a now well-documented 'explosion' of writings about the subject which has taken place since the 1970s, both within the social sciences and humanities and across a diverse range of cultural texts. The subject of masculinity, indeed, has become arguably one of *the* most written and talked about topics of the *fin de siècle* political and cultural landscape. Men's sexualities, subjectivities and desires, their hopes, aspirations and fears, men's power, aggression and vulnerabilities have each been discussed and analysed at length through reference to the concept of masculinity and, increasingly, masculin*ities*. Within the academy a body of scholarship has emerged, variously termed the 'new sociology of masculinity' (Carrigan et al., 1985), the 'critical study of men and masculinity' (Hearn, 1992; Hearn and Morgan, 1990; Morgan, 1992) and, more especially in North America, 'men's studies' (Brod, 1987), which together has produced numerous books, articles and journals and held seminars, conferences and other events concerned to explore the multifarious dimensions to men's lives. Diverse in terms of method, politics and underlying theoretical assumptions, there is no consensus to this work. What tends to unite such engagements with men *as men* is, however, whether it be from an overtly 'pro-' or 'anti-'feminist political orientation, a faith in the analytic purchase of the concept of masculinity and/or masculinities. Criminology has not been immune from this more general 'masculinity turn' in the social sciences, and a succession of books, articles and journals have appeared in recent years echoing this aim of 'taking masculinity seriously' (Carlen and Jefferson, 1996; Messerschmidt, 1993; Newburn and Stanko, 1994a). Indeed, judging by the frequent injunctions which have been made about the need for the discipline of criminology to address the 'masculinity of crime', be it in the context of criminological texts, conferences, seminars or workshops,[1] it might seem to the observer that something of a sea-change in, if not a wholesale transformation of, criminological thought is presently taking place. Criminology, for so long the target of feminist critique as the apotheosis of a 'masculinist' discipline in terms of its epistemological assumptions, methodology and institutional practices, might at last appear to be addressing its very own 'sex question' (Allen, 1989) by seeking to engage with the sexed specificity of its object of study – the fact that crime is, overwhelmingly, an activity engaged in by men.

In this book I shall argue that such an interpretation of recent developments within criminology would be both misleading and misplaced. What follows is, on one level, a contribution to the emerging debate which is taking place around the subject of masculinities and crime. However, and for reasons which will become clear as the book progresses, it is also a critique of some of the basic premises of this debate itself. The book seeks to question the present iconic status of this concept of 'masculinity' within such conversations and debates taking place about men and crime. It seeks to ask *why* it should be, at this particular moment, that a discipline which has failed so spectacularly in the past to address the sexed specificity of crime should now be turning (albeit tentatively) to an engagement with the 'gender' of men. A recurring theme in what follows will thus be a refusal, a questioning of, and intention to undermine, the presently privileged status of the gendered concept of masculinity over and above alternative – and I shall suggest preferable – readings of the relationship between men and crime based on an engagement with sexual difference, sex-specific corporeality and the idea of sexed subjectivity. As a 'gendered' attribute associated with the sex-class men, the concept of masculinity is, as some accounts from within sociology are now beginning to recognise (Hearn, 1996), both fluid, unstable and politically ambiguous. There may thus appear to be a certain irony in a book seeking to critique the concept of 'masculinity' itself then accommodating this problematic term in its own title. In light of the present seemingly pervasive status of the concept within the social sciences, not least its increasing visibility within criminology, an explicit engagement with masculinity does, at least, locate this book within the context of the debates with which it is seeking to engage. The exploration of sex, gender and the body which follows does not, moreover, imply that 'masculinity' is meaningless. The questions which need to be asked, I shall suggest (and which this book seeks to address), relate to the *ways in which* the terms 'masculinity' or 'masculinities' are presently being made to signify at particular moments and in particular ways. To deconstruct the 'masculinity' of 'criminology' is not to negate the discursive purchase of the concept:

> ... on the contrary deconstruction implies only that we suspend all commitments to that which the term [refers]. . . . To deconstruct is not to negate or to dismiss, but to call into question and, perhaps most importantly, to open up a term . . . to a reusage or redeployment that previously has not been authorized. (Butler, 1992: 15; Naffine, 1997: 86)

This book is about re-imagining or re-imaging men, not as the taken-for-granted norm of criminology, but from the perspective of 'other', of men as different (from women), of men as (sexed) specific subjects. It is, ultimately, about the social practices which produce 'men' and, of course, the idea of their 'masculinity'.

Masculinities, Crime and Criminology is, in one sense, a book about the discipline of criminology itself. It seeks to present the reader with an accessible and critical introduction to, and overview of, past criminological representations of the 'maleness' of crime. Chapters 1 and 2, for example, seek to place the present 'masculinity turn' within the context of criminology's own conceptual and institutional development, by exploring the epistemological, methodological and political foundations of criminology as a discipline. It has been suggested that criminology is at present seeking to (re)conceptualise the 'gender' of crime via an interrogation of the 'masculinity' or 'masculinities' of men. Yet in so doing, I shall argue, important aspects of the sex specificity of crime itself continue to be effaced. In seeking to 'unpack' the ways in which the 'Man' of a broader crimino-legal field has been a sexed (as male) subject (Young, 1996: 2; see below), this book seeks to integrate into an analysis of the relationship between men and crime a recognition of sexual difference and sex-specific corporeality, to move, ultimately, 'beyond' the paradigms of gender and heterosexuality which have, I shall suggest, in so many ways limited criminological understandings of the relationship between men and crime. In short, the chapters which follow focus on and seek to address elements of the men/crime relation which, I shall argue, continue to be hidden and negated within criminology's 'masculinity question'. This project will, in particular, involve an engagement with the *sexed bodies* of men, whether as offenders and victims (Chapters 3 and 4), as agents working within the criminal justice system, as academic criminologists seeking to 'explain' crime (Chapter 2), or as politicians seeking to 'control' crime (Chapter 6). This book is not seeking to 'bring masculinity into' the criminological gaze. It aims, rather, to shift or to disturb the gaze itself, to open up the conventional borders of the discipline and to question the very concepts, categories and systems of thought which rendered the sexed specificity of crime – the fact that crime is overwhelmingly an activity engaged in by men – invisible in the first place. It seeks to *see differently* the relationships between men and crime, masculinity and criminology.

In so doing what is required is a critical re-focusing on some ignored or misunderstood dimensions to the relationship between men and crime. The concerns of the book are thus not confined to a theoretical engagement with sex, gender and criminological discourse. What follows also aims to intervene in, and to speak to, a series of contemporary debates about the politics of crime, criminal justice and 'law and order'. The chapters which follow address issues of youth crime, schooling and urban disorder (Chapter 3), men's violences and the (hetero)sexed male body (Chapter 4), the relationship between 'family breakdown', fatherhood and crime (Chapter 5), and questions of criminal justice, crime control and crime prevention (Chapter 6). Among the recurring themes of the book will be the nature of the changing configurations of childhood, family and fatherhood, of heterosexual social practices and the sexed subject and, in particular, the relationship between the sexed (as male) body, corporeality and the crimes of men. What will emerge is, I shall argue, not so much an understanding of the relationship between men and crime in which men are seen to be 'accomplishing' or 'doing' masculinity through their involvement in crime (cf. Messerschmidt, 1993), but, rather, a position in which the mutual discursive constitution of crime, criminology *and* masculinity each emerge as historically specific, and interwoven, constructions of modernity. The present, much-heralded 'crisis' of masculinity, far from constituting a moment of 'truth' about particular changes taking place in the lives of men and women (be it in relation to their criminality, their family roles, their work, economic status, sexuality or emotional lives, and so forth), is in fact, I shall argue, emblematic of broader tensions surrounding ideas of heterosexuality, family and social (dis)order which have marked a reconfiguration of the idea of the 'social' itself within postmodernity. What appear to be conversations about 'masculinity', I shall suggest, can usefully be seen as attempts to tell other stories, to give voice and bear witness to other subjects and to speak of broader concerns, anxieties and tensions.

Masculinities, Crime and Criminology is not a traditional criminology textbook. It does not set out to discuss a pre-given body of issues and topics. Such a project is already well served by a range of other texts aimed at the student and teacher of criminology. It does not reproduce the now familiar 'history' of the discipline, that neat and compact linear narrative which traces a progression from the 'dark ages' of Lombrosian biologism through to the sociogenic Enlightenment of contemporary criminology. Nor does what follows seek to uncover a 'truth' about men and crime. Far from presenting any grand theory of men's criminality it begins from a wish to 'relinquish the traditional scientific desire to document exhaustively, to know fully and, hence, to master the individual as scientific object of investigation' (Naffine, 1997: 151). What follows is a series of readings which illustrate particular aspects of the ways in which the relationship between men and crime is constructed within and across a range of discourses. What emerges, we shall see, is something of the complexity of the ways in which specific ideas of masculinity, crime and heterosexuality have been discursively constituted through reference to each other. Far from 'explaining' men's crimes through recourse to an analysis of their status as 'masculine' phenomena, the readings which follow seek to deconstruct both crime and masculinity by locating representations of the men/crime relation within the particular discursive domains in which they are constituted (domains, that is, such as sexuality, the family, childhood and the social).

Given the potential scope of such a project in terms of the ubiquity and diversity of men's crimes, it has been necessary to be selective in the topics covered. Certain aspects or areas of the crimes of men are either not tackled or will be addressed only in passing. What follows has, moreover, a clear western orientation. Much of the engagement is with texts and debates from within British, North American and Australian criminology in particular. However, in seeking to place the production of criminological knowledge on a broader canvas, and in investigating how forms of knowledge about crime themselves become grounded in specific institutional practices, political movements and cultural settings, the concerns of the book necessarily transcend the topic of crime and the traditional remit of the discipline of criminology. What follows draws on scholarship and integrates questions from the fields of feminist theory, sociology, criminal justice and family law, cultural studies, geography, socio-legal studies and social theory. Its sources include a diverse range of representational practices, media and cultural artefacts, alongside the body of more 'traditional' criminological and socio-legal scholarship. The title of the book itself borrows from a text which remains one of the most influential and powerful in this field, Carol Smart's (1977) *Women, Crime and Criminology: A Feminist Critique*. To echo the title of such a justifiably celebrated work is, perhaps, to invite charges of over-ambition for this project. My intention is much more modest. Given the development of the topic of 'gender and crime' in the more than twenty years since the publication of Smart's book, and in light of the ways in which subsequent feminist scholarship has transformed the field of criminology, I believe the time is propitious to reassess and reconfigure the relationship between *men*, crime and criminology. I do not mean to invoke by this a 'man' who is pre-discursive and pre-given but, rather, to address the male *subject* of criminology: '. . . the term "man" should not be regarded as essentially dominant and self-contained; . . . in truth, it takes its meaning from the term "woman" [which] can now no longer be regarded as outside the concept of man, but [is] utterly central to it' (Naffine, 1997: 85). Carol Smart's own later work has been influenced (like this text) by developments around feminism/postmodernism and has, interestingly, explicitly sought to reject the discipline of criminology whilst continuing to engage with a discourse of masculinities (Smart, 1989: 86–7) and, more recently, heterosexuality/ies (Smart, 1996a, 1996b). In seeking to re-read the relationship between men, crime and criminology, what follows is, I hope, a useful contribution to a field of feminist and criminological scholarship in which a critical reassessment of the concept of the 'Man' and the 'masculine' subject is, I believe, long overdue.

Note

1. It is now commonplace for there to be, at the very least, a panel or stream organised around the theme of 'masculinity and crime' at major criminological conferences: see, for example, the programme of the British Criminology Conference, 1993, 1995, 1997. For some time, whenever 'new directions' or 'new agendas' in the discipline have been discussed, the topic of masculinity has surfaced in the context of 'breaking new ground' (see Heidensohn, 1995: 80–1). Unquestionably significant in raising the general profile of the subject was the conference *Masculinity and Crime: Issues of Theory and Practice* (1993), an international event held at the Centre for Criminal Justice Research, Brunel University, 14–15 September, and the subsequent book *Just Boys Doing Business? Men, Masculinities and Crime* (Newburn and Stanko, 1994a). In 1996 a 'Special Issue' of the prestigious *British Journal of Criminology* was devoted to the subject of 'Masculinities and Crime' (Carlen and Jefferson, 1996), a further sign of the growing 'mainstream' acceptance of the topic.

Acknowledgements

Masculinities, Crime and Criminology has been a difficult book to write, and in its completion I have incurred many debts. I would like to take this opportunity to thank, in particular, Gillian Stern at Sage. She has shown unwavering encouragement and understanding as each deadline passed. Her support, enthusiasm and kindness has been greatly appreciated. Earlier versions of arguments contained within this book have been presented in papers at many conferences and seminars. I would like to thank all who participated for their comments and all who have invited me to speak. I would like to acknowledge the financial assistance given by the British Academy (Small Personal Research Grant) and the University of Newcastle upon Tyne (Research Committee) towards this project. Chapter 4 includes material previously published in the *Journal of Law and Society*, 1997, 24 (2): 177–99, here reproduced by permission of Basil Blackwell. Chapter 5 includes material previously published in *Feminist Legal Studies*, 1996, 4 (1): 3–48, here reproduced by permission of Deborah Charles Publications.

Many people have provided friendship and encouragement at various stages during my time at Newcastle University. I would like to thank in particular, and acknowledge the support of, Mike Allen, Linda Anderson and all at the Centre for Gender and Women's Studies, Simon Blyth, Bea Campbell, Sara Fovargue, Tim Frazer, Robert Hollands, Nina Laurie, Ruth Lewis, Clare McGlynn, José Miola, Anoop Nayak, Mike Purdue, Pauline Purdue, Mark Thompson, Neil Ward and Rachel Woodward. Alastair Bonnett has been a constant source of support. I would like to thank him for listening, for his good humour and for making me laugh so much during countless escapes to the Hancock café. Elsewhere, I would like to thank the following: Lois Bibbings and all her colleagues at the Bristol Centre for Law and Gender Studies, Beverley Brown, Shelia Duncan, Nicola Lacey, Fiona MacMillan, John Morison, Anu Pylkkanen and all her colleagues involved in the 'Gendered Persons and Communities' project at Helsinki University, Shelly Day Sclater, Joe Sim, Sally Sheldon and everyone at the Keele Centre for Gender and Law, Carl Stychin, Louise Westmarland and Maggie Wykes. I would like to thank, in particular, Katherine O'Donovan and Carol Smart, who have supported and shaped my thinking through the years, and the influence of whose scholarship runs through this text. As ever, I would like to thank Les Moran. His friendship has been valued, his points about the 'complex economy of silence within the institution of academic legal studies' well taken. The following have, particularly during difficult times, helped in too many ways to mention: Beryl Graham, Gael Hardie-Brown, Val Nossiter, Andrew Pope and Graham Sutton. I would like to thank all at Murdoch Law School, Perth, for the support I was given and the kindness shown me during my time there, in particular Michael Blakeney, Jo Goodie and Chris Kendall. I would like to thank Margaret Thornton, who made me welcome at La Trobe University, and Ngarie Naffine, both of whose work has stimulated much of the discussion in this book. I would also like to thank Peter Rush and Alison Young, whose generosity and support made me so welcome in Melbourne. Especial thanks and love to Leanne, Russell and Rose Kingdom-Barron in Perth for their kindness and laughter, for putting me up and, most of all, for their friendship. I would like to thank my mother, Nancy Collier, and my aunt, Mag Collier, for all the support and encouragement they have shown me through the years. I would like to thank Fiona: without her understanding, patience and humour I am not sure that this book would have been completed. Finally, I would like to dedicate this book to Rosie, with all my love.

1   Sex, Gender and the (Criminal) Bodies of Men

Introduction: the new criminology of 'masculinities and crime'

This introductory chapter is an exploration of the diverse ways in which criminology's engagement with the 'spectre' of the question of sex – the recognition 'that [crime] is almost always committed by men' (Newburn and Stanko, 1994b: 10) – has historically been addressed via reference to the concept of 'masculinity/ies'. The chapter is in three sections. The first seeks to contextualise criminology's recent 'masculinity turn' by asking 'why now?' Why, at this present moment, should masculinity have surfaced on the criminological agenda as an issue deserving of analysis in its own right? The second section identifies and critiques the distinct strands to this engagement in terms of their underlying epistemological and methodological assumptions. Particular attention will be paid to the influence of the concept of 'hegemonic masculinity'. The third section seeks to progress the debate around 'masculinities and crime' by exploring what I shall suggest is an alternative and preferable perspective from which to approach the relationship between men and crime. Recent scholarship around sex/gender, sex-specific corporeality and the sexed subject has, I shall argue, served to destabilise and undermine the concept of 'masculinity' in ways which have important implications for developing understandings of the relationship between men, crime and criminology. At the present moment a debate is taking place around the subject of masculinities and crime which is seeking to address the historic failure of criminology to explain its own 'sex question' (Carlen and Jefferson, 1996; Newburn and Stanko, 1994a). In this chapter I shall argue that the contours of this debate in fact tell us much about the broader reconfigurations presently taking place not just in relation to crime but also around ideas of heterosexuality, childhood, the family and the social. In seeking to move beyond the paradigms of gender and heterosexuality, it is a concern with these questions which will constitute the subject matter of the remaining chapters of this book.

Let us be clear at the outset. The vast majority of conversations and debates around the issue of crime are, in fact, about the actions of men. This is not to claim that women and children do not commit crime or that the offending of women is not treated in ways very different to that of men. Nor, importantly, is it to claim that women and children are not the victims/

survivors of men's crimes. It is to recognise that men constitute the vast majority of all known offenders[1] and that the crimes of men are ubiquitous, the staple fare of newspaper headlines, television and radio reporting, films, novels and television scheduling. Men predominate not just as officially 'known' (and unknown) offenders but also as workers within the criminal justice system. From the upper echelons of state bureaucracies, where policies are devised for the management, control and regulation of crime, through to the 'front line' of the police and prisons, the criminal justice system is quite simply dominated by men (Martin and Jurik, 1996). To a large degree the well-documented public 'fear of crime'[2] is, in effect, a fear of men: of men as potential burglars, of men as physical attackers, of men who steal, deceive and kill, men who abuse, injure, harm and maim. It is a fear of the slow drip of men's violences against women, children and other men, the unforeseen (and foreseen) consequences of men's business and corporate actions. Most crimes remain unimaginable without the presence of men (Jefferson, 1992). The question is: What does this knowledge tell us about 'crime'? What, importantly, does it tell us about men?

This 'fact' can thus be identified, an empirical 'truth', a starting point. Men commit the vast majority of crime. Certainly, the statement may be qualified in different ways, moderated to account for problems associated with the construction and interpretation of criminal statistics,[3] the 'dark figure' of crime and the contingencies of type and frequency of crime (Heidensohn, 1994: 1001). However, and as criminologists have long recognised, it is sex-status which is, along with youth, the strongest predictor of criminal involvement. Men and boys perpetrate more conventional crimes and the more serious of these crimes than women and girls. Sex difference explains more variance in crime across nations and cultures than any other variable. In short, women commit fewer crimes of all types and proportionately fewer serious and violent crimes than men do. It is accordingly, Allen (1989: 19) has suggested, the capacity of criminology to explain this high sex ratio which 'might be posed as the litmus test of the discipline'; and it is a test which, it has been argued by a now voluminous body of feminist scholarship, criminology has failed quite spectacularly to pass.

The problem is not that criminology has failed to recognise that the object of its analysis has been, largely, men and crime. The target of the feminist critiques of the discipline which have emerged during the past twenty years has been with the nature of this recognition, *the way in which* the sex-specificity of crime has been conceptualised. Criminology, it has been argued, has been fundamentally flawed in (at least) two crucial senses. Firstly, it has failed to account for, in anything like an adequate manner, the nature of women's offending and, related to this, the treatment of women within the criminal justice system. This has been seen as a failure to address adequately both the causes of women's crimes and the specificities of women's experiences. Secondly, criminology has failed to address what has become known as the 'gender of crime' itself. It has failed to address the 'masculinity' or 'maleness' of crimes, the crimes of men *as men*; that is, what is it about men,

> not as working-class, not as migrants, not as underprivileged individuals but *as men* that induces them to commit crime? Here it is no longer women who are judged by the norms of masculinity and found to be 'the problem'. Now it is men and not humanity who are openly acknowledged as the objects and subjects of investigation. (Grosz, 1987: 6, quoted by Walklate, 1995: 169)

Addressing the former issue – the failure to account for the crimes of women – has been the topic of a now considerable body of feminist criminological scholarship (for example, Carlen, 1983, 1988; Carrington, 1993; Daly and Chesney Lind, 1988; Gelsthorpe, 1989; Gelsthorpe and Morris, 1988, 1990a; Leonard, 1982; Naffine, 1987; Smart, 1977; Walklate, 1995; Worrall, 1990). An explicit concern with the concept of masculinity, however, although frequently implicit in much feminist work, has become central to those more recent engagements with the question of 'gender and crime', which, though overlapping with and heavily indebted to feminist scholarship, have drawn on rather different political and intellectual traditions. By criminology's 'masculinity turn' I am referring to a body of work being undertaken by women and men which has been concerned to explore the relationship between men and crime via an explicit foregrounding of the concept of masculinity and/or masculinities (Carlen and Jefferson, 1996). In seeking to 'reconceptualise' (Messerschmidt, 1993) or 'take seriously' (Newburn and Stanko, 1994a) masculinity, these studies have sought to explore what analysis of the concept might tell us about such issues as the formation of the state (Liddle, 1996; Scraton, 1990; Sumner, 1990; see Chapter 6, pp. 165–7), police culture and policing discourse (Fielding, 1994; Sheptycki and Westmarland, 1993; Westmarland, 1997), schooling and youth crime (Messerschmidt, 1994), questions of 'race' and ethnicity (Bourgeois, 1996; Gibbs and Merighi, 1994), sport and culture (Jefferson, 1996), prisons (Newton, 1994; Sim, 1994; Thurston, 1996), men's violences (Alder and Polk, 1996; Kersten, 1996; Polk, 1994a, 1994b; Stanko, 1994), drugs and consumption (Collinson, 1996), victimology (Newburn and Stanko, 1994c), fear of crime (Goodey, 1997), media representations of crime (Sparks, 1996) and white-collar crime (Beirne and Messerschmidt, 1991: 54; Levi, 1994).

Two recent books, James Messerschmidt's *Masculinities and Crime* (1993) and Tim Newburn and Elizabeth Stanko's edited collection *Just Boys Doing Business* (1994a), exemplify this work. What unites these texts, beyond a considerable overlap in the topics they address, is a belief that the social meaning(s) of masculinity/ies are not 'given' or 'determined' (be it by biology or psyche). The subtitle of Messerschmidt's book captures well the intent of each text: this 'new' critical criminological engagement with masculinity is one of a *critique* (of criminology's 'masculinist' past) and of *reconceptualisation* (of what criminology's future may be once the 'sex question' is adequately addressed). What emerges is a complex, challenging and compelling picture of the ways in which diverse and differentially empowered masculinities are constituted through men's various engagements in criminal activity. In keeping with broader developments within the sociology of masculinity more generally, these analyses stress the plurality of masculin*ities*, moving away from the fixed model of a unitary masculinity (which had tended to frame earlier sociological accounts). What marks this work out as 'different' from what has gone before, therefore, is the question of *how* the sociality of masculinity is being theorised. Accordingly, and in Messerschmidt's terms, it is at the level of the theoretical reconceptualisation of the 'masculinity' of 'crime' that criminology is to be judged.

Two core objectives, or assumptions, underlie this masculinity turn. Firstly, there is a belief that there exists something distinct about men and the experience of 'being a man' which (at the very least) disposes men to criminality in a way which differentiates one sex (men) from the other (women). Men are no longer seen as de-sexed, neutral and universal subjects, the 'taken-for-granted' of post-Enlightenment knowledge formations. Men are to be taken seriously *as men*; that is, as 'gendered' beings. In this respect, criminology can be seen as 'catching up' with, or echoing, a more general concern to recognise the nature of the sexed specificity of the object of study well established in other disciplines. Secondly, and in terms of how this specificity is itself then conceptualised, it has been through the framework of 'gender and crime' and, specifically, through utilisation of the gender category 'masculinity/ies', that the relationship between men and crime is being explored. In a sense, therefore, the recent engagement with masculinity can be seen as a sub-division of a more general 'gender and crime' project. Thus, Walklate (1995) devotes a chapter of her book on the topic of *Gender and Crime* to what is seen as the 'new equation for criminology' represented by the study of masculinity. In keeping with the themes of the masculinity turn more generally, her analysis focuses on the heterogeneous nature of masculinities, the complexity, fragmentation and differentiation which exists between, alongside a concern with the continuities which unite, the lives of men (see further Morgan, 1992). What does 'unite' all men, it would seem, is this overwhelming propensity towards criminality relative to women, testified to by both criminal statistics and lived experience.

I shall argue in the remainder of this chapter that a number of epistemological and methodological difficulties underlie criminology's recent conceptualisation of the relationship between masculinity and crime. These problems relate, first and foremost, to a profound uncertainty as to 'what is exactly meant by masculinity' in the first place (Hearn, 1996: 213). Before beginning to address such questions, however, it is instructive to consider *why* it should be, at this particular moment, that a (generally) pro-feminist engagement with masculinity should have surfaced in that classically 'masculinist' discipline of criminology.

The 'masculinity turn': why now?

The emergence of the subject of men, masculinities and crime can be seen at a nexus of three developments, each with its own distinct political and intellectual trajectory. My concern in this section is to explore what each of these contexts share, and how they differ, in the ways in which masculinity is conceptualised. In order to ask what, if anything, may be different about the ways in which the masculinity turn is seeking to *re*conceptualise an already well-established sociogenic engagement with masculinity *in the light of feminist critiques* of the discipline, it is important to consider why it should be at this particular moment that the subject of masculinity should have begun to attract the attention of criminologists.

Feminism and feminist criminology/ies

The first, and most prominent, influence has been that of feminism. A concern with the diversity and deleterious consequences of men's offending has long been fundamental to feminist critiques of mainstream criminology. Whether it has been framed in terms of 'the generalizability problem' (do theories designed to describe men's offending apply to women?) or the 'gender ratio problem' (why do females commit less crime than males?) (Daly and Chesney Lind, 1988: 508), explaining the criminality of men has 'haunted criminology' (Allen, 1989). The masculinity turn begins with the feminist recognition of criminology's historic failure to adequately address the 'sex' of most crime. There is, of course, much more to the feminist critique of criminology than questions around masculinity. The very project and indeed possibility of a distinctive feminist criminology is contentious in terms of its epistemological foundation around a unified subject, 'Woman' (Smart, 1995: 70; see further Naffine, 1997; Smart, 1990; Young, 1996: Ch. 2, esp. 49–50). Nonetheless, it is clear that the concept of masculinity has been taken to have *some* kind of explanatory purchase at the levels of both feminist method and epistemology. Within the earlier perspective of liberal-progressivist 'first phase' feminist scholarship (Naffine, 1990: 3–6), or what Harding (1986, 1987) has influentially termed 'feminist empiricism', the 'maleness' of the criminological vision was depicted as having somehow 'distorted' the gaze of an otherwise neutral observer (Atkins and Hoggett, 1984; Sachs and Wilson, 1978). Maintaining a theoretically and politically tenable (sex-neutral) criminology nonetheless remained possible (for a critique of this position, see Brown, 1986, 1990; Naffine, 1990; Smart, 1990). Within later 'standpoint' (or 'second phase' scholarship) accounts, in contrast, the focus shifts to an analysis and valorisation of the experiences of women, for example as the victims/survivors of men's crimes. What emerges from this work are powerful and disturbing accounts which highlight and bring attention to the scale and diversity of men's violence, the untold pains of men's 'everyday' practices (Stanko, 1990), an awareness that women 'live in potential danger from men's violence as an ordinary part of their daily lives' (Stanko, 1994: 34; see also Kelly, 1988; Stanko, 1988, 1995).

Both of these strands of feminist scholarship have not only transformed the discipline of criminology and, to degrees, resulted in significant changes within criminal justice practices; they also gave a hitherto 'problem with no name' – the behaviour of men – a name at last: the problem of masculinity. Together, whether from the perspectives of 'feminist empiricism' or 'standpoint feminism' (Naffine, 1997: 30–7; Smart, 1990: 77), this work identified no less than an overwhelming 'masculinity', a 'maleness' or 'masculinism' of law, crime and criminal justice. This pervasive masculinity was itself conceptualised in different ways within the diverse strands of feminist thought (cf. MacKinnon, 1987; see below). Nonetheless what tended to be a consistent and recurring theme was the way in which some kind of correlation was being made between the power of men, their masculinity and their crime(s). Even in more recent postmodern-influenced accounts, in which feminism's 'Woman' has been displaced and (her)self rendered problematic, the concept of masculinity/ies has continued to be accorded a general heuristic purchase, to be understood to be telling us something about the multiplicity of ways in which men oppress women and construct women as other. In short, the significance of feminist scholarship – and the centrality of masculinity to these feminist critiques – cannot be underestimated.

The sociology or 'critical study' of men and masculinity

Feminist work has historically made considerable analytic use of a conceptualisation of 'masculinity' in seeking to address the relationship between gender and crime. It has not, however (for obvious reasons), tended to concern itself with progressing any idea of what this might mean in terms of specific analyses which foreground the experiences of men. I do not mean by this that feminist work has not engaged with men in multifarious ways, be it as offenders (Dobash et al., 1996) or victims (Stanko and Hobdell, 1993). Rather, the political project of feminism has addressed itself, first and foremost, to *women's* experiences, social position, status, and so forth (albeit that it has done so from diverse epistemological and methodological perspectives). Throughout the social sciences the relationship of men 'to' or 'in' this (these) feminist project(s) has been, and remains, contested and problematic (Boone, 1992; Bristow, 1992; Canaan and Griffin, 1990; Douglas, 1994; Jardine and Smith, 1987; Messner, 1997). The relationship between men and feminism is, some would say, an ultimately impossible one (Blyth, 1996). What has tended to happen has been that, in sociology, law and other disciplines (and now, we have seen, criminology), the questioning of men's masculinity has been seen as a matter best left for *men* to engage in. It is men, that is, who should 'put their own house in order'.[4]

The second context for the development of the masculinity turn in criminology is provided by a body of theoretical and empirical scholarship which has sought to do precisely that – to take up the feminist critique of masculinity and to explore the 'gender' of men (see Middleton, 1992). Identified variously as the pro-feminist 'new sociology' (Carrigan et al., 1985) or 'critical study' of men and masculinity (Hearn and Morgan, 1990), this work, which has expanded considerably over the last twenty years,[5] now constitutes a distinct body of scholarship and, for some, an academic discipline in its own right (Brod, 1987). The impact of this scholarship has been felt across disciplines such as sociology, anthropology, literary studies, psychology, history and law. In each, attempts have been made to reconceptualise the relationship of the discipline in question to masculinity. The resulting research has drawn on different interpretations, schools of thought, political allegiances and orientations (Messner, 1997), although amongst the recurring issues or core concerns have been, firstly, a (feminist-informed) focus on men's power relative to women (Brittan, 1989; Edley and Wetherell, 1996) and, secondly, a pervasive (and, I shall argue, questionable) notion that masculinity is in, or is at least approaching, a state of crisis (the 'crisis of masculinity' thesis: Brittan, 1989: 25–36; Carrigan et al., 1985; Hearn, 1987: 16–31; Sunley, 1996: see p. 175). This sociology of masculinity also, importantly, tended to focus on the experiences of heterosexual men (Carrigan et al., 1985; Dowsett, 1993). More generally, and beyond the academy, a growing concern with broader questions around men and masculinity has also been evident in a diverse body of journalistic and media accounts of changes in gender relations between men and women (what has been termed, in one popular phrase, the 'genderquake'). In accounting for these changes, once again, men's criminality has been accorded a central significance as somehow being emblematic of this broader 'masculine' or 'gender crisis'.

Public debates: crime, criminal justice and the politics of 'law and order'

If feminism and the critical study of (predominantly heterosexual) masculinities constitute two contexts for the masculinity turn in criminology, a third is provided by a development which, although it appears in some senses to be 'outside' the academy, has nonetheless profoundly impacted on the reassessment presently taking place of the men/crime relation. It also, importantly, shares many of the above concerns about what is happening around men, their 'gender' and social change. Contested meanings of masculinity have, in short, been central to a number of recent debates in Britain around a broad range of subjects which transcend any specific concern with crime and criminality. In relation to issues as diverse as the legal regulation of the family and sexuality, child care and child support, reproduction, parenthood, divorce and marriage, the behaviour of *men* is an issue which has been increasingly called into question (see, for example, Coote, 1994). Around issues relating to the changing nature of men's 'role' in the family, for example, a range of concerns around male sexuality, fatherhood, parenting and work have been addressed in terms of masculinity and a 'crisis' of gender relations (Collier, 1996a). Nonetheless, of all the areas in which this masculine crisis thesis has been articulated, the most prominent has been in relation to conversations around the social problem of crime and the potential criminality of men and boys. It has been, in particular, in a series of high-profile and controversial political debates about crime, criminal justice and the politics of 'law and order' that men (and in particular male youth) have assumed a central, iconic significance.

It is a concern to explore the nature of these debates around men and crime – to address what is, and what is not, being said about 'being a man' – which structures the chapters that follow. The issues which will be addressed are familiar features of current 'law and order' debates: for example, the 'trouble with boys' and young men, be it in terms of schooling, educational underachievement and drift into 'delinquency' (Chapter 3), questions of crime, parenting and familial socialisation (Chapter 5), the development of strategies of crime prevention (Chapter 6), the symbolic and seemingly inexplicable dimension to men's crimes (Chapter 4), and the failure of criminology itself to explain, to account for and to 'do something about' such crimes (Chapter 2). What unites each of these areas is the way in which some kind of association is being made across media, political and academic discourses between, on the one hand, contested and shifting forms of masculinity and, on the other, what are seen as changing (that is, worsening) manifestations of men's crimes and criminality. Within each of these conversations around crime, whether they are characterised as 'official' discourse (in the form of governmental policy, ministerial statements, and so on), 'public' debates (such as media representations) or academic scholarship (as within feminism and the sociology of masculinity), the concept of masculinity *is* being addressed. It is, however, I shall now argue, constructed in frequently contradictory ways. The kinds of issues which are being evoked under the rubric of the 'masculinity of crime' – questions about men's subjectivity and power, about men's bodies, desires, fears and privilege – are vast. Importantly, however, there remain certain problematic epistemological, methodological and political questions relating to the concept of masculinity itself which, ultimately, render it of limited use in seeking to analyse, understand and challenge the sexed specificity of the crimes of men. In a sense, the terrain of the 'masculinity of crime' can be seen to encompass all that might be said about 'being a man'. If criminology is now seeking to take this masculinity seriously, then it is necessary to ask at this stage just what is meant by 'masculinity' in the first place.

From sex roles to the sexed subject: (re)constructing 'masculinity'

The above section has identified something of the background against which criminology's present 'masculinity turn' is taking place. It also, of course, provides a context for the analysis to be presented in this book. In this section I wish to shift the gaze from criminology's *present* to criminology's *past* in order to trace and unpack what I shall suggest have been the 'three phases' of the discipline's engagement with the masculinity/crime relation. My concern in this section is with the underlying epistemological and methodological assumptions of the conceptualisation of masculinity within criminology and, more generally, sociology. What both criminology and sociology have tended to share has been an approach to masculinity based on a conceptual distinction between 'sex' and 'gender'. In contrast to this sex/gender perspective, it is from within the (potentially more productive) theoretical framework emerging from the interface of recent feminist and postmodern scholarship that, I shall argue, it becomes possible to integrate into the analysis of men and crime questions of sexed specificity. Accordingly, the remainder of this chapter as a whole seeks to develop the theoretical framework upon which the readings of men and crime to take place in the following chapters will be built. First, however, it is necessary to consider further the inadequacies of both traditional mainstream and feminist criminological accounts in terms of their underlying conceptualisation of the 'masculinity of crime'.

Phase one: 'traditional' or 'malestream' criminology: from biogenic to sociogenic accounts

Research into the relationship between masculinity and crime has a long history within criminological thought. Indeed, the discipline is replete with studies of crime which have utilised the term 'masculinity'. From late nineteenth- and early twentieth-century biogenic and psychogenic depictions of 'atavistic man', through mid-twentieth-century studies of gangs, sub-cultures and juvenile delinquency, and through to contemporary accounts of urban disorder and the 'underclass male', explaining the disproportionate criminality of men vis-à-vis women has been a foundational imperative for criminology. In order to understand the ways in which this concept of masculinity has been variously used in such accounts, however, it is first necessary to have some understanding of the scope and nature of criminology itself. How criminology has (and has not) engaged with masculinity depends in part, I shall suggest, on how criminology is itself conceptualised.

It has become standard practice in accounts of the history of criminology to trace the beginnings of modern criminological thought to the writings of the eighteenth and early nineteenth centuries. Modern criminology, Garland (1994) has argued, grew out of the convergence of two separate enterprises, a 'governmental project' and a 'Lombrosian project', which together continue to provide an intellectual rationale for the discipline at the end of the twentieth century. The former refers to a series of empirical inquiries into crime which, since the eighteenth century, have sought to enhance the efficient and equitable administration of justice by engaging in such activities as charting the patterns of crime and monitoring the practices of the criminal justice system.[6] The Lombrosian project, in contrast, refers to the development of criminology as an aetiological, explanatory science based on the premise that criminals can somehow be scientifically differentiated from non-criminals (Garland, 1985). It is from within this latter tradition that the engagement with masculinity has most obviously been addressed within criminology, in the form of investigations of such issues as the psychology of offending and the nature of criminal motivation. Modern criminology, therefore, can be seen as being marked by a number of characteristics: a scientific approach to crime; a concern with the individual criminal; an engagement with the causes of crime; and an investigation of the new pathological phenomenon of criminality itself (understood as the source of criminal behaviour). Each of these characteristics of criminology has raised particular questions about, and involved certain understandings of, men and their masculinity.

Scientific method   In relation to its dominant methodology, criminology can lay claim to being, from one feminist perspective, the epitome of a 'masculinist' discipline. Criminology has traditionally involved a scientific approach to crime, based on observation, measurement and inductive reasoning. The discipline continues to place considerable faith in the role of 'experts' in the administration of a range of social problems related to crime. Contemporary criminologists (the vast majority of whom are men: see Chapter 2) continue to be called upon by the media to pronounce on such issues as the motivation behind particular crimes, developments in crime control and related subjects. In terms of its underlying epistemology, criminology's status as a progressive scientific mission has encouraged a reading of the discipline in terms of a linear meta-narrative, a 'received history' based on the development of 'schools of thought' and key distinctions (such as positivism and classicism: Garland, 1994: 20–2; Rock, 1988). Whilst it has been generally recognised that 'the myth of an emergent criminology, progressing from ancient error to modern truth' does 'little to improve our understanding of the past or of the present' (Garland, 1994: 24), the correlation between criminology's status as an androcentric, positivist discipline and an association with its masculinist nature continues to be made in feminist work (Smart, 1990). In terms of methodology, and in marked contrast to feminist perspectives (Roberts, 1981; Stanley and Wise, 1983), criminology's historic association with scientific method and reason has been seen as implicating it with other phallocentric, totalising and oppressive knowledge formations in the way in which it has systematically effaced the sexed specificities of women's experiences. Like the criminal justice system itself, whose medicalising and pathologising regimes have served to negate women's rationality and choice (insisting women are subject to forces outside intellectual control: H. Allen, 1987; Smart, 1977: 146–77), within criminology men have been systematically accorded and associated with rationality and reason (Smart, 1977). This 'criminological man' has taken (his) reason for granted, regarding it as final authority and arbiter of criminological truth (cf. Seidler, 1995: 171; see further Seidler, 1989). The male offender (in marked contrast to women's offending) has been characterised historically as a rational, free-willed actor who engages in crime in a calculated, utilitarian way. It is he who will (or will not) be responsive to deterrent, proportionate penalties; it is he, a rational *male* actor, who has been historically central to the project of scientific criminology.

The individual (male) offender　Alongside this faith in an appropriately scientific method, criminology has focused on the individual criminal and the characteristics which have been taken to mark them (him) off as different from the 'normal' (non-criminal) population. Or, to 'sex' this statement, criminology has concerned itself with *individual* men at the expense of any engagement with the structural power of *all* men. Criminology has taken men as the norm (Naffine, 1997). In so doing, what has been routinely effaced is any questioning of what might link the purportedly 'pathological' with the 'normal-normatively' masculine (Hollway, 1981; Sunley, 1996). The implications of this cannot be confined to questions of how criminology has (failed) in relation to accounting for women's criminality. Taking men to be the (unspoken) benchmark has also had important consequences for understanding the particular ways in which men have been constituted – and sexed – within the criminological project.

Within the Lombrosian tradition, we have seen, criminology produced a distinctive science of the criminal. For Lombroso himself, the criminal was conceptualised as a naturally occurring entity, a fact of nature rather than a social or legal product. With the shift from biogenic to sociogenic accounts of crime which took place during the twentieth century, the vast majority of aetiological studies have subsequently de-emphasised the biological determinants which Lombroso took to be fundamental. Sociogenic criminology focused, in contrast, on issues such as the ecology of crime, the concepts of anomie, strain and subculture, social control and conflict. Nonetheless, an overarching positivist paradigm continued to inform much of criminology's search for the distinctive characteristics of the 'criminal man' (albeit that it was now looking to social background rather than bodily stigmata, educational underachievement rather than atavistic abnormalities, and so forth).

The general problems relating to these earlier biogenic and sociogenic criminological accounts have been well documented (Allen, 1989; Naffine, 1997, 1990). As situationally based analyses they involved no conception of men's power, their methodological individualism negating any engagement with social structure. When masculinity did appear it tended to be seen as something which could be measured or individually possessed (Bem, 1974; on 'masculinity theory' in criminology see Naffine, 1987: Ch. 4). Nonetheless, in seeking to engage with the concept of masculinity these (pre-feminist) sociogenic 'sex role' accounts did surface a number of themes which were to recur within later feminist and pro-feminist engagements with men and crime. Masculinity appeared, perhaps above all, as something which was fragile, precarious and marked by a range of anxieties, notably around (hetero)sexuality (Hartley, 1959). Masculinity was something to be 'achieved' and yet, simultaneously, something natural and taken for granted. It was, above all, defined through reference to what it was *not*: not feminine, not homosexual and not 'unmanly'. In straining to 'be' masculine, this first phase work established a criminological *dramatis personae* which in many respects has continued to inform later, ostensibly more 'critical' or 'radical', criminological critiques.

Part of the aim of the 'new' criminologies of the 1970s (for example, Box, 1983; Chambliss, 1975; Quinney, 1974; Taylor et al., 1973, 1975) had been to subject this traditional criminology in all its forms to a sustained critique. However, and notwithstanding the fact that questions of gender would later be integrated into (at least) some critical criminological texts within the broad tradition of 'left realism' (see Chapter 2), the 'sex question' continued to be effaced. By, in effect, 'feminising' a consciousness of 'gender issues' – by associating sex/gender with the pervasive 'woman question' (albeit at times in an ostensibly pro-feminist form) and *not* 'sexing' its own 'man question' – critical/Left criminologies continued to leave men as the unexplored, de-sexed norm. Just as women are sexed, the sexed specificity of men is effaced at the very moment that the subject of criminology – criminality – is being constituted. Later sociogenic accounts therefore, although rejecting biological determinism in favour of sociological explanation, have continued to associate women with the field of sex/gender, with all matters corporeal, whilst continuing to take men as the (de-sexed) norm (Allen, 1989; Naffine, 1997). An ideology of natural sexual difference has thus continued, albeit in a form more sophisticated than Lombrosian atavism, to locate women's criminality in relation to the distinctive features of their sexed ('female') corporeality and, in so doing, to evacuate 'sex' from consideration of men's criminality. In so doing, importantly, what has been left unquestioned is the relationship between the *sexed bodies* of men and accounts of their crimes: the 'female body was subjected to an intensive criminological gaze [whilst] the male body was evacuated, disallowed, disavowed' (Allen, 1989: 22).[7]

To recap: criminology largely remains bifurcated around a man/woman axis in which general universal theories of crime causation have been taken to apply to men whilst the crimes of women (and thus women generally) are assessed from, or in relation to, the male norm. Women have been seen as an aberration to this norm, to be as other, somehow less than 'fully' male. However, crucially, one result of this simultaneous focus on (a) the individual offender and (b) the constitution of men as the norm has been that the sex-class men have themselves been separated out into two groups: the *offending* (criminal) man and the *non-offending* (non-criminal) man. It has been feminist work, especially in the area of men's violences, which has challenged the subsequent pathologising of the crimes of men that results from such a division, by seeking to explore instead what men (as men) may share, as opposed to the attributes of the individual (criminal) man. Within mainstream criminology men considered to be 'deviant' or 'pathological' have been contrasted with the 'normal' and the 'law-abiding'. Whilst some criminologists may have sought to blur this distinction (Matza, 1964, 1969), it is a bifurcation between different types or categories of men which nonetheless remains the (unspoken) norm of criminological discourse. It has been in seeking to understand this issue of what men may share that, in the work of the second phase criminologists writing from feminist and pro-feminist perspectives, the concept of masculinity has been seen to have had a particular, and rather different, heuristic purchase.

Phase two: the possibilities – and 'limits' – of masculinity: sex, gender and social constructionism

Whereas a methodological individualism had marked the 'pre-history' of masculinity theory discussed above, within the range of feminist texts which began to impact on the discipline during the 1970s and 1980s the question of power – specifically, the structural power of men – was to be accorded a central status. Within contemporary sociology more generally, the term 'masculinity', Hearn (1996: 203) has argued, would itself come to serve as 'a reference point' against which a diverse range of behaviours and identities could be evaluated from within frameworks seeking to accommodate this feminist awareness of men's power relative to women. The meanings of 'masculinity' in this work, however, are by no means clear. At times masculinity has encompassed such attributes as the psychological character-istics of men, men's experiences as 'gendered' beings, their gender 'identity' and aspects of sex-role socialisation, as well as psychoanalytic and power-based accounts and analyses of men's gendered behaviour in institutional practices (Hearn, 1996: 203; see also McMahon, 1993: 690). The roots of the concept of masculinity within sociology can be found in the kinds of social psychological research on 'sex roles' and identity which had informed the earlier criminological engagements discussed above (see Connell, 1987). However, unquestionably the key distinction which has marked the twentieth-century shift from predominantly biogenic to sociogenic con-ceptualisations of masculinity has been that of sex/gender. It is this distinction which continues to inform social constructionist accounts of masculinity, whether feminist or otherwise.

The sex/gender distinction Situated in the philosophical foundations of the Cartesian dualism, of body/consciousness (Gatens, 1996: 7),[8] the distinction between sex and gender has been traced back (at least) to Freud (see Connell, 1987). There appears some agreement that the precursor of the current sociological usage – that which has framed the subsequent investiga-tions within criminology – can be found in the work of Robert Stoller (1968). Stoller, drawing on studies of biological anomalies and trans-sexualism, argued that biological sex augmented, but did not determine, the appropriate gender 'identity' for each sex (that is, masculinity in the case of the male sex, femininity in the case of female sex). Crucially, a person's gender *identity* – his or her sense of maleness or femaleness – was seen by Stoller to be a result of post-natal psychological influences which were able to completely override the biological 'fact' of a person's genital, chromosomal or hormonal sex (resulting in, for example, the phenomenon of the transsexual). Within this model, 'sex' and 'gender' are thus conceptually differentiated. 'Sex' is deployed to describe the innate biological characteristics of humans. Sex is 'of the body', denoting physical differences between 'men' and 'women'. 'Gender', in contrast, relates to social characteristics and usages which are understood to be socially/culturally associated with one sex or the other: the qualities or characteristics deemed to constitute their 'maleness' (masculinity) or 'femaleness' (femininity).

This sex/gender axis remains the key binary pair through reference to which the vast majority of criminological engagements with masculinity and crime have been constructed. That is, it has been from within this overarching paradigm of 'gender' that feminist criminology has tended to conceptualise masculinity. As such, the adequacy of these feminist conceptualisations of masculinity in terms of the sex/gender distinction serves as a useful (and arguably under-explored: see Allen, 1989) case study of the more general failings and conceptual limitations of the sex/gender binary.

It is difficult to overestimate the present ubiquity of the 'gender' frame within criminology. The feminist criminological engagement with gender has been largely unequivocal. Gelsthorpe and Morris capture the nature of this 'gendered' critique of criminology:

> Gender blindness is not a trivial oversight: it carries social and political significance. Moreover, theories which do not address gender are not merely incomplete; they are misleading. (1988: 98)

The concept of gender has been, and remains, central to feminist critiques of both criminology and law (see, for example, Carlen and Worrall, 1987; Daly, 1993; Edwards, 1989; Gelsthorpe and Morris, 1988; Gregory and Lees, 1994; Gwynn, 1993; Heidensohn, 1994; Walklate, 1995). It continues to be used as an analytic tool which, it is presumed, 'yields high explanatory returns (as opposed to the barren category of 'sex': Gatens, 1996: 3). Indeed, at the present moment gender is, within Anglo-American feminism, 'a central explanatory and organising category for accounts of the social, familial and discursive construction of subjectivity' (Gatens, 1996: 4). In many ways this 'gendering' of crime debate has itself been presented as being at the 'cutting edge' of the discipline, a 'new direction', a subject in need of serious study. For example, a chapter of the *Oxford Handbook of Criminology* (Heidensohn, 1994) is devoted to the subject of 'Gender and Crime'. Walklate's (1995) book *Gender and Crime* similarly explores the project of 'gendering criminology', which is seen to involve questions of 'gendering sexual violence', 'gendering police work', 'gendering criminal justice policy' and, importantly, in a chapter concerned explicitly with 'the masculinity of crime' (a 'new equation for criminology': 1995: 160), 'gendering the criminal'. Elsewhere, the book *International Feminist Perspectives in Criminology* (Hahn Rafter and Heidensohn, 1995) similarly makes its originating paradigm clear in the use of the subtitle 'Engendering a Discipline'. The concept of gender is, in short, ubiquitous.

As Gatens (1996) notes, the appeal of the use of gender for a progressive politics such as feminism is understandable. Stoller's work appeared from the outset to be a breakthrough in the areas of sexuality and socialisation. Across disciplines, social scientists located in the sex/gender distinction a theoretical justification for women's right to claim equality independently of presumed biologically 'natural' sex differences (Chodorow, 1978; Dinnerstein, 1978; Millett, 1971; Oakley, 1972). However, in so doing, feminist studies were not only reconceptualising women's oppression; in developing analyses of the 'problem of men' throughout the 1970s and 1980s a re-engagement with the concept of masculinity was itself becoming increasingly central to a feminist political project premised on the validity of the social constructionist frame of sex/gender. With varying degrees of determinism, men were seen as being subject to the control of their 'gender' (cf. MacKinnon, 1987, 1989). The men's 'anti-sexist' studies and practices of the 1970s and 1980s, which had emerged as a direct response to second wave feminism, drew on, rarely contesting, these feminist social constructionist accounts of masculinity (Carrigan et al., 1985; Hearn, 1987; Metcalf and Humphries, 1985; Reynaud, 1983; Rowen, 1987; Tolson, 1977; see also, generally, Middleton, 1992). However, and in seeking to question whether understandings of crime 'can be completed at all ... through an understanding of masculinity' (Walklate, 1995: 180), it is becoming increasingly clear that the wholesale adoption of the gender category 'masculinity' also brought with it certain problems.

Before exploring further these conceptual limits of 'masculinity' a proviso is required. I do not wish to argue that the gender category 'masculinity' has been politically ineffective in conceptualising aspects of the 'problem of men' from a feminist perspective. In the very act of *naming men* as being 'the problem' in relation to crime the subject matter of criminology has been transformed. The politics of crime can no longer be collapsed into the familiar politics of class, capital and/or race. In giving voice to those who had hitherto been silenced within criminology, the use of the term 'masculinity' or 'masculinism' has appeared to capture well and chime with the stifling, suffocating nature of a unitary male voice, the oppressive silencing of the experiences of women and children. More recently, and in stressing the provisional, historically and culturally specific nature of masculini*ties*, sociological work has sought to conceptualise men's 'gender' not simply as an individual possession (as in the sex-role framework discussed above) but in terms of institutional practices located in structures of power (Connell, 1987). In a development which has reached a particularly sophisticated form in the work of Connell (1995), this scholarship on masculinities has begun to fuse questions of theory with biographical and life history work whilst also integrating an awareness of historical and global perspectives (on the 'gender' of men, see Hearn, 1996). Nonetheless, and notwithstanding the above strengths, the more general project of 'gendering' men in criminology, of applying the same (or similar) analyses to men's lives as those which have traditionally been related to women, continues to leave unaddressed many questions. What concerns me at this point are the ways in which the concept of masculinity is itself, if not fundamentally flawed, then at least limited in several important respects in seeking to develop an understanding of the relationship between men and crime.

The conceptual 'limits' of masculinity   'Masculinity', Hearn has suggested, has become

> a symbolic icon for the more general increase in interest in the study of men, critical or otherwise. It is as if this concept exemplifies the field of concern and even, possibly, distils the aggregation of activity of men in the social world into one neat word. (1996: 202)

As a 'symbolic icon' which 'distils the aggregation of activity of men . . . into one neat word', the present masculinity turn within criminology illustrates many aspects of more general problems with the concept of masculinity. There are a number of elements to these (conceptual) 'limits of masculinity', each of which needs to be unpacked.

Firstly, masculinity is politically ambiguous. Specifically, it is used in different ways within different discourses and perspectives. This stems from the open-ended nature of the concept itself and relates to the ways in which an underlying essentialism, an ontological assumption about the status of the men/masculinity relation, is itself mobilised to different ends and at different historical moments. Politically divergent perspectives such as feminist, men's liberationist, mytho-poetic and neo-conservative discourses have each, for example, at various moments utilised an essentialist conception of masculinity in seeking to account for the relationship between men and crime (see Chapter 5).

Secondly, and relating to this political ambiguity, masculinity is conceptually imprecise. Such are the wide variety of its uses in different contexts (Hearn, 1996: 203) that the concepts of masculinity and masculinities each stand in an ambiguous relationship to culture. Within certain social constructionist accounts, for example, the existence of a unitary 'masculine' cultural form has been presumed to frame (biological) men's endeavours to become (real) 'men'. Implicitly, an underlying and essential cultural norm is here presumed to exist to which all men can, or should, aspire. Masculinity is, in effect, understood as a generalised form of culture. It is transcultural and, for some, transhistorical (within one strand of feminism, for example, masculinity *is* patriarchal culture). Yet at other times masculinity is utilised in a very different way in seeking to account for the diversity of men's experiences. It is not uncommon to find masculinity being conceptualised in different ways, frequently within the same text. Thus, for example, Scraton

(1990) presents a powerful account of the 'masculinism' of criminological discourse. Yet, whilst recognising the limitations of 'false universalism' in relation to women (1990: 15, 21), a universal*ising* conception of masculinity as oppressive is also embraced (cf. Sunley, 1996). Masculinity thus appears both as a specific form of culture *and* as something which varies within and between broader cultures (Hearn 1996: 205). It is generalisable; it signifies a cultural phenomenon which encompasses a range of expressions of men's 'gendered' beings and gender identities. Yet the question remains as to whether engaging with such a multiplicity (or multiplicities) of masculinities ultimately subverts the whole enterprise of a sociology of 'masculinity' itself (Morgan, 1992). The use of the plural 'masculinities' does not, by itself, address these questions.

Thirdly, and a point which has a particular salience in relation to debates around men and crime, it is unclear how 'in terms of ageing and movement through the life-course – what is thought of as personal time – ... masculinity might be thought to figure' (Hearn, 1996: 210). One of the most familiar and controversial questions in debates around crime has been whether individuals 'grow out of' crime. If they do, then at what age? Yet one thing which has emerged clearly from life-history research on men is how the meanings of masculinity differ and how masculinity is accorded different significances, at different moments, during the life cycle. One of the principal concerns of criminology, as we shall see in more detail in Chapter 3, has been with the transition of boys 'into' adult masculinity. Many contemporary debates around youth criminality continue to focus on the crimogenic dimensions of the processes whereby boys are (or are rather not) 'initiated' into 'manhood'. What remains unclear, however, is at what point the relationship between masculinity and crime per se is understood to become synonymous: Is it when a child is born? Or is it during adolescence? The former is compatible with a host of essentialist accounts, feminist or otherwise, which relate crime to a range of inherent qualities of 'maleness', of 'being a man'. The latter looks to questions of the socialisation of male youth into their 'disorder'. Each, however, conceptualises *masculinity* as something which impacts on men so as to induce *criminality*. What remains unanswered is why the impact of masculinity should take place at the time it does. The recognition that the meanings of masculinity may vary over the life course serves to highlight the ways in which so much of the 'masculinity of crime' debate has, in fact, been concerned with particular masculinities: not men in general but, specifically, with the masculinities of young men, their 'wild', 'dangerous' and 'maverick' subjectivities (on which, see Chapter 3). Other masculinities, or men at different stages of the life cycle, are constituted in very different ways. What is not addressed, therefore, is the question raised by Jefferson (1994a): how, and why, do men choose particular actions, to 'become' particular kinds of men? To state that diverse masculinities are 'offered up' for men within particular socio-cultural, structural locations does not, by itself, fully answer this question (Walklate, 1995: 180; cf. Messerschmidt, 1993; see below, p. 29).

The ubiquitous (and problematic) concept of hegemonic masculinity   The current status of the concept of hegemonic masculinity is indicative of the ways in which a faith in the viability of the concepts and categories of modernist criminology continues to frame understanding of the crimes of men. Its present ubiquity also illustrates, in a particularly clear way, each of the problems noted above around the conceptual limits of masculinity per se.

The concept of hegemonic masculinity is presently pervasive, in both work on masculinity and crime and, though perhaps to a lesser degree, feminist criminology. In the introduction preceding the collection of essays in *Just Boys Doing Business?*, for example, Newburn and Stanko (1994b) note that, of all the current theorisations of masculinity/ies, it is that by the Australian sociologist Bob Connell – the concept of 'hegemonic masculinity' – which has been the most influential and frequently cited: '. . . indeed this is illustrated by the number of references to his work throughout the chapters in this book' (1994b: 3). Connell himself, writing the foreword to James Messerschmidt's *Masculinities and Crime*, praises the text as 'part of a conceptual revolution in the social sciences, reflecting profound changes in our understanding of everyday life . . . a time when questions of gender and sexual politics, femininity and masculinity, have been brought out of obscurity and seen as key issues in our society' (Connell, 1993: vii).

The concept of hegemonic masculinity is certainly appealing. It addresses what had by 1987 (the year of publication of Connell's *Gender and Power*) become the pressing question noted above: '. . . how are we to conceptualise relations among men, especially when class and ethnic and generational relations are included?' (Jefferson, 1994a: 15). How, in other words, is it possible to recognise diversity of men's lives whilst also recognising the existence of a culturally exalted form of masculinity? For Connell, the answer lies in the concept of hegemonic masculinity, which 'is always constructed in relation to various subordinated masculinities as well as in relation to women' (1987: 183). Central to hegemonic masculinity is the idea that a variety of masculinities can be ordered hierarchically. Gender relations, Connell argues, are constituted through three interrelated structures: labour, power and cathexis. What 'orderliness' exists between them is not that of a system but, rather, a 'unity of historical composition'. What is produced is a 'gender order', 'a historically constructed pattern of power relations between men and women and definitions of femininity and masculinity' (Connell, 1987: 98–9). Hegemonic masculinity is central to this hierarchical ordering of gender relations within the context of their complex interaction with social structures. Following Gramsci (1971), the resulting 'hegemony' is always incomplete (Connell, 1987: 184), the relation between domination and subordination never fixed or final. Indeed, the very politics of gender arise from this *always contested* nature of men's power, the ever present possibility of resistance and contestation (see, for example, on men in prison, Sim, 1994: 111). Hegemonic masculinity, therefore, must be constantly produced and reproduced. The gender regime is, at any historical moment, always in a dynamic process of constitution: '. . . structures identified by analysis . . . exist only in solution, they are not absolutely prior to the subject but themselves are always in process of formation. Social and personal life are practices' (Middleton, 1992: 153). It is Connell's contention, therefore, that hegemonic masculinity is never finally closed, fixed or resolved. The politics of masculinity cannot be confined to the level of the personal (matters of choice, conditioning, human nature, and so forth). They are also *embedded* in the gender regime, part of the organisational sexuality of institutions and society generally. As Segal puts it, capturing key elements of Connell's approach, masculinity

> is best understood as transcending the personal, as a heterogeneous set of ideas, constructed around assumptions of social power which are lived out and re-inforced, or perhaps denied and challenged, in multiple and diverse ways within a whole social system in which relations of authority, work and domestic life are organised, in the main, along hierarchical gender lines. (Segal, 1990: 288)

It is important to bear in mind, therefore, when considering the ways in which hegemonic masculinity has been subsequently embraced within criminology, that the concept arose from within an analysis of gender concerned with social structure, action and the interrelation between gender systems and social formations. To repeat: the central idea, drawing on the concept's Gramscian origins, is one of *contestation*. What is interesting, however, is the way in which hegemonic masculinity is presently being used within accounts of men and crime in a rather different manner. Specifically, hegemonic masculinity has been utilised in such a way that it can be taken, on the one hand, as referring to a certain set of characteristics or traits, which are then made to signify 'the masculine' in particular contexts; and, on the other, as explaining, the *cause* of, the crimes of men. This point, and the tension between the two interpretations, requires clarification.

Hegemonic masculinity has been taken as referring to a selective range of categories culturally associated with the masculine: specifically, such qualities as aggression, 'macho', pride, competitiveness, duty, feelings of insecurity, failure, and so forth. As Walklate (1995: 181) notes, however, the 'maleness of crime' covers a vast range of activities. Hegemonic masculinity has been routinely associated within recent work on men and crime with those characteristics which depict men as being unemotional, independent, non-nurturing, violent and dispassionate (whilst at the same time being, on occasion, inappropriately passionate: McMahon 1993; see, generally, the accounts in Newburn and Stanko, 1994a). There is, however, a profound problem here. As Gilmore (1993) and others have shown, cultural ideas of manhood can also encompass qualities which might be deemed (from a certain feminist perspective) 'positive'. That is, to encompass behaviour on the part of men which is not always 'self-serving, egotistical and uncaring' (Gilmore, 1993; 229). Moreover, geographical, cross-cultural and anthropological studies attest to the ways in which the concept of 'masculinity' itself may be inapplicable to certain cultural situations (Connell, 1995: 30–4:

Gilmore, 1993). This raises, Hearn (1996) has suggested, some far-reaching questions about whether masculinity is itself 'an ethnocentric or even a Eurocentric notion'. It is, for example, misleading to state that masculinity varies historically (and therefore the masculinity/crime relation also varies historically), when in some societies and situations the concept of masculinity is, quite simply, not present. In the nineteenth century a concept of 'manliness' was used rather than that of masculinity (Mangan and Walvin, 1987; cf. Roper and Tosh, 1991). Yet this, as historical research has shown (Rotundo, 1993), was itself a class-based notion. The 'dangerous classes' of the time, the object of Lombrosian scrutiny, would in all likelihood not have recognised themselves in such terms (see Chapter 5, p. 29). As Hearn notes, '. . . in some historical structures the contexts of masculinity may be irrelevant or misleading' (1996: 209).

Such (at the very least) provisos have a number of implications for seeking to understand the men/crime relationship in terms of the concept of masculinity. Within accounts of men 'accomplishing' masculinity through their involvement in crime (Messerschmidt, 1993; Newburn and Stanko, 1994a), men are seen as 'doing' their gender (masculinity) through engaging in such diverse crimes as burglary, rape, the sexual abuse of children, the taking of motor vehicles without consent, corporate crime, football 'hooliganism', state terrorism, traffic offences, 'road rage', violence towards other men, and so forth (each of these has been the subject matter of recent analyses). To account for such a diversity is, clearly, asking a great deal of the concept of masculinity. What men are not seen as 'doing', however, is a masculinity which might in any sense be interpreted as 'positive'; not so much in the sense of the undoubted 'seductions' of crime when seen from the perspective of the men themselves (Jefferson, 1992; Katz, 1988), but in terms of an engagement with the complexity of the ways in which a 'masculine' subject is constituted through relationships to women and other men. For example, Walklate (1995: 181) asks, '. . . what women want . . . is important . . . do women really want their men to be "wimps"? And if "their man" turns out to be a wimp, how do they deal with this?' (see also Coward, 1994). Raising the question is, she states, not to imply that women are to blame for men's behaviour (though it is possible it can be read this way). It is, rather, to suggest the need to recognise a psychologically complex subject for whom the meanings of 'masculinity' cannot be confined to the (generally oppressive and negative) list of traits seen above.

The concept of hegemonic masculinity, I wish to suggest, is of limited use in seeking to engage with such a complex male subject. What we are dealing with here is a description, a list of 'masculine' traits (Hearn 1996: 207), each of which conjures up powerful images about men and crime (and which, importantly, has social effects). In theory, each of the characteristics associated with hegemonic masculinity could apply equally to women as to men. Not *all* crime, it would seem, is to be explained by reference to hegemonic masculinity. Whilst some crimes shock (murder, rape, violence against children, the elderly), others are equated with essentially harmless human traits (for example, some motoring offences are seen this way). Does this mean that the concept of hegemonic masculinity is only to be of use in explaining some crimes? If so, then some criteria for selection are required. Is it only to be those crimes which are violent and/or destructive which bespeak their origins in masculinity? Yet men, we have seen, dominate all crimes, though some crimes appear to escape being 'gendered' in ways in which others do not. It has been largely as a result of feminism, for example, that so-called 'private' harms have been depicted as gendered crimes (in contrast, for example, to corporate and political crime: Beirne and Messerschmidt, 1991). However, and regardless of the categories of crime which are to be seen as being capable of explanation in terms of hegemonic masculinity, another serious problem remains.

The concept of hegemonic masculinity has been used both as a primary and underlying *cause* (or source) of particular social effects (in this case, crime) and, simultaneously, as something which is seen as *resulting from* or which is 'accomplished' through (Messerschmidt, 1993), recourse to crime: '. . . not only does this reflect a failure to resolve fully the tendency towards universalism, it can also be read as tautological' (Walklate, 1995: 181). What is actually being discussed in accounts of (hegemonic) masculinity and crime is, in effect, a range of popular ideologies of what constitute ideal or actual characteristics of 'being a man' (Hearn, 1996). Hegemonic masculinity appears to open up an analysis of the diversity of masculinities (subordinate, effeminate, non-capitalist?) whilst simultaneously holding in place a normative masculine 'gender' to which is then assigned the range of (usually undesirable/negative) characteristics. What remains unclear, however, is what the relationship is between these structured masculinities: 'how many structures are needed to think this series of relationships? . . . if structure is simply the outcome of prior practice, albeit constrained practice, how does practice produce, and continually reproduce, something as systematic as the gender order?' (Jefferson, 1994a: 15). If hegemonic masculinity is in 'transition' (Hanke, 1992), what qualities 'maintain' the masculine in such a way that it continues to be of a 'hegemonic' kind? Hegemonic masculinity does not afford a handle on the conflicts generated between material and ideological networks of power. Nor, importantly, does it address the complexity and multi-layered nature of the social subject.

Ultimately, such issues around the ambiguities of hegemonic masculinity lead to difficult questions about what it means to engage with a politics of masculinity per se. What is to be the object of the study of masculinity (whether it is in relation to crime or not)? Is it to challenge all 'hegemonic' masculinities, whilst leaving other (subordinated) masculinities well alone (cf. the reading of crime presented by Sumner, 1990)? If so, then such an approach would be to misread Connell's (1987) original point about the ways in which all men are empowered by hegemonic masculinity. It has been argued that theories (criminological, legal) and institutions (criminal justice, the legal profession) have been vehicles for the promotion of a particular ideology of 'hegemonic masculinity' or 'masculinism'. Yet such an analysis does not address 'the theories or institutions as such, nor the significance of such statements within their specific discursive contexts' (Brown, 1990: 47). What it *does* do is conflate, by reference to a *pre-constituted definition* of the ideological or cultural meanings of 'masculinity', a number of biologistic 'myths'. The construction of hegemonic masculinity as a unifying and all-encompassing ideology of the masculine envisages an image of men's beliefs and interests which is then seen as somehow intruding 'into the "sacred" realm of theoretical or institutional practices' (Brown, 1990: 48–9). Yet, in so doing, both criminological theory and criminal justice institution are each seen as being linked together in a systematic unity of shared assumptions; they are thus depicted as being, variously, 'sexist', 'masculinist' embodiments of 'the masculinity of law' (Brown, 1990: 41). In effect, a distorted set of beliefs about the bodies of women and men is thus seen as maintaining an oppressive social order which ascribes essential (bodily) differences to women's and men's natures. Yet, crucially, these (sexed) bodies are, throughout, pre-given, pre-discursive, taken for granted.

To recap this point: within the sex/gender(ed) frame in which the hegemonic masculinity/crime relation is presently being addressed within sociogenic criminology, a recognition of diversity and difference (that not all 'masculinities', and therefore not all men, are the same) is reconciled with an approach which simultaneously purports to 'explain' the criminality of all men by reference to their (socially constructed) 'hegemonic' gender (their masculinity understood as 'a behavioural response to the particular conditions and situations in which we participate' [Messerschmidt, 1994: 88]). A recognition of the dangers of false universalism has led to the occasional (though generally rare) allowance that some qualities presently associated with 'manhood' may not necessarily be negative in all instances. Qualities which women can be seen as possessing or aspiring to (such as generosity, independence and, in certain contexts, self-sacrifice) are 'without' the frame of this masculine as it is here being constituted. However, the argument that 'real men' (that which is ascribed the status of 'hegemonic' masculinity) are inherently oppressive continues to override any investigation of the complexity of the behaviour of men in their everyday relations with women and other men. Hegemonic masculinity imposes an a priori theoretical/conceptual frame on the psychological complexity of men's behaviour. What continues to be evaded, however, are the ways in which each act of aggression or kindness, sensitivity or independence, self-sacrifice or selfishness is itself encoded at particular moments and locations as a 'masculine' or 'feminine' attribute. Ultimately, the use of the concept of hegemonic masculinity within recent accounts of men and crime serves to illustrate the more general uncertainty which surrounds a reductive conception of masculinity. This problem relates, I shall now argue, to the way in which 'masculinity' has itself been conceptualised in terms of the sex/gender distinction. It is at this point that the analysis shifts from a specific focus on masculinity to those recent attempts which have sought to reject, or transcend, this sex/gender distinction.

Phase three: sexed bodies, corporeality and the sexed subject

Identified above were three contexts in relation to which, I suggested, criminology's recent masculinity turn might usefully be located: feminism, the 'critical study' of masculinity and, more generally, a series of public debates around crime and social order in which the 'problem of masculinity' has assumed a particular significance (albeit in relation to certain crimes and contexts). At this stage I wish to add one further issue which, although it has not necessarily framed the ways in which criminology is presently seeking to address the question of the masculinity of crime, can nonetheless be seen as forming the backdrop against which the 'sex question' is presently being played out in the discipline. In seeking to surface the epistemological crisis presently facing both aetiological criminology and feminism as a consequence of wider developments in social theory (notably, around postmodernism and postcolonialism), what concerns me in this section are the implications of rethinking criminology's own modernist episteme in terms of reconceptualising the relationship between men and crime. On the one hand, there now exists within the sociology of masculinity a distinct strand of scholarship which has been influenced by these developments within postmodernism (notably, it must be said, in relation to the theorising of male subjectivity and identity: Gutterman, 1994; Jefferson, 1994a; Middleton 1992: 131–45). Within what I shall suggest is tentatively emerging as the 'third phase' of criminological work on masculinity, however, one of the primary influences has been a body of explicitly feminist postmodern and poststructuralist scholarship which has sought to rethink such key 'gender' concepts as identity, subjectivity and the 'sexed' body (Benhabib et al., 1995; Butler and Scott, 1992; Flax, 1990; Fraser and Nicholson, 1990; Fuss, 1989; Nicholson, 1990; Spivak, 1987; Weedon, 1987). Within this work, I now wish to argue, and albeit implicitly, the 'masculinity' of modernity has itself been challenged and displaced within what has become a broader, and rather different, questioning of understandings of the body, corporeality, sexual difference and sex/gender.

There is, in a sense, a 'pre-history' to these concerns, and earlier warnings of the problem of sex difference, gender and the body within criminology can be found in the work of writers such as Cousins (1980) and Greenwood (1981). Greenwood, for example, sought to question the ways in which feminist critiques of men's 'sexism', which had evolved during the 1970s, had themselves somehow passed over the underlying structure of criminological thought, with the result that an ostensibly progressive feminist politics 'might end up as a sort of laundry service, validating not only the general problematic of conventional criminology but also its specific definitions of issues concerning women, once purged of their sexism' (Brown, 1990: 45–6). The danger, Greenwood suggested, was one of feminist criminologists coming to resurrect one of the central themes of malestream criminology – the association of women and conformity and, of course, men with criminality.

In more recent years some specific concerns and engagements with questions of the role of the body and sex difference in the construction of subjectivity have become central to the work of feminist scholars (Butler, 1990, 1993; Gatens, 1983, 1996; Grosz, 1990, 1994; Grosz and Probyn, 1995; on women's bodies as the object of penality, Howe, 1994). This work has sought (among other things) to investigate how subjectivity, as the lived experience of a psychical and libidinally mapped body which gives meaning to subjects, is itself socially and culturally inscribed. In one of the first engagements with this perspective in the field of criminology, Judith Allen (1989) sought in her article 'Men, Crime and Criminology: Recasting the Questions' to relate the earlier work of Grosz and others (Leng, 1995) and, in particular, the emerging critique of the sex/gender distinction, to a re-reading of some 'classic' criminological texts. In the years since Allen's article this kind of investigation – what Daly (1997) has subsequently termed the 'sexed bodies' approach – has emerged as a distinctive perspective, both within feminist theory generally and, more recently (albeit tentatively), in criminology (Collier, 1996b; Daly, 1997). Central to this approach, and in contrast to the focus on the 'gendering' of crime through recourse to the concept of masculinity which had marked Phases One and Two discussed above, can be seen to be a concern with the sexing *and* criminalising (a sexed-criminalising?) of the bodies of men.

In the remainder of this chapter I shall seek to fuse some of the general themes of postmodern thought with some of the questions raised by this developing 'sexed bodies' perspective. I shall argue that a number of themes or issues emerge, each of which have important implications for seeking to understand the sexed specificity of crime (that is, criminology's 'sex question'). In rejecting the sex/gender distinction in view of its conceptual and political failings, the gender category of 'masculinity' itself is not simply thrown into question as a meaningful concept from which to approach the men/crime relation. An alternative, and very different, approach emerges based on a rethinking not just of the philosophical relationship of the mind/body distinction, but also of *all* those binaries which have marked modernist thought and constructed understandings of 'men' and their 'masculinity'. Disturbing or 'bursting' (Murphy, 1996) these binaries results, I wish to suggest, in some very different questions about, and in a very different conceptualisation *of*, the relationship between men, sex difference and crime.

The passive, neutral body   The sex/gender distinction, Gatens (1996) has argued, polarises accounts of the human subject characterised as being either predominantly (or wholly) determined by the influence of social or familial relations (environment/society/gender) or by biological forces (heredity/the body/sex). In so doing a neutral, pre-social, pre-discursive body is presumed.

The strategy of 'degendering' within social constructionist feminism has entailed, it is argued, a particular reading in which the body has been seen as the passive recipient of certain gender 'roles' or 'messages' (as in, for example, the social scripts or cultural expectations of 'masculinity' which informed certain criminological readings discussed above). The *sexed specificity* of the male body, however, is in effect rendered completely irrelevant in determining 'masculine' consciousness. In assuming that the body is a passive *tabula rasa* upon which social lessons are inscribed, such an approach denies what has been called the sexed specificity of subjectivity. 'Biology', understood as the complexity of products and capacities of the organism, is thus re-positioned: 'If the organisms called human beings produce culture, language, subjectivities and criminalities, these must be "in the nature of human biology" ' (Allen, 1989: 34), the use of biological here denoting 'of the animal' (Frye, 1983: 37, quoted by Allen, 1989: 34). Such a sexed body is neither brute nor passive but is 'interwoven with and constitutive of systems of meaning, signification and representation' (Grosz, 1990: 18). The questions which are asked of this body address the ways in which sexual difference *is made to signify* hierarchically:

> ... what, ontologically speaking, is the body? What is its 'stuff', its matter? ... do bodies, all bodies ... have a specifically sexual dimension which is psychically and culturally inscribed according to its morphology? Is sexual difference primary and sexual inscription a cultural overlay or rewriting of an ontologically prior differentiation? Or is sexual differentiation a product of the various forms of inscription of culturally specific bodies? Do inscriptions produce sexual differentiation? Or does sexual difference imply a differential mode of inscription? (Grosz, 1994: 189)

Or, as Butler puts it:

> ... is there a political shape 'women', as it were, that precedes and prefigures the political elaboration of their interests and epistemic point of view? ... Is 'the body' or 'the sexed body' the firm foundation on which gender and systems of compulsory sexuality operate? Or is 'the body' itself shaped by political forces with strategic interests in keeping that body bounded and constituted by the markers of sex? (1990: 128–9)

The implications of these questions for criminology are profound. By locating social practices and behaviours as being embedded in the *subject* rather than 'in consciousness' or 'in the body', this approach has the important repercussion that the subject which emerges (the 'men' of criminology, for example) is always a sexed subject (Gatens, 1996: 8–9). That is, this approach valorises *sexual difference* and leads to analyses of the specificity of female and male experiences (which in this context must mean the specificity in the experiences of men's criminality). It does so in a way which seeks to take account of the specificities of male and female bodies. Importantly, to valorise sexed specificity is not to imply a fixity/essence to the social signification of bodily functions, events or experiences (for example, the experiences of work or sexual differences in the transition from adolescence to adulthood so central to accounts of youth crime). Indeed, Gatens (1996: 9) notes, it is the importance of signification and its constitutive role in the construction of subjectivity which is actually absent from the writings of proponents of social constructionism (as we have seen above, all too clearly, in relation to the limits of hegemonic masculinity). To recognise that active processes are involved in becoming a signifying subject is also to recognise that some bodily experiences and events, though they may lack any *fixed* significance, are likely in all social structures to be privileged sites of significance. Thus, as anthropological, ethnological and historical evidence shows, 'the body can and does intervene to confirm or to deny various social significances' (Gatens, 1996: 10).

Within the terms of the dominant divisions through which criminology has framed its engagements with masculinity (such as sex/gender, man/woman), biology has been cast as fixed and immutable in much the same way that Gatens suggests. It has been seen as static, deriving from outside culture. The bodies of 'men' and 'women' thus appear as pre-theoretical constructs. Specifically, it is the bodies of men which, as the primary object of criminological knowledge, have been ascribed at different historical moments a changing set of 'gender roles' (or, in the language of the moment, masculinities) which themselves somehow 'float free' of the body. It is these 'masculinities' which are then seen as being open to contestation, resistance and cultural challenge (for example, in the form of re-socialisation and re-education programmes: see Chapter 6, p. 171). Yet, implicitly, the male body of criminology remains a passive body. Both the social constructionist and egalitarian feminist accounts discussed above (Grosz, 1990: 15) have negated the sexed specificity of the body via recourse to the argument that a number of 'sexist' myths or 'masculine' ideologies have somehow 'contaminated' the (otherwise 'pure'?) areas of criminological thought or legal decision-making in which they are to be found. And yet, as Brown (1990: 47) suggests, in so doing a set of 'distort*ed* ideas' have been read as having correspondingly 'distort*ing* consequences'. Criminology has been committed to a mind/body variant on the sex/gender opposition in which the body has been conceived of as biologically determined, fixed and ahistorical. For the social constructionist criminologist (whether of feminist, pro-feminist or other orientation) the essential shift which must take place is at the level of 'gender' ideology (challenging 'masculinism', 'taking masculinity seriously'), which is then seen to result in the body and its functions having different meanings (see, for example, Sumner's [1990] reading of hegemonic masculinity). Yet, crucially, such an approach does not involve any rethinking of the body or, importantly, any transgression of the sex/gender distinction itself. Rather, the body continues to be conceptualised as a biological reality which is then offered up as a passive surface to gendered inscription.

Sex-specific corporeality   In contrast to the above, I shall argue that it is necessary to address the specificity of the sexed (as male) body in particular cultural and historical locations. The recognition of such specificity is not to argue that men have a physically determined nature that makes them inherently different from, or superior/inferior in any sense to, women. Nor is it to embrace a wholly semiotic or cultural account (which is, ultimately, no more tenable than a biological reductionist one).[9] It is, rather, to transcend what Gatens (1996) refers to as the 'tired and tiresome' charges of essentialism and biologism so often levelled at theories of sexual difference. The intention here is not to prioritise the body *over* 'gender'; it is to rework the dualism between mind/body so that it becomes impossible to think *only* in terms of the 'mind' or the 'body'. To recognise sexual difference is not, crucially, to abrogate the field of the social and the political. Nor is it to resort to a reductionist, essentialist biologism (Grosz, 1994). Indeed, it is these very associations with reductionism, essentialism and determinism which must be seen, Allen (1989: 34) has argued, as part of the legacy of knowledges such as modernist criminology. To make reference to 'male' biology is not necessarily to subscribe to a major biologistic premise, and thus all the deduced implications of that premise (Brown, 1990: 44). It cannot be assumed that what is being said about the bodies of men is operating from a foundationalist universal premise about men's 'essential' nature (Brown, 1990: 52). Biologism, Brown (1990) has suggested, means something more than any simple hierarchy of 'male' and 'female'. This is, we must remember, a hierarchy in which men have been associated with such ideas as paternity and the public realm, sexual activity and uncomplex, unproblematic sexual urges, pathological stability and rationality. 'Female' nature has, in contrast, been attributed with some very different, and deemed inferior, attributes and modes of conduct: the maternal and the domestic sphere, passivity and an excessive (or repressive) sexuality, tendencies to hysteria and pathological instability, and so forth. What is at issue ultimately is, Brown suggests, not the essential or ontological basis of such a hierarchy but, rather, the way in which such a

> categorization of women has come to be located entirely in the realm of nature while men are placed on the other side of the boundary that separates nature from culture, determinism from freedom of will, emotion from reason. (1990: 41)

Men, it is now becoming clear, have also been constructed in particular ways – as being outside the realm of nature, as being outwith the body, as apart from the (their) bodies. The social 'reality' of the relationship between men and crime is itself always mediated (Game, 1991), the very term 'images of masculinity' problematic (Hearn, 1996: 213) in that these 'masculinities' do not pre-exist their imaging (see Hearn, 1995; Hearn and Melechi, 1992). The assumption within criminology, we have seen, has been *and continues to be* (as in the debates around 'hegemonic masculinity') that all discursive constructions of the categories of Men can be known in advance through a study of representations of masculinity/ies, read from within an invariant set of meanings and fixed oppositions. However, representations of men and women, male and female do not have such invariant and acontextual meanings. They do not have any set of readily identifiable effects (Brown, 1990: 47). To be 'rational' or 'emotional', for example, has different meanings in different contexts. A young man's 'enthusiasm' for sex over an emotional relationship might, for example, be seen as indicating a lack of rationality because of an essential biological sexual urge. In accounts of men's confrontational interpersonal violences (Polk, 1994b), men certainly do appear to have little problem expressing their emotions. The problem, as it were, is that these emotions are themselves violent, destructive and have frequently fatal consequences. There is thus a contingent, *though not arbitrary* (Gatens, 1996: 15),[10] relation between the male body and characteristics which are deemed masculine. To state as much is not to make an essentialist claim but is, rather, to recognise the importance of:

> complex and ubiquitous networks of signification to the historically, psychologically and culturally variable ways of being a man or a woman. To deny these networks and the specificity of historical forms of femininity and masculinity in favour of a conception of the subject as essentially sex-neutral will lead to the reproduction of present relations between the sexes. (Gatens, 1996: 13)

Such questionings of the bodies of men have been, I will seek to illustrate, generally avoided as a subject of theoretical engagement within both sociogenic feminism and criminology. Indeed, when biologism has been addressed, Brown (1990) notes, it has frequently been marked by a wilful misreading of criminological texts resulting from an inability to transcend the framework, concepts and reasoning of the dominant modernist epistemology. Masculinity and biologism have each been fused in a series of feminist representations of 'myths, stereotypes, images, propositions, beliefs, assumptions – about women that allows all the different critical [feminist] resources to be mobilised against the defined target' (Brown, 1990: 43). Thus, as we have seen above, the target of feminism has been the 'gender' of crime and law, a project in which the characteristics of masculinity, masculinism, and so forth, have been, in effect, equated with the power of men. In so doing, masculinity has itself been reified within feminist discourse. What a reframing of this socially constituted masculine does, in contrast, is facilitate a recognition of how the 'life of the body' can itself be seen as another source of diversity and variation in the lives of men. This does, however, raise difficult questions for criminology about 'personal space and ontology, paralleling societal space and culture', in which it becomes unclear how the concept of 'masculinity might relate to the embodied social selves of men', and how 'the body might be perceived through the leaving of traces following previous events . . . or the body might be perceived through the inscription of the social on the physical' (Hearn, 1996: 210). To begin to address such questions, what is required is a very different conceptualisation of the social subject.

The fragmented subject In seeking to challenge conventional understandings of the standpoint of the knowing subject (objectivity, neutrality, distance), postmodernism has, in turn, disturbed the subject at the heart of the traditional modernist, post-Enlightenment project. We have seen above a male criminological subject who appears as a rational, free-willed actor, a subject who engages in crime in a calculated, utilitarian way. Recent theories of the subject have, however, focused on the ways in which social identities are themselves complex and heterogeneous, and the ways in which this social subject is in fact composed of multiple and contradictory positionings or subjectivities.[11] To carry this over to a reading of the masculine subject of criminology, the point is not simply that male 'identities' are precariously achieved and never fixed; this, in itself, is broadly compatible with the notion of 'fragile' masculinity which appeared within the sociogenic accounts seen above. Rather, what we can see in those earlier positivist and frequently functionalist accounts is the presumption of an implicitly normative masculinity. Within recent accounts informed by theorising of the (postmodern) subject, in contrast, to talk about the 'masculinity' of the subject is itself, in a sense, to miss out on the ways in which perception cannot be regarded as passive but is in fact (always) an active process (Gatens, 1996; Jefferson, 1994a). From this perspective, perception can be reduced to neither the body nor consciousness but must be seen as an activity of *the subject* (see Chapter 3, pp. 89–90; Chapter 5, pp. 149–51).[12]

To clarify: postmodern accounts of subjectivity, in rendering contingent notions of 'identity', have undermined the 'natural' and 'normative' status of a dominant 'heterosexual matrix' in which particular subjectivities are constituted (Butler, 1990). From diverse perspectives – deconstructive feminism, identity politics and anti-essentialist views, 'poststructuralist . . . discursive and postmodern psychologies' (Walkerdine, 1995: 312) – 'gender' now appears as 'performative construction' naturalised through repetition (Butler, 1990, 1993; Fuss, 1989). Gender is thus understood not as singular but as a repetitive act:

> . . . the repeated stylisation of the body, a set of repeated acts within a highly rigid regulatory frame that congeal over time to produce the appearance of substance, of a natural sort of being. A political genealogy of gender ontologies, if it is successful, will deconstruct the substantive appearance of gender into its constitutive acts and locate and account for those acts within the compulsory frames set by the various forces that police the social appearance of gender. (Butler, 1990: 33; see also Probyn, 1993: 2)

The focus of analysis becomes not the nature of any one fixed, unitary masculine identity, but, rather, the way in which sexualities themselves become codified, and how this in turn informs the subjectivity of a sexed self (Probyn, 1996).

In this section I have outlined some of the problems with the sex/gender conceptualisation of masculinity. I have suggested that a different approach, that which has been termed 'sexed bodies' (Daly, 1997), may be potentially more productive in seeking to address the sexed specificity of crime and integrate questions of sexual difference. This leads us to, importantly, a very different kind of engagement with masculinity from that which had informed both traditional sociogenic and later feminist accounts within criminology. It is not to presume the existence of a pre-discursive 'masculine' subject. It is, rather, to seek instead an engagement with sex-specific corporeality in developing an understanding of the crimes of men.

(Hetero)sexualising crime and criminology

The arguments to be presented in this book draw on the work outlined in this chapter in seeking to enunciate a 'deconstructive moment' beyond the 'heterosexual matrix' (Butler, 1990). It seeks not to 'solve' a 'crisis of masculinity' but to 'elaborate the contemporary forms that this crisis is taking, and to suggest what the consequences of this might be' (Young, 1996: 2). What is taking place at the moment at the interface of feminism/ postmodernism is, I have argued in this chapter, a privileging of sexuality and the sexed body rather than concept of gender per se. Deriving from a diverse range of theoretical positions gender has been reconceived as a 'performative' construction (Butler, 1990, 1993; Fuss, 1989; Sedgwick, 1994). To be clear at the outset where these arguments have been coming from, within academic debates around sexuality and gender it has been an aim of one, arguably increasingly influential, strand of feminist and queer theory[13] (Bower, 1994; Grosz, 1994; McIntosh, 1993; Stychin, 1996; Warner, 1993) to 'disruptively resist', 'transcend' or 'subvert' the range of binary divisions through which the idea of modern 'sexuality' has been constituted. The chapters which follow will, in keeping with this general project, not take it for granted that 'gendered' power relations are in any sense primary between males/men and females/women. Rather, the readings to be presented will seek to question the discursive constitution of this heterosexual matrix, to crosscut categories and relations and to explore, importantly, the (much neglected) *mutuality* of men's hetero- and homo-sexualities (Edwards, 1994; Sedgwick, 1994; Wittig, 1992). In so doing, what follows is, in part, an investigation of how the category of 'masculin-ity' has itself served to reinforce a dominant ideology of (hetero)sexuality:

> ... to assume *a priori* that masculinity/masculinities exist is to reify the social construction of sex and gender, so that the typical dimorphism is assumed to be natural. Qualities (of masculinity/femininity) are assumed to complement other dimorphic structures of men/women, male/female or the masculine/the feminine. (Hearn, 1996: 212)

Criminology's 'masculinity', I shall argue, suggests just such a heterosexual dimorphism, part of a process which reproduces the dominant hetero-sexualising of social arrangements. Criminology is, ultimately, just one among the many discourses which have mapped multifarious bodily actions

through reference to hierarchical bi-polarities (notably those of active/
passive, hetero/homo[sex] and man/woman). Legal language and culture, for
example, through denigrating and denying legitimacy to active sexual
desires expressed outside the restrictive frames of compulsory heterosexuality (Collier, 1995a, 1996a; Moran, 1996), can similarly be seen as being
central to the reproduction of a heterosexual imperative in which 'active'
sexuality has been historically linked to the hierarchical, phallic and heterosexist polarities of the masculine gender. What is ultimately at stake in this
challenge to the (hetero)sexuality of criminology's subject becomes no less
than the shattering of all fixed gender identities and sexualities premised on
the dualisms of modernity; that is, the undermining of a heterosexual matrix
premised on a

> hegemonic discursive/epistemic model of gender intelligibility that assumes that
> for bodies to cohere and make sense there must be a stable sex expressed through
> a stable gender (masculine expresses male, feminine expresses female) that is
> oppositionally and hierarchically defined through the compulsory practice of
> heterosexuality. (Butler, 1990: 15)[14]

In the chapters which follow I shall seek to utilise these theories of
subjectivity, identity and agency in order to rethink the ways in which
cultural values are ascribed to particular gendered identities at particular
moments (identities such as those of 'criminal' or 'delinquent', the 'family
man' and 'the homosexual, the 'single parent' and the 'spree killer'). This
enterprise, crucially, addresses issues of intervention, social change and
personal experience. In focusing on the instability and multiplicity of social
identities, both the cultural scripts of 'the masculine', and the ways in which
social practices such as criminology constitute bodies as masculine/male, are
themselves rendered contingent, socially accountable and open to change.
This approach 'writes in' to the analysis of men and crime the agency of the
social subject. The notion of 'identity' with which we are working here
emerges as always partial, uncertain and fragmented, constituted through
reference to its dependency on that which is defined as 'other' (Gutterman,
1994: 221) (and that which, we shall see, might always reappear). What
follows in this book is about the 'other' of men's criminality – about that
through reference to which men are constituted as criminal, are criminalised
and, importantly, resist criminalisation. This criminal(ised) subject is a
social agent constituted by an ensemble of 'subject positions' that can never
be totally fixed in a closed system of differences, constructed by a diversity
of discourses among which there is no necessary relation but a constant
movement of over-determination and displacement. The identity of such a
multiple and contradictory subject is, I have suggested, always contingent
and precarious, temporarily fixed at the intersection of subject positions and
dependent on specific forms of identification (Mouffe, 1992: 372).

It is necessary to be clear, at the outset, as to the limitations of this project.
To 'deconstruct' the heterosexual man of criminology is not, in itself,

sufficient to understand the contours of the formation of individual subjective commitments in any particular instance. It does not, for example, explain *why* fragmented positionings may be held together by individuals in such a way as to produce the subjective experience of 'identity': '. . . what is the relationship of the discursively produced subject to how the subject is "lived", in relation to historicity and materiality? How is a non-unitary, non-rationalist subject held together?' (Walkerdine, 1995: 313). Nor does it address 'how potential subject positions become actual subjectivities . . . what motivates people to "choose" to invest in or identify with one discursive position rather than another?' (Jefferson, 1994a: 25). What would be required to begin to address such questions is a concept of subjectivity which, as Jefferson suggests, cannot be reduced either to the intentions of consciously choosing subjects nor simply to the effects of language/ discourse. Between 'society, structures and discourses, the subject, personality and life-histories; the question of conceptualising their interpenetration in a non-dualistic, non-deterministic fashion remains' (Jefferson, 1994a: 29).

Such questions are beyond the remit of this book. What this book seeks to present is a perhaps more modest exploration of subjectivity understood as embodiment, subjectivity as the lived experience of a (specifically masculine) body as it is socially and culturally inscribed;[15] that is, an engagement with the (re)production of the male subject of criminology in such a way that it becomes possible to render political and accountable the very categories with which we are operating when we seek to talk about the 'masculinity of crime'.

Concluding remarks

It is difficult to see how criminology can resolve the debate presently occurring around 'taking masculinity seriously' by evoking a foundationalist conception of gender which separates out men's masculinities (their gender) from their (sexed) bodies. Ultimately, it is not difficult to see where the questions raised by this debate are leading: '. . . for by increasing the complexities of the categories of men, the possibility is raised that all foundations of knowledge are flawed' (Hearn, 1996: 211). To dismiss the postmodern-influenced 'feminosceptic' strand within contemporary criminology (Heidensohn, 1994: 1029) as simply a trend *within* an otherwise 'intact' aetiological discipline is to misread the challenge taking place to a subject which appears incapable of escaping its own positivist legacy (Smart, 1990; see Chapter 6). In exploring the conceptual foundations of the way in which a relationship between 'masculinity' and 'crime' has been constructed within and beyond criminological discourse, I have argued that it is, by itself, misleading to claim that academic criminology has hitherto 'failed' to engage with the crimes of men as 'gendered' beings. An engagement with masculinity has been long present within criminological thought. At issue, however, is *the ways in which* masculinity has been conceptualised. The theoretical framework I have outlined in this chapter, and which will inform the rest of this book, is concerned to address the ways in which ideas of the body, sexual difference and subjectivity are presently being silenced in these debates around the relationship between men, masculinities and crime.

The project of corporeal feminism (Leng, 1995) or 'sexed bodies' (Daly, 1997) has, I have suggested, exposed the production of discourses of masculinity as a process of sexual division or exclusion. Recent feminist theoretical practices have sought to locate an absence of sexual difference within dominant modes of knowledges and representations. Criminology is one such mode of knowledge which has sought to collapse all subject positions into one 'humanity'. Feminist practice, in contrast, has unearthed a sexually specific subject (male, masculine) lying beneath the supposedly universal and neutral human category. The perspective of sexed bodies offers a way forward 'outside', or beyond, the confines of the sex/gender distinction. It promises new understandings of the men/crime relation. The focus of feminist concern, Gatens (1996) has suggested, should be an engagement with sex(ual) difference, and not masculinity, femininity, and so forth, at least as conceived in social constructionist terms. If one accepts the notion of this sexually specific subject, it then becomes necessary to dismiss the notion that 'patriarchy' or the power of men can be characterised as a system of social organisation which systematically and unproblematically valorises the masculine gender over the feminine gender. Rather, it is to see the particular sexed bodes of men as being valorised within a particular system of signification, as the focus turns to the activity of signification rather than behaviourist-oriented conceptions of the passive subject. This is not, importantly, to depoliticise men's crimes. Far from it. It is to see the body as a 'political object par excellence'. The current locations of the (male) body are, as we shall see, contestable and redefinable. Ultimately, as Hearn notes, 'the materialist deconstruction of masculinity is necessary as one part of the materialist deconstruction of the category of sex' (1996: 214). In so doing, we have seen in this chapter, in the analysis of the relationship between men and crime the concept of 'masculinity may not be the most appropriate or relevant' place from which to begin (Hearn, 1996: 210).

Notes

1. Men constitute between 80 and 90 per cent of all known offenders. When compared to their proportion in the population, women are under-represented amongst those cautioned or found guilty for indictable offences in England and Wales. Women constitute a small proportion of the prison population. Four out of five known young offenders are male (Home Office, 1993). There now exist a range of breakdowns of criminal statistics based on sex (for example, Heidensohn, 1994; Naffine, 1997: 6). One in sixty of a sample of men had a conviction by the age of forty for some type of sexual offence (Marshall, 1997).

2. 'Fear of Crime': Research study conducted by LORI for October Films, August 1995, quoted in *Ten Key Messages About Crime* (NACRO, 1996). One in five adults questioned for the British Crime Survey 1996 stated they were 'very worried' about being burgled, mugged or having their car stolen or broken into (Audit Commission, 1996: 5).
3. Notwithstanding the limits of arrest data, criminalities measured by other means, such as victim and self-report surveys, generally confirm the sex differential, though disclosing rates of female criminalities higher than officially recorded (Heidensohn, 1994: 1005). Taking data on 'private' harms perpetrated in the home into account, it is likely that the gender ratio would be adversely affected for men since it is men who are largely, though not exclusively, the offenders in such crimes.
4. Heidensohn (1995: 81) notes how the move towards privileging of the concept of masculinity 'poses major problems for feminists', who, she states, do not, and cannot, share such a standpoint.
5. The expansion in the literature has, in particular, been marked in the period since 1987 (the year of publication of Connell's *Gender and Power*).
6. The legacy of this project is, Garland (1994) suggests, evident in the growth of more pragmatic, policy-oriented administrative projects which seek to use science in the service of management and control. The distinction between these two traditions is not meant to be hard and fast. It is Garland's argument that the combination of the two has been essential to criminology's claim to be sufficiently 'useful' and 'scientific' to merit the status of an accredited, state-sponsored academic discipline: on which, see Chapter 2.
7. See further, on law and non-consummation, Collier (1992).
8. The following section borrows from the reading of Gatens (1996).
9. Connell has argued that 'social constructionist approaches to gender and sexuality underpinned by a semiotic approach to the body provide an almost complete antithesis to socio-biology. Rather than arrangements being the effects of the body-machine, the body is a field on which social determination runs riot' (1995: 50). Connell's concern is that 'with so much emphasis on the signifier, the signified tends to vanish' (1995: 50–1), resulting, he suggests, in a 'disembodying' of sex. Gender, moreover, 'is hardly in better case, when it becomes just a subject-position in discourse, the place from which one speaks, when gender is seen as, above all, a performance; or when the rendering contradictions within gendered lives become "an instatement of metaphor" ' (Connell, 1995: 51).
10. '. . . modes of defensive behaviour that utilise culturally shared phantasies about biology . . . these traits are manifestations of and reactions to the (conscious and unconscious) ideas which we share about biology. . . . Masculinity and femininity as forms of sex-appropriate behaviours are manifestations of a historically based, culturally shared phantasy about male and female biologies' (Gatens, 1996: 13).
11. See, for example, Bell and Valentine (1995); Butler (1990, 1993); Fuss (1989); Hollway (1989); McRobbie (1994, Ch. 4); Pile and Thrift (1995); Probyn (1993, 1996). The section follows the argument of Jefferson (1994a).
12. Corporeal feminism maintains that if one wants to understand sex and gender – or, that is, a person's biology and the social and personal significance of that biology as lived – what is ultimately required is an analysis of the imaginary body. In the work of Grosz (1994), Gatens (1996) and others, and drawing on feminist re-readings of Freud, this project involves developing a theoretical description of the process whereby male and female biologies become 'lived' as masculine and feminine subjectivities; that is, the development of an understanding of the emotional and libidinal investment obtaining between the subject and her or his body (see Daly, 1997; Leng, 1995): 'The imaginary body

is socially and historically specific in that it is constructed by a shared language; the shared psychical significance and privileging of various zones of the body (for example, the mouth, the anus, the genitals); and common institutional practices and discourses (for example, medical, juridical and educational) which act on and through the body' (Gatens, 1996: 12). Criminology, and the crimino-legal domain more generally, provide just such institutional practices and discourses. Such analyses of the imaginary body show it to be the site of the historical and cultural specificity of particular ideas of masculinity and femininity. Thus 'it is to the imaginary body that we must look to find the key or the code to the decipherment of the social and personal significance of male and female biologies as lived in culture, that is, masculinity and femininity' (Gatens, 1996: 12).

13. Queer theory and politics has been identified as a stance which is generated from a position of dissent, set up in resistance to attempts at rigid categorisation (for example, hetero/homosexual) within both dominant culture and, importantly, sexual subcultures (see further Stychin, 1996).

14. 'The heterosexualization of desire required and institutes the production of discrete and asymmetrical oppositions between "feminine" and "masculine", where these are understood as expressive attributes of "male" and "female" ' (Butler, 1990: 17); see also Wittig, 1992.

15. It is Grosz's (1994) argument that human subjects give meaning to their biologies, to their bodies and their existence, have investment in their bodies. The body always means something. See also Butler: 'We may be tempted to think that to assume the subject in advance is necessary in order to safeguard the agency of the subject. But to claim that the subject is constituted is not to claim that the subject is determined. On the contrary, the constituted character of the subject is the very precondition of its agency' (1990: 12).

2 Boys' Own Stories? Law, Criminology and (Un)Sexy Bodies

Masculinity, I have argued in Chapter 1, has been conceptualised within sociogenic criminology primarily through reference to the sex/gender binary. As a result the male body has been seen as neutral and pre-discursive, a *tabula rasa* on which various ideas of 'masculinity/ies' – the cultural scripts of 'being a man' and so forth – are then inscribed. Within the emerging repositioning of the idea of the sexed body which is presently taking place within postmodern feminist and queer theoretical scholarship, however, I have suggested that these sociogenic understandings of 'masculinity' are themselves challenged and disturbed. In this chapter I shall seek to develop this analysis and explore some of the implications of the 'sexed bodies' approach via an investigation of what has been, and remains, one of the most neglected areas of the criminological enterprise: the sexed/gendered relationship between what might be termed the 'subjects' and 'objects' of the criminological gaze. For the criminologist, the majority of whom we shall see are men, the recognition that the subjectivity of the 'researcher' is formed like that of those who are 'researched' has many implications. The analysis presented in Chapter 1 sought to question the nature of criminological reasoning. In order to progress this investigation of what it means to speak of the 'masculinity' of criminology in the first place, in this chapter I will seek to explore further what it means to 'do' criminology in terms of gendered or sexed performativity. This chapter, in short, seeks to develop the conceptual critique of masculinity introduced above by focusing not on criminological reasoning, but on the 'making of men' within two particular areas of the crimino-legal[1] field. It seeks to bring this discussion of the 'masculinity of crime', at the outset, somewhat 'closer to home' by focusing not on the (male) offender or victim, but on a rather different category of men – those 'other' men who have been concerned with the regulation, control and explanation of crime. The specific focus of this discussion is the representation and reproduction of the ways in which a range of categories of men's subjectivities are presently encoded as masculine (and, specifically, heterosexual) within the institutional and organisational contexts of, firstly, the legal profession and, secondly, the 'social world of British criminology'.

Criminology, law and the 'sexing' of men

A word of explanation is required at the outset for the choice of these two institutional and discursive fields. Criminology and law are, of course, different discourses and, given the diverse range of institutions and practices which comprise the crimino-legal, a focus on the areas of law and academic criminology is necessarily selective. Other aspects of crimino-legal practice might equally have been chosen: for example, the way in which the subjects of 'men' are constituted within media representations of crime, within the practices of the probation service, the police, the prison system, the courts, and so forth. The criminal justice system itself is made up of a diverse array of institutions and personnel, each with differing and frequently competing norms and internal cultures. Indeed, it is difficult to talk of a coherent criminal justice 'system' at all (Cavadino and Dignan, 1997). Its components embrace (at the very least) law enforcement, the courts and the prison system, a concern with the prevention and detection of crime, and the apprehension, adjudication, sentencing, punishment and rehabilitation of offenders (Lacey, 1994; Martin and Jurik, 1996: 4). In such a context, to focus narrowly on academic criminology and legal practice is to leave this discussion open to the charge of tackling questions of men, sex and gender in areas which may have little to do with the everyday 'reality' of crime and criminal justice per se. In the case of law this problem is compounded. In an increasingly bifurcated legal profession, the worlds of the corporate commercial multi-national law firm (Galanter, 1983), the high street practice and the criminal legal aid firm appear increasingly distinct. An engagement with criminal justice is but a small part of the work of the legal profession when seen as a whole, and the sexed cultures of law/legal practice might thus seem a marginal consideration when seen in the context of a discussion of men, masculinities and crime.

Notwithstanding the purchase of the above points, I shall argue in this chapter that a *mutual* analysis of both law and criminology – of what they share as much as how they differ – can in fact reveal much about the ways in which the 'sexing' of men outlined in Chapter 1 relates to the constitution of social, cultural and economic capital as a gendered phenomenon within the crimino-legal field more generally. The principal reason for looking at these seemingly distinct, though I shall argue in fact overlapping, areas relates to the ways in which both law and criminology have been depicted as 'masculine' domains within feminist scholarship at the levels of both theory and methodology. Both law and criminology represent areas of the broader crimino-legal field in which a gendered critique has been particularly well developed within feminist scholarship. With regard to each, importantly, the concept of masculinity has been accorded a central significance in seeking to understand and challenge the power of men. Both law and criminology have been represented within feminist theory as 'masculinist', as being suffused with an ideology of 'masculinism', as reflecting or embodying a dominant 'masculinity', and so forth.

A number of dimensions have informed the characterisation of law, criminology and criminal justice as somehow being quintessentially masculine. Empirically, men dominate the upper echelons of both the legal profession and the academic institutions concerned with the production of knowledge about law and crime. Women remain a small minority in the realms of law-making, criminal justice and in the upper echelons of higher education. In terms of theory, within both law and criminology the charge of being 'masculinist' has been equated with the discipline's historical association with positivist, androcentric and scientific reasoning, as discussed in Chapter 1. In respect of each, that which is 'feminine' has been seen to have been excluded, marginalised and/or effaced. Whether it is in relation to the legal profession (conceptualised here as encompassing both legal practice and the law school: Thornton, 1996a), criminal justice practices or the criminological academy, theorising 'masculinity' and 'masculinism' has thus been central to the development of feminist understandings of and attempts to challenge the processes whereby men and women are (or are not) constituted as members of the jurisprudential and criminological communities. Women's entry into hitherto male-dominated spheres, whether it be criminal justice occupations traditionally held by men (Martin and Jurik, 1996), the legal profession or the academy (Thornton, 1996a, 1996b), has been constructed as the 'exception', as the 'problem', the issue which is to be discussed under the rubric of 'women and . . .' law, 'women and . . .' crime, 'women and . . .' criminology, and so forth (Martin and Jurik, 1996). What has been less explored is the question of *why* this should be the case and, crucially, what the framing of the debate in such a way tells us about the sexed bodies of men. Theoretically, the focus on these two areas provides an ideal opportunity to explore what insights, if any, may be derived from the scholarship outlined in Chapter 1 on the relationship between identity, subjectivity and corporeality in seeking to reconceptualise what it means to speak of 'masculine' cultures of criminology and law. In what follows I shall, accordingly, advance the methodology based on sexual difference by way of seeking to ground an account of men and women's 'gendered' existences in a constitutive analysis of law and crimino-legal institutions. In so doing, I shall argue, new light is shed on the nature of these purportedly 'masculinist' exclusions. When the focus shifts away from 'masculinity' and towards questions of sex-specific corporeality within the processes of production of criminological and legal knowledge, both the 'man of law' and 'criminological man' – the *criminologist as a man* – themselves appear as sexed, specific and contingent subjects. This, I shall suggest, has far-reaching implications for understanding the 'masculinity' not just of crime, but of criminology itself. In shifting the gaze from the offender to the criminologist, in turning *to* the mainstream – to the men of law and criminology –, what is opened out to analysis is an examination of the transmission of 'official' sex/gender codes through systems of management, instruments of discipline, and institutional values and rituals within institutions which have historically been concerned, as we have seen, with the production of knowledge about men, masculinities and crime. When it comes to the ways in which the bodies of men have been empowered through an encoding as masculine, the worlds of the legal profession and academic criminology have, I shall suggest, much more in common than might otherwise at first appear to be the case.

The structure of the argument

The argument to be presented in this chapter is divided into four parts. The first seeks to unpack the ways in which the male body has been conceptualised within feminist scholarship concerned to challenge the masculinism of both criminology and law. The second explores the iconography of men's legal 'professionalism' via an engagement with the masculine body 'at work' and, in particular, the ways in which the relationship between men, child care and conceptions of 'parenting' and 'career success' has been understood in the fields of law and the legal profession. The third addresses these same questions in the context of the social world of British criminology, drawing on a range of texts in which criminology has recently sought to reflect back to itself on its own project, its social and institutional infrastructure and practices. These sections, together, draw on a reading of the sexed male body in seeking to develop an understanding of the links which exist between the social worlds, institutional relationships and practices of law and criminology, and the ways in which, with regard to each, feminist critiques continue to be marginalised. The fourth section brings together the arguments presented thus far in a discussion of the ways in which shifting organisational/institutional, social, economic and cultural contexts are, at the end of the twentieth century, presently reconfiguring the subject positions available to men within the domains of both the legal profession and academic criminology. Conclusions address what some of the implications of this shift within the theoretical framework in which masculinity is conceptualised might be for seeking to understand these changes, what it means to engage with the politics of 'doing law, doing criminology' in terms of the problematisation of 'masculinity'.

Reframing the 'problem' of 'women and . . .' law, criminology and criminal justice

That a correlation exists between the characteristics of masculinity and the ethos, organisations and skills associated with working in the fields of law and criminal justice has been central to feminist engagements, both at the level of theoretical scholarship and with regard to 'practical' interventions designed to undermine, and challenge, what has been seen to be the pervasive 'masculinism' of those fields. Whilst the topics and issues addressed within the field of feminist jurisprudence have been broad, encompassing such subjects as the family, sexuality, reproduction, parenting, ethics and legal reasoning, a concern with (men's) crime and criminal justice has also figured prominently as exemplifying the more general argument that law is a masculine/ist discourse. In some accounts, it is the state itself which has been presented as masculine/male (for example, MacKinnon, 1987). The 'overlap' between feminist jurisprudence and criminology, as it were, has thus been considerable. Notwithstanding the changes which have taken place over the last twenty years in the gender profile of both the legal profession and the field of criminal justice, both in Britain and elsewhere, the picture which emerges from a now extensive body of feminist research is, across jurisdictions, one of legal and criminal justice professions, institutions and organisations in which discrimination and inequality in the employment of women is commonplace at the levels of recruitment, promotion and career advancement (on law see: McGlynn, 1996; McGlynn and Graham, 1995; Podmore and Spencer, 1982; Somerlad, 1994; Thornton, 1994, 1996a). As repeated and high-profile examples from different areas of the crimino-legal domain illustrate, they are also fields in which sexual harassment is pervasive.[2]

To 'describe' and recount the existence of such treatment – which is, explicitly it must be remembered, about behaviour on the part of men – takes the analysis so far. Certainly, at present in Britain 'women and the law' is itself a high-profile and contested political issue.[3] However, a body of recent feminist research has sought to build on and develop this focus on 'describing' the features of women's treatment by moving towards, instead, a conceptualisation of the social dynamics whereby such discrimination is reproduced and legitimated on a daily basis; in, that is, the 'everyday' interactions of men and women, men and other men.[4] This has entailed recourse to a theoretical framework in which 'Women' have been depicted as other to the (masculine) norm, be it in relation to crime, criminal justice or law. From this perspective, far from assuming that transformative change will follow women's 'acceptance' into these domains, it is the gendered encoding of social, cultural and symbolic capital within the specific field in question which has been seen to result in the masculinist character of those cultures and practices which, intimately intertwined with their functional and facilitative role in advanced capitalism, 'prevent[s] women from being regarded as authoritative members of the . . . community to the same extent as their male counterparts' (Thornton, 1996b: 2; cf. Menkel-Meadow, 1986).[5] Traditional theories of human capital, hierarchy and structural organisational analyses have, it is argued, systematically failed to address the dimensions of sex, gender and power which are, in contrast, central to the emerging feminist scholarship (Thornton, 1996b: 21).

By locating both the legal field and the domains of criminal justice and criminology within the broader context of the social, economic and cultural processes whereby men's discrimination of women is both reproduced and legitimated, a rather different set of issues and questions have emerged from those which have framed the liberal-legal equality model (the following list is by no means exclusive). First, the concept of a 'masculine career mode' has been identified as, alongside the social structuring of child care in terms of sexual division, locating men as 'unencumbered' beings whilst confining women to the 'double-shift' (the 'women don't have wives model': on lawyering and 'family life' see Mossman, 1994). Secondly, the related 'fast-tracking' of men (whether as academics or lawyers) and 'feminisation' of bureaucratic environments has been seen as ascribing to women 'caring' (for example, pastoral) roles which, whilst crucial to promulgating the appearance of a humanising ethos within the workplace, nonetheless work against women in terms of career advancement (Somerlad, 1994). Thirdly, and drawing on a phenomenon well documented within the sociology of masculinity, the existence of homosocial bonds and cultures has been identified as both excluding women and militating against women's progression within a range of organisations (Bell, 1995; Collier, 1991; Thornton, 1989). Fourthly, central to women's marginality has been seen to be the pervasive *sexualising* of women's corporeality in the workplace, resulting in a negation of women's authority and status as legitimate legal 'knowers' in the public domain. Like nature, women by virtue of their sexed specificity are 'natural, marked by fecundity and growth ... apparently uncontrolled and uncontrollable' (McDowell, 1995: 80).

In each of the above four areas, of course, something is being said about the behaviour of men and the 'structured relations of hierarchic heterosexuality' (Hearn, 1987: 114). Something is also being said, I now wish to argue, about the sexed specificity of *men's* bodies as characterised in Chapter 1. In revealing the sociality of this 'imaginary' masculine ideal as a discursive construct, the ostensibly 'natural' quality of the subject to which women have been constituted as other – the actions of the 'benchmark man', the 'man of law', the men who act in discriminatory ways – is itself rendered problematic. If women's corporeality has been sexualised in the workplace, what, in short, does this say about the bodies of men?

In order to take the analysis further and develop an understanding of the ways in which these complex configurations between sex, gender and power are reproduced and played out, it is necessary to reconfigure the sexed specificity of men's subjectivities within the specific organisational and institutional contexts of, firstly, the legal profession and, secondly, the criminological academy. Institutions do not merely 'reflect' a dominant sexual ideology; they are, crucially, sites for the active production of gender divisions. Indeed, what is presently emerging from the growing literature on the gendering of organisations and bureaucracy (Adkins, 1995; Collinson and Hearn, 1994, 1996; Davies, 1996) is something of the complexity of the processes whereby practices have been historically constituted through reference to a 'masculinist' vision of 'professional' work; and, inter alia, with the implications of the 'sexing' of professionalism for women and, increasingly, for men (Collinson and Hearn, 1996). Notwithstanding contradictions, ambiguities and tensions in the process of their constitution, both law and criminology can thus be conceptualised as domains for the 'making' of masculine subjectivities. As 'deeply gendered and heterosexual regimes, [which] construct relations of domination and subordination' (Mac an Ghaill, 1994: 4), they function to constitute and regulate, to varying degrees, a range of subject positions available to men.

To recap the theoretical underpinning of the analysis which follows: an engagement with the sexed specificity of men's subjectivities is not possible without an adequate conceptualisation of the ways in which the bodies of men are themselves sexed as 'masculine' in specific contexts (Waldby, 1995). What is necessary here is an understanding of men's corporeality, as depicted in Chapter 1. To focus on the 'fictive feminine' and the 'imagined masculine' as cultural constructs is not to argue that 'real' men's and women's bodies do not exist (Thornton, 1996a). It does not follow that sexual difference has no meaning. Rather, it is to valorise – rather than negate – the processes whereby the bodies of women and men are constituted at particular moments and contexts as having differential access to 'knowledge' resulting from their embodied social locations in a gendered world (Gatens, 1996; Grosz, 1990, 1994). Positioning within a particular gendered scene of vision does not mean that all men will necessarily have that vision. However, it does mean that, as men, a particular (but non-reductive) relationship will be established with cultures and discourses of 'the masculine'. What is clear from research on discrimination against women in the legal profession and the academy generally, let alone in the criminal justice field, is that the *potential* situations of men and women are different because of the ways in which the existing distribution of social, cultural and symbolic capital is presently configured. As such, the constitution of suitably 'professional' and 'masculine' bodies and subjectivities can be seen as important factors in the production and maintenance of normative constructs of social, economic and cultural capital which have, in turn, served to marginalise and discriminate against women in a range of areas of employment. Discrimination does not just 'happen'. It is a significance attached to the (inter)actions of sexed individuals in specific contexts.

In the following section I shall explore and expand on the contours of this 'sexing' of men via reference to a range of representations of men as legal professionals. I shall seek to answer the following questions: How do these subject positions make claims to authority? How – as distinctly 'masculine' identities – are they empowered (or, at times, disempowered)? The gendering of cultural, symbolic and economic capital in the legal field has been secured, I shall argue, via a two-fold process involving, firstly, a dissociation of men from child care (premised on the public/private dualism); and, secondly, a 'de-sexing' of men's corporeality in such a way that rationality, authority, the capacity to be objective and distant, and so forth, have each been evoked as 'key' masculine qualities. If there is a recurring theme in what follows it is, we shall see, not so much the 'hegemony' of one form of masculinity as the contingency, fragility and instability of ideas of 'normal' male heterosexual identity per se; and, related to this, the sociality of those binaries which, as we have seen in Chapter 1, have been (and remain) central to (but unspoken of in) debates around the masculinism of law and crime.

'Men in suits': authority and sexed representations of legal professionalism

> Sitting across from a man in a business suit, it is as if they did not have a body at all, just a face and a voice.
>
> (Charles Reich, quoted in Reynaud, 1983: 24)

> men in suits during heatwaves
> men in suits being cologne cool in heatwaves
> men in suits walking with precision during heatwaves
> men in suits wearing distinguished ties in heatwaves
> men in suits with tight collars in heatwaves . . .
> sons of men in suits rolling forward towards those days when
>   they will become men in suits allowing nothing to
>   get in the way: undeterred by any kind of weather
>
> (excerpt from Joanne Burns, 'Genetics')[6]

The gender regimes of both law school and legal practice can be seen as microcosms of broader employment structures in which a particular (hetero-)familial frame has ascribed social meanings in such a way that terms like 'career', 'parenting' or 'child care' have become entwined within a dualism of sexual difference. Indeed, both associate public, visible displays of 'availability' to work long hours with an individual's personal commitment to the institution and to the development of an appropriate 'professional' attitude. In the case of the legal practice the primary reduction of lawyer's work to an economic nexus via the commodification of time captured in the dominant culture of 'billing' hours can be seen as emblematic of a career structure in which success is premised on 'visible commitment' and 'paying dues' (in the form of working long hours, being 'seen' to 'be there': Somerlad, 1994). This is a career structure with which academics are, of course, becoming increasingly familiar (Wills, 1996) and which pervades many areas of employment. It has been via reference to the cultural norms of the post-war business and corporate world that the 'professional style' of the practising lawyer has been constituted (Mort, 1996; Roper and Tosh, 1991). Yet the sexed specificity of this style has, in marked contrast to the growing literature on the corporeality of women in the profession, remained largely unexplored. What I shall term the resulting 'de-sexing' of men's bodies within legal practice has been dependent, however, on certain deeply problematic assumptions.

To clarify: feminist scholarship has explored at some length the representation and regulation of the disciplinary controls exerted over women's dress in legal practice and the law school. What has emerged has been a complex picture of the multifarious dimensions to the processes whereby women are regulated within parameters which constitute 'being feminine' as, per se, a sexualised state (Thornton, 1996a: 224-5). This 'sexing' of women, however, begs a number of questions about the status of 'being masculine' in this context. Consider the following. If it is argued that women's bodies inappropriately 'eroticise' a courtroom, that women are tolerated in a rational space as legal professionals only if they consciously 'suppress' the 'feminine' 'non-rational elements perceived to be corrosive of legality' (Thornton, 1996a: 226–7), does this then mean that the 'masculine' body somehow 'naturally' embodies rationality, legality and order? If overt messages of corporeality suggest a woman's presence in a courtroom is eroticising an otherwise rational public sphere, what does this say about men's bodies? Does this mean that a court consisting solely of men is without, or beyond, the erotic? Such an argument would presume, firstly, that intra-male relations are asexual (thus revealing the presumptive hetero-sexism which frames understanding of men's social relations: Edwards, 1990); and, secondly, that as 'sexed' beings, men's eroticism is confined to the private, affective sphere (in keeping with the depiction of men's 'unencumbered' relation to child care discussed above). It is not simply that the implicit, and apparently rigid, hetero/homo dualism sits uneasily with the existence of the pervasive and well-documented homosociality of the legal and political worlds (and, indeed, of academia). It also begs the question of why the maintenance of these dualisms should appear to be so central to securing the stability of the normative masculine subject in the first place. With this in mind, and in seeking to relate this 'professional' 'asexuality' of men to the mobilisation of forms of cultural and symbolic capital as a sexed/gendered phenomenon, what might the 'return of the feminine' mean for a subject which has been encoded – by virtue of being 'male' – as an authoritative speaker within the legal field?

There exists considerable variation among men lawyers in term of their dress, style and deportment. The worlds of the corporate commercial multi-national (Galanter, 1983), the high street practice and the criminal legal aid firm are so different they belie the idea that the legal profession is a homogeneous entity (Cain, 1994: 26–7; Hagan and Kay, 1995; Sugarman, 1994). The 'aggressive masculinity' which has been identified as informing social practices in corporate City firms, epitomised by 'tough' negotiating styles and excessive 'macho' behaviour (McDowell, 1995), certainly appears of a different order to the workplace cultures of high street legal practice. A very different political orientation, interpersonal style and work commitment may inform the lives of the City and criminal legal aid lawyer. There is, moreover, a great diversity to men's bodies. Different shapes, ages, ethnicities, class backgrounds and physical abilities all mark the body in different ways. The body 'at work' may also not be what it seems. Behind the suit may lie transgression, in the form of tattooing, body piercing, of a subject 'passing' as one thing but 'really' being another (Bell and Valentine, 1995). Notwithstanding the above, however, it is possible to identify a broadly hegemonic masculine style of the lawyer which corresponds, by and large, to Connell's description of professionalism as a historically constituted form of masculinity:

> ... emotionally flat, centred on a specialist skill, insistent on professional esteem and technically based dominance over other workers, and requiring for its highest (specialist) development the complete freedom from child care and domestic work. (Connell, 1987: 181)

It is, generally, the style of the corporate, business and governmental world and its central icon is the business suit.

This 'smart' or 'distinguished' outfit is neither complicated nor very varied, encompassing a two- or three-piece suit in a (very) dark colour, black or dark coloured shoes, a pale shirt, white and, more often or not, dull socks and underwear (Reynaud, 1983: 23).[7] Thornton similarly depicts the man in the dark suit, plain shirt and unostentatious tie as 'most commonly equated with the image of impersonal authority' (1996a: 223). He is the epitome of Connell's disembodied, rational worker. In the organisational context of the legal profession, in which the marketing of personal attributes is widely seen as part of the product of good effective lawyering (the ability to interact with clients for example), the wearing of the business suit does more than 'impersonalise' men's appearance. It serves the crucial function of desexualising the male body, not in the sense of rendering men in suits beyond erotic attachment (far from it), but rather in terms of erasing the sexed specificity of the individual male body. Whereas women lawyers, like other business and professional women, 'are expected to look like women – that is, *sexed* – although the code requires that they do not look *sexual*' (Thornton 1996a: 226–7), men do not look 'sexed' for what is here considered to be 'sexual' would deflect from the establishment of authority. By constituting the wearing of the business suit as cultural and symbolic capital, the women lawyer can only be 'a pale copy of her male counterpart in both appearance and style' (Thornton, 1996a: 223).

Such a regulation of feminine and masculine forms of embodiment does not just serve to maintain a traditional gender ordering in the workplace. It also constitutes men, as paradigmatic agents of legality, as

> a neutral conduit of ... knowledge. To obtrude one's bodily persona detracts from the neutrality, the objectivity, and the universality of law. The male body is invisible in the business suit that disguises both primary and secondary characteristics. And this body is normative within the public sphere, it has come to represent neutrality and *dis*embodiment. (Thornton, 1996a: 216)

This is a male bodily persona which is, within the public sphere generally, constituted as an authoritative 'knowing' subject. The man who speaks with a suit takes up a position of authority. The occasional (socially licensed) 'dressing down' simply betrays the hegemony of this cultural norm, particularly when it is itself institutionalised (in the form of 'Casual Fridays' for example). Men are 'seen' in the context of the business and government world by virtue of wearing a suit. To dress otherwise is, in a sense, not to be 'seen'. At the individual level it denotes maturity, progression and acceptance into institutional/organisational norms. A senior colleague in my own institution, a university where dress codes might seem (on the surface at least, as we shall see) more liberal and relaxed than within the profession, made quite explicit his conscious choice, as his academic career progressed, that it would be appropriate for him to change his dress from the casual wear (corduroys, jumper) of his 'youthful' days to the regular wearing of the business suit. This was, he stated, the only way to be 'taken seriously' by those (men) in positions of authority in the university. He 'felt more powerful, more authoritative' and responded to others accordingly. It is not by chance that comic figures wear bright, ill-fitting or stylistically archaic suits.

I am not arguing here that the processes whereby professional codes are inculcated into the legal initiate work on a *tabula rasa*. The point is that men have already absorbed the messages and, importantly, appear able and willing to discipline themselves in terms of appropriately masculine dress, voice and authoritative demeanour. The male legal recruit appears to face few of the disciplinary twists and turns faced by women (Seron and Ferris, 1995; Thornton, 1996a). Notwithstanding the complex codes of 'manly aesthetics' and pervasive cultural commodification of the male body which has marked advanced capitalism (Mort, 1996), it continues to be taken for granted that, at least in the business and corporate domain, the body is of 'secondary' importance. The suit thus enables a man's body to 'blend in to uniformity and to use dress as the symbol of his power. ... Masculine elegance provides a good example of the way man asserts himself through standardisation and through control over his body' (Reynaud, 1983: 22).

The degree to which individual men seek, consciously or unconsciously, to efface that which is culturally coded as feminine, with all its connotations of dependency and passivity, may relate to the contingencies of life history. Certainly, it would seem that the emotional costs of the 'high-pressure' stressful career in law play out differently within and between the sexes. Political persuasion, sexuality, physique, accent and social background might each render individual men more or less comfortable accommodating the style of the 'benchmark man'. A man's voice which comports with a feminine standard (and is thus associated with homosexuality) may, for example, also diminish his authority in the eyes of other men (Thornton, 1996a: 221). Others, by virtue of ethnicity or class, may never be in the privileged position to face such decisions in the first place, having already been excluded as 'players' in the legal field. However, and notwithstanding the fact that they are also disciplined by the regulatory codes of legal professionalism, men have available to them cultures of *resistance* to these dominant cultural norms in the form of a range of material and discursive spaces which have been constituted within a social frame which has ascribed to men, as men, power by virtue of the gendering of social and cultural capital. For example, as Thornton notes, while men may display character traits of various degrees of 'unattractiveness' (for example, aggression, poor personal hygiene, few interpersonal skills, overbearing arrogance), these failings 'will rarely constitute an impediment to their becoming authoritative knowers' because 'the parameters of public conduct have always been broader for men than women' (1994: 62). There is also, she suggests, some evidence that regional dialects may be acceptable in men at executive levels but not in women. There is, in short, no one masculine subject here but, rather, a rich diversity of subject positions. However, and in turning to what may initially appear to be the very different world of academic criminology, it is my concern in the remainder of this chapter to explore what these ostensibly diverse 'masculine' subjects may, in fact, share.

'An organised way of seeing': the 'social world of British criminology'

The above discussion of the law may seem, on the surface at least, far removed from the traditional concerns of criminology. This has been a discussion of 'powerful' men, of cultural styles far removed from the usual subjects of criminology: lower/working-class, frequently young, male offenders. It is with this latter group that criminology has associated the traits of what is now called hegemonic masculinity (aggression, hyper-heterosexuality, group-bonding, a casual sexism, macho attitudes, and so forth). Criminology has, of course, considered 'powerful' men in one particular context; and in analyses of white-collar/corporate crime there are signs that a gendered study of 'professional' men 'as men' is now beginning to shed new light on the ways in which sex difference has informed questions of criminal motivation, corporate/business organisational cultures and institutional hierarchies (Levi, 1994; Messerschmidt, 1993; cf. Box, 1983; Nelken, 1994). Such men may also, of course, be extensively involved in a diverse range of crimes traditionally deemed 'private'; they may abuse, maim or injure in countless ways those with whom they live or otherwise share their lives.

In this section I wish to shift the focus away from the legal profession and turn towards another group of 'powerful' men traditionally neglected by criminology; towards, that is, the institutional practices of 'doing' criminology itself and, specifically, to what has been called the 'social world of British criminology' (Rock, 1994). This is a world which appears, at first, very different from the legal/business culture depicted above. Without in any way underestimating the scale of influence of criminological scholarship associated with a right-wing or neo-conservative politics, much of British, North American and Australian academic criminology has assumed a broadly liberal, frequently Left-leaning political orientation. Indeed, key debates within recent British academic criminology, such as those which took place during the 1980s between Left realism and Left idealism, can themselves be seen in terms of a playing out of broader debates which were taking place at the time within British politics (Lea and Young, 1984; Young and Matthews 1992; cf. Scraton, 1987). With regard to such matters as specific organisational and cultural styles, the dress codes of the academy generally appear more 'relaxed' than the private sector. The 'men in suits' model discussed above may apply in certain contexts and locations within academia; academic 'professionalism' is certainly encoded at certain moments in such a way, for example in interactions with the, increasingly significant, category of 'Research Users' within government and private sector business. It is not, however, generally associated with the style of the academic (or at least not in the context of criminology: on the legal academy, see Collier, 1997b; Thornton, 1996a).

It is at this point, therefore, that a rather different question arises. We have seen above something of the nature of the 'masculinity' of law which feminist scholarship has sought to challenge, the 'sexing' of women and 'de-sexing' of men. In relation to criminology, however, how has it been that the purportedly 'relaxed' liberal (progressive?) world of academic criminology has also resulted historically in a dominant association of women *with* sex/gender and a systematic effacing of the sexed specificity of men (resulting, ultimately, in the negation of the sex of crime itself)? Here the picture becomes more hazy and in many ways more complicated. Liberal, non-commercial, 'middle-class' masculinities, Connell (1987) has argued, also 'profit' from the masculinist 'shock troops' of hegemonic masculinity. Central to Connell's thesis is a belief that hegemonic masculine traits cut across social groups (although they continue to be largely associated with one social class). How these issues are then mediated closer to home within criminology raises some very different, and possibly more disturbing, questions about both men and criminology, about the nature of the relationship between the 'criminological man' and the men who 'do' criminology

Sexing women, effacing men: a 'standard issue kit of collective terms and shared values'

Modern criminology, David Garland has recently written, 'like any other academic specialism, consists of a body of accredited and systematically transmitted forms of knowledge, approved procedures and techniques of investigation, and a cluster of questions which make up the subject's recognised research agendas' (1994: 25). Within these questions and research agendas one recurring figure has been the Lombrosian myth of the born criminal: 'it is he who is subsequently debunked, the reference point for future histories' which, as Garland puts it, have proceeded to provide contemporary criminological practitioners with 'a standard issue kit of collective terms and shared values' (1994: 21). In seeking to trace the contours of this 'standard issue kit', British criminology has recently experienced a number of historical 'overviews' or 'brief histories' of its own 'theoretical development' (Garland, 1994) and 'social organisation' (Rock,

1988, 1994; see also Radzinowicz, 1994). What has emerged is, in effect, an image of how British criminology 'sees itself' as written by some of its 'leading figures'. These overviews are worth taking seriously, not just for what is being said about the discipline of British criminology per se and how its 'social world' has been constituted and reproduced. They are also revealing of the ways in which the 'standard issue kit', the 'shared values' which are 'handed down' from generation to generation of criminologists, have failed, so spectacularly, to address the relationship between the criminological researcher and the men who are research*ed* in terms of sexed specificity, sex difference and the sex of crime itself (Groombridge, 1997; Naffine, 1997).

What has been said about British criminology? Garland (1994: 25) has depicted criminology as a discipline marked by a range of epistemological and methodological prescriptions. These include (among others), he states, 'appropriate norms' of evidence and argument; mechanisms for the evaluation and dissemination of research findings (which, in turn, result in historical revisions of theoretical and empirical knowledge); organised supervision and training of students (the socialisation of new recruits into the criminological canon); and the distribution of status and authority among criminology's 'accredited practitioners'. All of these processes take place within a material infrastructure which, Garland argues, carries out various disciplinary functions through a range of means. Particular significance is accorded in this regard to the need to publish in 'respected' professional journals (a consideration heightened by the impact of the Research Assessment Exercise in Britain), through involvement in appropriate professional associations (such as the British Society of Criminology) and through institutes and university departments, professional appointments, the processes of peer review, letters of recommendation, training courses and, of course, in criminological textbooks, conferences, funding agencies, and so on (Garland, 1994: 250). What emerges from Garland's overview is, ultimately, a picture of criminology as:

> a socially constructed and historically specific organization of knowledge and investigative procedures – a particular style of reasoning, representing, and intervening – *which is grounded in a particular set of institutions and forms of life*. It is a 'discipline', a regime of truth with its own special rules for deciding between truth and falsity, rather than the epitome of right thought and correct knowledge. (Garland, 1994: 24; my emphasis)

The boundaries of 'criminology' itself are, it is recognised, contestable. Its methods, conceptions of 'right thought and correct knowledge', are not given. Other 'problematizations', ways of conceiving 'crime' and 'deviance', are always possible beyond the established conventions. Indeed, it is noted, 'in recent years our historical understanding of the subject' has been considerably advanced by a range of "outsiders" . . . *who owe no allegiance to the discipline* and whose work is driven *by quite different historical and critical concerns*' (Garland, 1994: 24; my emphasis). Within the cast of such 'outsiders' are placed feminists who, it is made clear both in this and other disciplinary overviews (Rock, 1988, 1994), are not – at present – considered part of the criminological orthodoxy or mainstream. Feminism, that is, does not owe the same 'allegiance to the discipline' that others do; it is 'driven by quite different . . . concerns' (compare the argument of Smart, 1990; Young, 1996). Notwithstanding the undoubted impact of feminist thought within the discipline, Rock (1994: 147) concurs that criminology remains 'a masculine discipline' in a representation of the 'social world' of British criminology which is not dissimilar to that of Garland. Criminology is 'an institutionally bounded community, a tradition, a set of practices, a market-place, a network of communication, and an organised way of seeing the world' (Rock, 1994: 125). This 'world', it is acknowledged, is dominated by men and a pervasive masculine ethos. It is 'untouched by feminism': '. . . criminology is a masculine discipline, and the other big idea of the 1970s, feminism, has not spread very far within it' (Rock, 1994: 147). Academic criminology, therefore, like the male-dominated criminal justice system and the legal profession we have discussed above, also continues to constitute men as the universal norm, the benchmark, whilst women are ascribed the status of *other*.

The general 'maleness' of institutional criminology has thus been acknowledged (for a very different reading, see Naffine, 1997). Yet the recognition itself, I wish to suggest, has a number of important implications for understanding the 'gendering' of a discipline which is now, albeit tentatively, beginning to address its 'sex question' in terms of developing a critique of masculinity (the sex question which remains, we have seen, the 'litmus test' of a discipline concerned ultimately with explaining crime). To recap the argument at this point: we have seen in Chapter 1 that it has been feminism which has (largely) raised the 'gender question' within criminology. In the late 1990s 'we know a vast amount about women and crime viewed through the prism of gender. *Far less is known about men and crime*' (Heidensohn, 1994: 1031; my emphasis). There may be some agreement that feminism has impacted on British criminology, as in other jurisdictions (Hahn Rafter and Heidensohn, 1995), but it is also clear that contemporary British criminology nonetheless continues to be primarily concerned with the study of men. From without, from outside 'the prism of gender', none of the male criminologists in Rock's (1994) survey claimed in their current research to be working on the particular 'problems of women' (whatever these might be), while 14 per cent of the women criminologists did so (Rock, 1994: 138). The majority, it may be inferred, were working on 'problems of men'; that is, men are here writing about and researching men (as ungendered beings), women are writing about women (understood, implicitly, as 'gendered' beings). Rock's survey notes the existence of a 'continuing divide' in criminology between those who 'studied women' and those who did not. However, as we have seen in Chapter 1, what is all too clear is that the bulk of this research on men is *not* an engagement with the sex-specificity of crime. In terms of developing a gendered reading of crime as propounded by sociogenic feminism, it is not 'taking masculinity seriously'. It is, more accurately, a matter of criminological 'business as usual', supporting the conclusion that 'criminology is a masculinist discipline' largely 'untouched by feminism'.

If criminology is not addressing the sex-specificity of its object of study (criminal man), it should perhaps not then surprise us that the kinds of self-reflection around the object/subject relationship which have been evident in (at least) some sociological work on men (Hearn, 1987; Jackson, 1990; Morgan, 1992) should be similarly absent. This absence of any gender reflexivity is itself, on one level, ironic given that criminology is replete with accounts of crime in which 'lived experience' of the offender is valorised. Through naturalism, phenomenology and more recently accounts of anxiety and fear of crime, the 'truth' of the experiential has been accorded a central significance (the problem, in a sense, has related to whose 'experience' this has been). At other times, of course, the criminolog*ist* has indeed sought to address the relation between his own (heterosexual) masculinity and that of those whom he researches (for example, Cohen, 1955: 138; Whyte, 1943). He has done so, however, primarily in terms of class location. Consideration of the lived experience of the producers of criminological knowledge themselves as (hetero)sexed subjects (as men) would, however, raise a number of questions about the nature of the institutional infrastructure, the 'social world' depicted above. What, for example, does it mean for the (largely) white, educated middle-class men who constitute the majority of British criminologists to study men of other classes and ethnicities? Crucially, how do these diverse 'masculinities' interact (Groombridge, 1997; Naffine, 1997: 9–10, 38–42)? Subjectivity, as we have seen in Chapter 1, cannot be reduced to 'lived experience'. If the social relations of criminal justice organisations and occupations are not to be conceptualised as sex-neutral (Acker, 1990) but, rather, as operating 'according to ideologies, customs, and practices that produce and reproduce gender inequality' (Martin and Jurik, 1996: 17–18), how does this relate to the afore-mentioned – and acknowledged – 'masculinism' and 'male dominance' of criminology?

It is possible to make a number of points about the 'social world' of British criminology in the light of the above. First, the 'set of institutions and forms of life' which ground criminological knowledge (Garland, 1994: 24) are organised within an institutional matrix which has been marked historically by a homosocial subtext of patronage. This is perhaps epitomised by the ubiquity of the 'male pantheon of proper names', reflected in the tedious and self-regarding 'most influential' criminologists 'in the English-speaking world' debate (Cohen and Farrington, 1994) and the 'curious doxa' of 'male critics referring primarily to each other', albeit occasionally referring to the rarity of women's speech (something which is all too clear in the way in which Garland and Rock construct their social and theoretical histories: Morris, 1988): 'It is this doxa that leaves a woman no place from which to speak, writing her out of the history of philosophy once again'

(Leng, 1995: 50). How might these homosocial dynamics of a discipline, where progression is so clearly marked by patronage (being 'in the know', obtaining the 'right' reference), then inform understandings of the 'proper research agenda'? In such a context it is perhaps unsurprising that the insights of queer theory and gay and lesbian scholarship should remain such a notable absence in much of the work emerging on men, crime and criminal justice, even though, as I shall argue in later chapters, it is the *hetero-sexualisation of crime* which is itself crucial to understanding the constitution of men's subjectivities in many areas of life.

Where, therefore, does this leave understanding of the relationship between subject and object within criminology? It has been a recurring theme within postmodernism that claims to objective knowledge have been based on an elite, white, heterosexual, Eurocentric and androcentric perspective (Weedon, 1987). In short, as 'traditional boundaries between subject and object have broken down', what has surfaced is a recognition 'that our own subjectivity is formed like that of those we research' (Walkerdine, 1995: 310). The implications of this for a reflexive criminology are vast. The criminologist may ask why a young man 'chooses' crime. Yet the question may be turned on its head. Why 'choose' criminology? Why write about crime? What one writes about, or chooses to study, is influenced by the social location of the writer. Indeed, some critics have suggested, writers should identify themselves in terms of gender, race, sexual orientation, social class and any other relevant biographical information which might then enable readers to better evaluate the truth claims attached to the knowledge that is being presented (Martin and Jurik, 1996: 18; cf. Women and Geography Study Group, 1997). On one level there is a rich tradition of self-reflection within criminology in which researchers have sought to address their own social position relative to that of those being 'researched' (for example, Becker, 1973; Cloward and Ohlin, 1961; Whyte, 1943; see further Naffine, 1997: Ch. 2). Notwithstanding such reflexivity in terms of class position, however, the connections in terms of sex/gender have not been carried over to a consideration of *who* is enforcing the various disciplinary practices identified by Garland. What counts as 'knowledge' is not, after all, independent of the social and political position of the person who 'knows'.

What comes into view at this stage is a perception of what has been at stake in the ways in which, historically, criminology has systematically effaced its own sex question. For what is at issue here are the ways in which the constitution of the *criminologist* (him)self, as a particular (sexed, specific) man, has related to *criminology's* dominant constructions of both 'crime' *and* 'masculinity'. What we are and have been dealing with are his fantasies, his stories of class, of 'dangerous' boys and 'underworld' villains, his accounts of resistances, rituals and struggles. What comes into view at this stage, therefore, is the important question of how this sexed subject(ivity) of the criminologist and the conceptualisation of the maleness of crime may themselves be interrelated; how, that is, ideas of 'masculinity' have themselves informed the production of knowledge about the phenomenon of 'crime' (which is, it is to be remembered, a social construct) *at the very moment* that any engagement with the sex-specificity of crime has itself been effaced. It is, perhaps, no wonder that a division should be made between the 'masculinity' of the researched and researcher; for what would come into view if the feminist insights around the unities which exist between men were to be embraced? Like the men whom he studies, in what ways does the 'taking up' (however insecurely or momentarily) of specific identities encoded as 'masculine' constitute the sense of self of the criminologist? As hero, as rebel, as 'one of the boys' or 'riding in the cop car', in what ways is he a subject who, like the criminal men who are the object of his study, has been constituted via a systematic negation of corporeality and vulnerability alongside a valorisation of the promise of (hetero)sexual potency associated with crime? In terms of method, what masculine 'thrills', what 'seductions' (Katz, 1988) does the researcher share with the boys 'hanging out' on the street corner? How, in short, is the 'man question' silenced at the point of knowledge production? Addressing such issues is not 'about objectivity or bias, but about how certain stories get told and how they too can fulfil fantasies, be defences' (Walkerdine, 1995: 329).

The 'fortunate generation': constructing the in/outside of criminology

An illustration of how this silencing takes place can be found in the ways in which the social histories of criminology discussed above have sought to depict the boundaries of the in/outside of the discipline. In particular, a distinctly masculine narrative has informed a reading of an academic life course in which a youthful 'taking on' of the criminological establishment has been seen as giving way to a 'maturing' into middle age in the context of theoretical and political reassessments of criminological 'schools of thought' in 'the British tradition'. Criminology, we have seen, is an 'organised way of seeing the world' (Rock, 1994: 125). In Rock's review of 'the present state of criminology in Britain' he presents what in many ways is, in effect, something of a 'biography of the boys' or, rather, what Rock refers to as that 'fortunate generation' of teachers and researchers appointed to posts in criminology in and around the 1970s (Rock, 1988: 60). These are described as the 'prime generation' of criminologists, the product of a 'golden age' (Rock, 1988: 62). Their average age (in 1986) is said by Rock to be the early forties, which would locate this generation as the 'fortunate' beneficiaries of a context of post-war social mobility and belief in meritocracy. This is a context which saw the expansion of a tripartite system of education designed to find the brightest among the working class (but which, Walkerdine [1995: 321] suggests, was in fact to produce the middle-class student resistances of the late 1960s). This history of the 'fortunate generation' is indicative of the way in which the canon of critical or radical criminology had, by 1988, become so formalised that it is not just accorded a historical overview; it appears as somehow 'telling the story' of British academic criminology. Thus, Rock argues, it is still this 'fortunate generation' of academics which 'remains the major executor of the British Tradition'. These are the previous 'Young Turks' who, in Young's words, attacked the 'Sultanate of establishment criminology' (Young, 1988: 169) with their 'bravura pieces ... produced by graduates who had worked in some intellectual isolation' (Rock, 1988: 62). The work they produced was the 'bold creations of lone autodidacts who forged new, venturesome, eccentric and sometimes precarious syntheses' (Rock, 1988: 62). A few of the Young Turks may have 'lost none of their combativeness' (Rock, 1988: 63), whilst others have 'matured' into middle age. However, the point is that these are criminologists who 'know one another, they educate one another, they sometimes marry one another, they read each other's work and they gossip about each other. ... *They form a social world*' (Rock, 1988: 67; my emphasis).

The depiction of this 'social world' is open to a number of interpretations in terms of who is, and is not, considered to be a 'member'. Quite where this history leaves a presumably 'unfortunate' generation of younger academics is far from clear. The claim that the 'golden' generation had, by 1988, 'not been effectively challenged from behind' is certainly questionable, considering the scale of feminist scholarship which existed at the time. Nor can it be said that 'it is about the margins that skirmishes are now being fought' (Rock, 1988: 63) when, as we have seen in Chapter 1, the very modernist foundations of the criminological enterprise have come under sustained critique from feminism and postmodernism. What we have, rather, is a picture of a discipline in which, as Garland suggests, a particular 'regime of truth' is being established and in which criminological knowledge is 'accredited and systematically transmitted'. Certain questions do – and others do not – 'make up the subject's recognised research agendas' (Garland, 1994: 25). This is not simply a matter of the ways in which questions of 'authority' and 'influence' play out in terms of what is taken to constitute an 'established' research agenda (who edits the journals and writes the books, who secures the funding contracts, and so forth). Such issues are, of course, common to all academic disciplines. What we have here is, importantly, the question of sex difference in the formation of what is taken to be criminological knowledge. In criminology, as we have seen, the majority 'playing the game' are men. The relationships which are then presented as being hierarchically ordered are, it follows, largely relationships between men. It is the fact that the fortunate generation are now empowered by their academic seniority which informs Rock's observation that the young men and women criminologists appointed in the late 1980s and early 1990s 'find themselves not yet organised, massive, and confident enough to supply *their own* theories, politics, institutions, and meeting-places' (Rock, 1994: 144; my emphasis). The implications are clear: secure experience working with established scholars (and all that attends the academic apprenticeship), develop a track record in securing external funding,[8] and the career in British criminology, and admission to the 'social world', might follow (on this mixture of an 'aristocratic tendency' and 'iron law of oligarchy' in British criminology see Sheptycki, 1997; on what happens when criminologists 'fall out', see the *British Society of Criminology Newsletter* No. 29, 1997). However, the problem with this, of course, is that – *no less than in the case of the legal profession discussed above* – social, cultural and economic capital themselves continue to be constituted in terms of sexual difference. From the outset, as we have seen, one subject is identified as the 'ideological concern' or 'specialist interest' of an 'outsider' (such as feminism). The other is the 'recognised research agenda', the work of a 'most influential figure', the work which continues to at best marginalise, at worst efface entirely, the political and theoretical significance of criminology's sex question.

Reproducing 'gendered woman, ungendered man': the case of the Oxford Handbook

Perhaps one of the most glaring illustrations of the ways in which criminology has historically avoided the 'man question' has been the way in which the concept of 'gender' has been equated with, or seen as relating to, women and/or issues relating to women's lives. This association has, in turn, fed into a broader marginalisation and institutional negation of feminism and what has become known as 'gendered' perspectives. The first edition of *The Oxford Handbook of Criminology*, published in 1994, exemplifies this general approach (Maguire et al, 1994). This text has been (rightly) singled out for critique as exemplifying the ways in which feminism is, more generally, marginalised within criminology (Naffine, 1997: 2; Young, 1996: 49). The *Oxford Handbook* is a book of 1,259 pages and, drawing on the considerable expertise of its contributors, it seeks to provide a scholarly yet readable introduction and guide to the current state of criminology. The editors, following the general approach adopted by Rock and Garland, note in their Introduction that a 'high proportion' of a 'new generation' of women criminologists have 'established their reputations' within an overlapping set of 'relatively new specialist interests' (Maguire et al., 1994: 11). What these 'specialist interests' are is then clarified. Women are said to have had a particular influence 'in areas such as gender and crime, sexual and domestic violence, victimisation, and fear of crime, which were previously neglected by male criminologists' (Maguire et al., 1994: 11) (neglected by the male criminologists who, it must be remembered, Rock has argued continue to dominate the discipline). The editors asked themselves at the outset 'should gender and race be addressed in every chapter? Or should they be assigned to chapters for "specialist coverage"?' (Maguire et al., 1994: 11). The result is an account of the 'specialist interest' of 'Gender and Crime' (Heidensohn, 1994) which is the twenty-first chapter in the book. In effect, the *Oxford Handbook* appears as a book about men without sex. It is, certainly, difficult to see how the concept of gender has informed the preceding twenty chapters.

Men thus remain the 'proper' subject of criminology, though the 'gender' of their crimes does not. The index to the first edition of the *Oxford Handbook* does not list 'men' or 'masculinity' as separate subjects. 'Women', in contrast, is afforded a lengthy listing which covers, amongst other issues: 'chivalry, focus of', 'courts, in', 'criminal justice system, in', 'recorded offences, increase in', and so forth. Rock's overview of the social organisation of British criminology, a variation of which is contained in the *Oxford Handbook*, also contains two pages devoted to a discussion of 'Women in Criminology'. There is no consideration of whether what had preceded this discussion had been about 'Men in Criminology' (Rock, 1994: 137–9). Garland's (1994) theoretical overview in the *Handbook*, meanwhile, speaks of the 'whole gamut' of theoretical perspectives on which criminology has drawn. These are stated as including 'psychoanalysis, functionalism, interactionism, ethnomethodology, Marxism, econometrics, systems theory, postmodernism, etc.' (Garland, 1994: 26). Feminism is deferred (or confined) to another list, identified not as a 'theoretical perspective', but as one of a range of 'ideological concerns' which are said to have sought to 'influence' criminology: 'welfarism ..., the radicalism of the 1970s, feminism, left realism, etc. etc.' In effect, a hierarchy is set up in which feminism is dealt with as an 'ideological concern'.

There is now an established tradition within criminology whereby texts seek to acknowledge, in their second editions, an awareness of gender and, in particular, that feminism has had some impact on the discipline (see, for example, Downes and Rock, 1988; Lilly et al., 1995). It is revealing, therefore, that the second edition of the *Oxford Handbook* (Maguire et al., 1997) reflects the growing visibility and status of 'the masculinity turn' (Chapter 1) in the form of a chapter devoted entirely to the subject of masculinities and crime (Jefferson, 1997). The question remains, however. What is the objective here? Is the task to make mainstream criminology or, for some, (socialist) political movements 'aware' of feminism? Is it a matter of re-educating (presumably male?) criminologists and socialists to the inequalities of sex/gender?[9] Is it to discuss 'masculinity' only as it relates to the terrain of the sex crime, sexual offences and men's violences? Or is it to reconfigure the nature of the criminological project itself, to reassess the mutual discursive construction of men, masculinity and crime? (cf. Naffine, 1997: 139–53).

The accounts of British criminology discussed in this section seek to have it both ways. They embrace a (grudging?) recognition of feminism's presence and impact on the discipline whilst, simultaneously, carrying on much as before ('business as usual'). Yet this negation of sex difference has profound implications for the possibilities of developing, within such a rigorously policed discipline, an adequate theoretical and conceptual basis for approaching the men/crime relation. Though it is recognised as having been 'previously neglected' by male criminologists, the 'special interest' of gender continues to be marginalised by this nod of recognition; a chapter here, a footnote there as, at last it appears, feminism is (women are) welcomed into the fold. Given the nature of the institutional structure of British criminology which emerges from such accounts however (and which certainly tallies with my own experience), it must be open to question whether a criminological orthodoxy which is suspicious of, if not overtly hostile to, feminism will then seek to 'take masculinity seriously' at the level of its own institutions, methods, practices and theoretical assumptions. In a context where, for example, a critical recognition of the social and psychological dynamics of homosociality would seem an anathema to a heterosexualized norm, the insights of queer theory and gay and lesbian scholarship remain a notable absence in the lists of 'present influences' on criminology. Again, we can see some of the implications of how the (sexed) inquiring subject has in turn constituted the 'gendered' subject of (his) study in particular ways and to particular ends.

To summarise the argument of this section: just as the field of legal practice discussed above can be identified as a location for the production of sexed subjectivities, within the criminological academy a range of material, social and discursive practices have also been salient features in the making of gendered 'academic' subjectivities. Much is known about such matters as where criminology is taught in Britain, what the academic background of its practitioners is and 'who are the most influential criminologists'. Rather less is known about how the production of criminological knowledge is itself gendered when conceptualised as a *situated* knowledge, as something which is produced – largely – by men. At the present moment, and bearing in mind the disciplinary imperative to seek out new subject matters, new disciplinary terrains – to boldly go where no criminologist has gone before – there are shifting organisational/institutional, epistemological, social, economic and cultural factors which are pushing criminology towards an engagement with masculinity and which, in so doing, are reconfiguring the subject positions available to men within the criminological academy. Feminism clearly *has* impacted on criminology, if only in necessitating either a distancing from its critiques of men and what men 'do' or else in a partial acceptance of 'gender' as being a 'women's' issue. In the more general context of what has been seen as the 'third phase' of post-war criminology, however, marked by a lower level of theoretical intensity but a greater attentiveness to method and project management, and to policy as well as political issues (see further Young, 1994), this has meant that any theoretical engagement with 'masculinity and crime' would itself appear, in one sense, to be going against the grain of criminology's present direction. Whilst some have embraced the bureaucratisation of the academy, managerialism and technical rationality which has marked the restructuring and restratification of British higher education in the 1990s, others have resisted such moves and sought to explicitly defend and promote a theoretical, critical and politically committed scholarship (note, for example, the recent publication of the journal *Theoretical Criminology*: Beirne and Sumner, 1997). It is in the context of such debates internal to criminology that the masculinity question would appear to breathe new life into a discipline which has seemed bereft of the *critical* moorings of its (relatively) recent past (after all, the 'Young Turks' are now 'the establishment'). However, as has been argued in Chapter 1, the problem with any such masculinity turn, when seen in the context of the social world of British criminology discussed in this section, is not just a question of methodology or politics. It is not, as Smart (1990: 72) puts it, 'a simple problem of party membership': it is epistemological. At issue is the nature of, and what counts as, knowledge of crime produced by a 'social world' which continues to systematically fail to face up to its own inherent positivism and which remains unable or unwilling to tackle the sex of crime. This problem relates, I have argued, both to the structure of criminological thought *and* to the ways in which men are constituted as the norm at the very moment that their sexed specificity is erased.

Beyond the frame of (hetero-)'masculinity': identity and change in law/criminology

Thus far in this chapter I have explored two aspects of the crimino-legal field, legal practice and academic criminology, each of which has been characterised as 'masculinist' within feminist scholarship. What becomes clear at this point is not simply that these 'masculine' cultures are hetero-geneous, but that there are, in fact, a plurality of diverse 'masculine' subjectivities. In order to challenge the continued presence of cultures and practices which are inimical to women's acceptance into and progression within the jurisprudential and criminological communities it is necessary to address, I have suggested, what these diverse subjectivities *share*. This project involves, crucially, disturbing the sociality and contingency of a masculinity/femininity binary which is 'not necessarily congruent with the sexed bodies of men and women but contingent' (Thornton, 1996b: 5). In 'naming' the sociality of men's subjectivities as problematic it becomes possible to move beyond the models of 'women and the law', 'women and crime' and, with it, the associated simplistic conception of the 'masculinity' of law and crime as being a homogeneous entity.

   What unites these diverse masculinities is, I have suggested, a social positioning which, by virtue of being a sexed man, is then constructed as having at least the potential to make claims to the status of 'authoritative knower' within these particular social fields. This is not, I have argued, to claim that men inherently or necessarily embody, display or manifest the particular values society deems 'masculine' at any point in time. It is, in support of Fineman (1994, 1995), to advance a methodology based on sexual difference: not by way of arguing that women and men are 'essentially' (biologically, reductively) different, but rather by way of seeking to ground men and women's gendered existences in a constitutive analysis of law and crimino-legal institutions. Subject positions which are coded as masculine ascribe to men certain qualities and, in so doing, replicate familiar dualisms associated with the masculine/feminine divide. It may be argued, for example, that individual women in any particular institutional setting (legal practice, academia, politics) can be equally as competitive, ruthless, ambitious, self-seeking and careerist, as generally 'unpleasant' as the men with whom they work. That, however, would be to miss the point about the ways in which that which is constituted as cultural, economic and symbolic capital has itself been constructed historically within an over-arching cultural frame that has systematically privileged the values deemed masculine over the feminine.

The ways in which diverse 'masculinities' are lived is more complex, the body encoded more ambiguously, than simply by reference to the hegemonic 'benchmark' masculinity of either the 'man in a suit' or the 'liberal' academic. There is, importantly, more to power relations amongst hetero-males than straightforward hierarchies based on age, money, status, and so forth. It is from an already empowered subject position that these claims to authority, and the power to judge the validity of the knowledges of others, is taken up and assessed. Feminist agendas, we have seen in relation to the 'social world' of British criminology, may be conceptualised by men, who may or may not be generally sympathetic to feminism, as 'adding' something to another distinct, broader political or intellectual project; or, bearing in mind the bureaucratisation of the academy in which legal and criminological research takes place, feminism and 'gender issues' may be integrated into an academic agenda within the terms of 'a managerialist pedagogical frame with its emphasis on technicist explanations and solutions' (Mac an Ghaill, 1994: 8). 'Sex/gender' research may be thus supported instrumentally as 'good' in terms of research assessment. In the legal profession, as in the academy, sexual harassment and (un)equal opportunities remain 'problems' which can be 'solved' by the institution, 'women's issues' ('women and . . .' law, 'women and . . .' crime) easily subsumed into some broader political or theoretical project. The relation of the 'problem' itself to the material and discursive reproduction of a phallocentric frame continues, however, to be negated as an issue.

In the remainder of this chapter I wish to investigate that frame and to bring its foundational assumptions about men, sex, gender and difference into view in a more focused manner. The ways in which the differential constitution of male subjectivities in specific contexts has been informed by notions of race and ethnicity, and mediated by structures of class, sexuality and physical ability, has been well documented within the masculinity literature (see, generally, Connell, 1995). In relation to the British state and the iconography of the legal-governmental system, a normative benchmark masculinity has historically been bound up with trappings of nationhood, empire and authority. The subjective empowerment of this masculine norm is illustrated by a further consideration of what the subject positions discussed above, whether in the domain of legal practice or the criminological academy, share.

Naming the 'other': heterosexual(ising) subjectivities

The notion of professional 'asexuality' outlined above in the context of the legal profession has been constituted within a heterosexual frame (or 'heterosexual matrix': Butler, 1990) which represents normative (hetero-) masculinity as benchmark. The ways in which readings of the differential empowerment of men's diverse subjectivities are understood is profoundly disturbed once this over-arching frame of 'playing it straight' (Nayak and Kehily, 1996) is disturbed. In terms of hierarchic heterosexuality, who cooks, cleans and 'takes care' of the law firm senior partner or academic criminologist who works a ninety-hour week? Who is the primary child carer? One of the fundamental decisions facing women in these contexts has been the question of how to balance a 'career' and child care. How is it that men become 'unencumbered' from such decisions? Why is our primary response to a range of masculine typologies not 'but where are the children?' but rather some other assessment of 'masculine' status (such as authoritative demeanour, material and/or sexual 'success', cultural confidence)? Each of these questions is framed by, and only makes sense in terms of, the dominant dualisms of sexual difference and heterosexuality, exemplified by the way in which workplace social relations are frequently coded as familial or, rather, as a simulacrum, a perversion, of the familial 'proper'.

The range of subject positions available to men each make claims, albeit in different ways, to quite traditional notions of masculine authority. Central to their encoding as culturally 'masculine' has been this notion of normative heterosexuality. What analysis of these heterosex assumptions which frame this constitution reveals are two key discursive moves which, together, construct a resultant normative (hetero-)masculinity via the hierarchical mapping of sexual difference and the familiar negation or disavowal of that which would appear as other (the feminine, the homosexual). Firstly, normative (hetero)masculinity has been constituted on a foundational disavowal, a denial of the feminine and femininity which secures the dualism of sexual difference. Men are not like women. From this stems the mapping of what 'being a man' is, which, we have seen, is subject to historical and cultural variation. It is 'not being womanly', not being 'sexed' in a culture which equates the feminine with the sexual and the masculine with rationality, reason and authority. It is this difference which produces dominance. Any 'crisis' which is engendered for men by women's increased participation in the legal profession, or for criminology by women's challenges to what counts as criminological 'knowledge', results from women's increased presence in a sphere from which, it is clear, women are not retreating but are, significantly, establishing their own professional and frequently powerful networks (Benoit-Scott, 1996). To reframe the question of gender and/in law and crime as *other* than a 'woman's problem' is to ask *why* it should be that, for so many men, actually 'being' (working) in a social situation with women is considered 'not normal' and (for the individual man) frequently psychologically problematic. Far from constituting a crisis of masculinity, this relates to the ways in which men generally are no longer in workplace environments which shore up, defend and fortify masculine subjectivities which had in any case been constituted in key respects as always *outside* a world shared with women and children; that is, as simultaneously within and beyond the terms of the heterosexual frame in which men's relation to women's corporeality in the workplace continues to be bifurcated as either surrogate-familial (wife, daughter, partner, mother), or sexual and sexualising other, as essentially (sexed) 'Woman' as opposed to (de-sexed) 'Man'.

Secondly, and somewhat less explored, is the related negation of the homosexual alongside the profound privileging of homosocial cultures and organisation, cultures which pervade both the legal profession, academia and the crimino-legal field more generally. The crimino-legal domain is structured internally in terms of power relations, not only between men and women, but also between men. The cultures deemed masculine which have surfaced in work on 'women and the law' highlight, though they do not tend to analyse, the complex relation which exists between male hetero- and homosexualities. It is the taboo on homosexuality which informs and mediates much of intra-male social relations. Through a rich diversity of male homosocial heterosexual interactions a norm is reproduced to which men are held accountable, notwithstanding the considerable variation within individual conceptualisations of masculine subjectivities which depart from that norm (Bird, 1996: 120). Nonetheless, and crucially, non-hegemonic masculinities fail to influence structural arrangements significantly because their expression is, as Bird (1996) argues, either relegated to heterosocial settings or else suppressed entirely. This is the unspoken subtext of the social world, the institutional matrix and forms of life discussed by Garland et al.

Each of these themes – the negation of the feminine and the (homo)sexual – will be taken up, and explored in depth, in the chapters which follow. At this point, it is sufficient to note that the reason both women and homosexual men continue to transgress the erotic norms of hetero-masculine culture relates to the ways in which the heterosexual bodies of men have themselves been understood as, a priori, outwith or beyond the sexual: as, that is, de-sexed, *dis*-embodied neutral conduits of authoritative knowledge, as *un*sexy bodies.[10] The erotic ambiguities of homosociality are thus effaced. In the context of the legal profession, the saturation of City workplaces and practices with heterosexist imagery and behaviour can thus be seen as framing a conformity to heterosexual social practices which 'demand . . . of women a physically impossible performance' (McDowell, 1995: 75). They also, importantly, demand of men a watchful eye. These presumptions of heterosexism derive meaning through reference to a dualism of sex difference central to the articulation, reproduction and management of which have been notions of a normative male (hetero)sexuality. This is, however, as fluid, fragile and vulnerable as it is seemingly pervasive and all-encompassing. The benefits for men of identification with the dominant modes of the masculine – whether as lawyers or academics – 'derive from the social power it confers, the various attributions of mastery it solicits from others' (Waldby, 1995: 271). In terms of the ways in which these masculine subject positions are ascribed cultural and social capital, the ostensibly more 'liberal' and relaxed disciplinary codes of the criminological academy have, I have argued, much more in common with the apparently more rigid regulatory practices of the business and corporate world than might otherwise at first appear to be the case.

Concluding remarks: 'just (more) boys doing business?'

> What we are observing is the reign of an often unreflective science of criminology, which neither examines its own particular ideologies (its own specific world view) nor speculates about the consequent intellectual and ethical value of the criminological enterprise (why it is doing what it is doing). We see, instead, a preoccupation with the scientific study of criminal man and how to correct him, much as the scientific men of the nineteenth century saw their task. But the gaze is unidirectional. Criminologist examines criminal man but does not look back at himself to discover the nature of his own identity and how it shapes the very nature of the scientific process, including the very identity of criminal man himself.
>
> (Naffine, 1997: 28–9)

Concluding his review of criminology in Britain in 1988, Paul Rock stated his belief that an 'intellectual and political generation in their late thirties and early forties dominates the sociology of crime and deviance' (1988: 68). Writing in the previous year, Heidensohn asked of this generation, 'Have they taken [gender] seriously? Have they changed their minds, their research studies or their institutional practices?' (1987: 21). I have argued in this chapter that the male subject implicit within a strand of criminological and legal thought is, in fact, anything but the universal, neutral, objective and rational subject who is frequently presumed. This subject is not a 'disinterested knower', unhinged from lived experience and from the particularity of his position in the world. We have seen a motivated subject whose 'universal' truths have been generated in relation to a specific, embodied and sexed position in the world. He is a subject who has constructed a criminology in his own image, a discipline replete with his fears and desires, anxieties and projections. Ultimately, it should not surprise that this subject should have failed to 'take gender seriously' in the way Heidensohn suggests. For, we have seen, it has been of the essence to this subject that he is de-gendered, unsexed, his corporeality effaced as he is constituted as norm, the benchmark, as it becomes his knowledge which is that against which all others are to be judged and, ultimately – and inevitably – found wanting.

It is, in the light of the above, possible to make a number of concluding remarks. The stories of criminology's psychic life – the fantasies of its makers, the return of their 'others' – have yet to be written. This discussion has just hinted at what the criminologist and the subjects of his criminological gaze may in fact share. In his recent discussion of urban disorder, Pitts has drawn attention to the ways in which for 'working class young men, who, *like other men*, are evaluated by their peers on the basis of their power to make an impact upon the world "out there", adolescence is characteristically a period of heightened status frustration' (1996: 280; my emphasis). 'Status frustration' and 'making an impact upon the world "out there"' may be no less keenly felt by academics and other professionals, albeit from their positions of 'relative advantage' and not disadvantage. Ultimately, as Walkerdine suggests, 'perhaps the love/hate fantasy about the working class always said more about the desire of an intellectual Left for the masses to do the transforming, the dirty work as usual, while they could write, think and lead' (1995: 318). The defences which take place against the routine pains, insecurities and vulnerabilities of 'being' a man in contemporary society may, I have argued in this chapter, take different forms.

In this chapter I have sought to address the absence of the 'bodies of men' from accounts of 'what men do' in relation to both 'doing law' and 'doing criminology'. I have engaged with some of the ways in which a dualism of sexual difference has framed the ways in which the corporeality of men has been variously conceptualised in terms of differential access to social, economic and cultural capital. The chapter has, ultimately, only begun an exploration of the demands which inform the construction of the masculine within particular sub-sections of the economy and crimino-legal fields. I have argued that, in seeking to address the idea of the 'masculinism' of law and crime, it is necessary to engage with the ways in which men's subjectivities remain predicated on a dualism between 'public' masculinities and 'private' domains (Hearn, 1992). Within both the criminological academy and legal practice the discursive power of this public/private dualism has been fundamental to the mobilising of subjective commitments to institutional goals and values (working harder, putting 'work' first, 'getting on'). What actually constitutes social, cultural and symbolic capital may vary between the discrete fields of the academy and law firm. However, in each domain this 'capital' is a gendered, coded heterosexual phenomenon. Each has, like the 'public' world of work generally, been historically shaped in men's image and organised by institutions which have reflected the perspectives of men.

It is, as we have seen in Chapter 1, in many ways an archaic and yet still resonant, always negotiable masculine identity bequeathed men which is encapsulated by the ubiquitous concept of 'hegemonic masculinity' (Connell, 1987). At the present moment men of all classes are sharing environments with women that were once shared only with other men. In this process, different demands are being made on the multifarious heterosexual performances of men which are far more complex than simply variations on the hegemonic style or professional masculinity of the 'men in suits'. The fact that this should be seen as 'problematic', a 'woman's issue' or as the cause of a 'masculine crisis' is testimony to the rigidity of dominant cultural conceptions of 'masculine' and 'feminine' as sexed, hierarchical signifiers, each constituted via a dualism of sexual difference. Accordingly, strategies seeking to improve women's position based on individual rights and entitlements will be of little use so long as the social edifice which valorises these notions of gendered capital remains in place. It is for this reason that, at the present moment, debates around such topics as 'women and law' and 'women and criminology' face something of a paradox. For, at a time when there is a general acceptance of an ideology of gender 'equality' and 'equal rights' (few organisations would not claim to be equal opportunity employers), cultural reconfigurations of men's power and privileges are taking place which seek, quite explicitly, to evoke, defend and celebrate traditional notions of sexual difference and hetero-masculinity (see Chapter 5). So long as the sexed specificity of men is effaced within debates around sex/gender and power, it remains likely that the 'problem of men' will continue to be turned on its head and, in a neat discursive twist, the 'masculinism' of 'law', 'crime' or whatever will become, like so many other issues, a 'women's problem'.

Far from conceptualising Woman as 'other' to a masculine (legal) norm in such a way, this chapter has sought to unpack the nature of the 'norm' – the 'masculinism' of law and criminology – via an exploration of the ways in which sexed subject positions are understood at particular moments and locations to be 'masculine'. I have been concerned with the ways in which the 'taking up' (however insecurely or momentarily) of specific identities constituted as masculine has played out in terms of, and depended upon, what I have suggested has been a systematic negation of men's corporeality. This project has involved disturbing and fragmenting a range of binary divisions (such as man/woman, hetero/homosexual, public/private) which continue to pervade representations of the 'masculinism' of criminology, law and legal culture. In rendering social, accountable and contingent both the corporeality and behaviour of men – what men do, as opposed to the qualities of an abstracted signifier of their gender ('masculinity') – this chapter has sought to reconfigure the relationship between the crimino-legal field and men's 'identity', understood here as a social construction involving

> a process of exclusion, negation and repression ... a process which, even if successful, results in an identity intrinsically unstable. This is bad news for masculinity one of whose self-conceptions is stability, and whose function is to maintain it socially and psychically. (Dollimore, 1986: 6–7)

To conclude: I have argued that particular notions of the masculine are affirmed and valorised via a range of ideologies, discursive representations and material practices which, together and individually, systematically privilege those men with the capacity to claim social and cultural capital. Socio-economic background (education, the inheritance and/or financial support, the style and deportment promoted by private education, the 'right' accent and intonation) remain, for example, key gate-keepers into the legal field. It 'pays' for men to be closely associated with the cultural norms of 'professionalism' in these particular areas (instrumental rationality, ambition, competitiveness, aggression) rather than others (empathy, care, compassion). Nonetheless, and notwithstanding the fact that both women and men are subject to disciplinary practices, the bureaucratic and epistemological scripts are profoundly different for individuals whose bodies have been 'sexed' (that is, constituted as 'sexual') in different ways. A central argument of this chapter has been that the dominant construct of women as 'other' (to be 'let in' to the masculine(ised) world of law, criminology, crime, and so forth) is dependent on, firstly, a denial of men's sexed corporeality and, secondly, and related, an evacuation of men from the domain of child care and, more generally, from relations of 'dependency' (Fineman, 1995). It should not surprise that considerable ideological regulation then goes into ensuring that men's *hetero*sexual bodies do not surface as problematic entities. Notwithstanding contradictions, ambiguities and tensions in the process of their constitution, both legal practice and academic criminology can be seen as domains for the 'making' of professional legal masculinities. As 'deeply gendered and heterosexual regimes, [which] construct relations of domination and subordination' (Mac an Ghaill, 1994: 4), both university and law firm function to constitute and regulate, to varying degrees, the range of subject positions available to men. Further research might usefully explore the diversity of men's heterosexualities and the complex dynamics of men's resistances to and (re)negotiations of hegemonic norms. Certainly, more work is needed into the deeper structure and significance of everyday practices in the crimino-legal field, into the multifarious ways in which heterosexuality is performed and related to understandings of 'lawyers' work' and 'criminologists' work'.

One thing seems clear. Without the will to address, let alone institute, questions of transformative social and economic structural change, it is likely that debates about men, women, criminology and the legal profession will continue to be marginalised and peripheral issues, their inclusion on conference programmes and agendas, in journals and books, marking a tokenistic deference to a climate of 'concern' about a problem which can be identified and experienced (there is something happening 'out there') but seldom analysed. In seeking to surface the sexed bodies of men within a 'situated knowledge' (Harvey and Haraway, 1995) and to relate the personal and political in an account of the mutual constitution of heterosexuality and masculinity (Robinson, 1996: 124), this chapter has sought to 'bring home' to the politics of 'doing' law and criminology the question of what it means to speak of the 'maleness' of this field. For all recent, and welcome, attempts to address the 'gender' order of crime, law and criminology, at the end of the day one important question remains unanswered: how is it possible to talk about the 'masculinity' of 'law' and 'crime' when, I have suggested, we remain so unclear and unsure as to what the term 'masculinity' actually means in the first place?

Notes

1. My use of 'crimino-legal' here delineates, following Young (1996: 2), more than simply 'criminology' or criminal justice' or 'criminal law' but, rather, 'all of these together with the popular discourses that are manifested in the media, cinema and advertising, in order to convey the sense that "crime" has become (been made?) a potent sign which can be exchanged among criminal justice personnel, criminologists, politicians, journalists, film-makers and, importantly, (mythical) ordinary individuals'.

2. In 1995 an unpublished Bar Council Working Party Report found that women Bar students in England and Wales were being regularly offered pupillages in return for sex. This reflected, it stated, an 'unacceptably high' level of 'misconduct' (*The Guardian*, 4 May 1995). The issue of discrimination and harassment has been particularly evident in relation to the police and armed forces ('Wren Sues for Sexual Torment', *The Guardian*, 3 February 1997; 'Police Make Big Sex Bias Payouts', *The Guardian*, 18 September 1996).

3. Notably during the period in which Martin Mears held office as elected President of the Law Society. During his tenure, and in a series of highly publicised pronouncements on what he saw as the iniquities of the 'sex discrimination industry', Mears was reported as describing women as 'the enemy', 'feminist zealots' who 'thrive on grievances and use minorities as raw material for their whinge factories' (quoted in *The Guardian*, 22 April 1996; see further Pembridge 1996; M. Mears, letter to *The Independent*, 1 May 1996; 'Women Set to Oust Law Society Chief', *Mail on Sunday*, 28 April 1996).

4. Margaret Thornton's powerful book *Dissonance and Distrust: Women in the Legal Profession* (1996a) exemplifies this trend.

5. My use of cultural, social and symbolic capital is here drawing on the work of Bourdieu (1977, 1984; see further Jenkins, 1992: 85).

6. In S. Lever (ed.), *The Oxford Book of Australian Women's Verse*, Oxford: Oxford University Press.

7. The young hero in John Grisham's novel *The Firm* is told to buy 'dark grey or navy wool suits, white or blue cotton button down, medium starch, and silk ties'. On 'the suit theory' in the novels of Grisham generally, N. Walker, Review, *The Guardian*, 3 May 1996.

8. Securing research council funding has become of growing significance throughout the academy in Britain. Certainly, Economic and Social Research Council (ESRC) stress on policy issues and Home Office concern with 'policy relevant' research has impacted on the field of criminology.

9. '... under the impact of the Women's Movement socialists quite correctly began to realise the problems of violence against women and their sexual harassment' (Lea and Young, 1993: 262).

10. This term is adapted from Grosz and Probyn's (1995) use of 'sexy bodies'.

3   The 'Trouble With Boys'? The Child, the Social and the Dangerous Other

> The schoolboys on the top deck of the No. 50 bus were as loud and boisterous as any bunch of 13-year-olds can be. Twenty years ago they might have put their feet on the seats and cheeked the conductor. Last week in Streatham, south London, they followed a fellow passenger from the bus, pointed a handgun at his stomach and forced him to hand over the £10 in his wallet. Armed robbery by children, once something that happened only in New York's South Bronx, has arrived in Britain.
>
> ('Britain's Daily Diet of Crime', *The Sunday Times*, 28 February 1993)

> Some deaths are emblematic, tipping the scales, and little James [Bulger's] death – green fruit shaken from the bough, an ear of grain sown back in the earth – seemed like the murder of hope: the unthinkable thought of, the undoable done. . . . Those nameless boys had killed not just a child but the idea of childhood, all its happy first associations. No good could grow up from the earth.
>
> (Morrison, 1997: 21)

Introduction

This chapter is an exploration of the 'death' of childhood referred to above by Blake Morrison. It is, specifically, about the gendering of a debate around youth and crime which has taken place in Britain during the 1990s. It seeks to challenge the ways in which an idea of 'masculine crisis' has informed a series of conversations about the relationship between male youth, crime and criminality. It will be argued, drawing on the theorisations of corporeality, subjectivity and the sexed body outlined in Chapters 1 and 2, that there exist both continuities and revealing differences in the ways in which cultural mappings of a relationship between the 'masculinities' of boys, male youth and crime have historically informed the constitution of specific criminal(ised) subjects and populations. In seeking to uncover the ways in which the sexed bodies of male youth and boys have been encoded *as* masculine at particular moments, this chapter is about the discursive production of the category of the 'dangerous' male child. The argument will be developed via an analysis of two areas in which the debate around youth, crime and criminality has recently assumed a particularly high profile in Britain: firstly, in relation to boys and schooling and, secondly, in the context of representations of urban disorder and the 'riot'.

The chapter is structured around five sections. The first contextualises the argument to follow by exploring some of the recent associations which have been made between boys and disorder. Particular attention will be paid to the way in which these representations have drawn on and evoked what I have identified above as the 'masculine crisis' thesis. The second section explores the cultural iconography of the offending boy via a re-reading of some 'classic' criminological texts. The aim here is to surface the way in which particular – and, I shall argue, problematic – conceptualisations of both class and heterosexuality have each functioned to constitute a discourse of these 'dangerous' youthful masculinities at specific historical moments. Just as the construction of the working-class body as an object of social-scientific knowledge was itself central to those strategies which used its creation as a mode of classification and regulation, I shall argue in this chapter that a particular manifestation of the idea that there is a crisis 'within' or 'of' young men's masculinity has, at the present moment, become emblematic of some more general changes and anxieties surrounding questions of stability, integration and the social bond within the conditions of late modernity/postmodernity. These changes have resulted, I shall suggest, in a heightened form of criminalisation and vilification of specific populations.

The third and fourth sections seek to illustrate this central theme by focusing on, firstly, contemporary debates around the 'crisis' of boys and schooling and, secondly what has been called the 'crisis of masculinity' made evident in recent incidents of urban disorder. In respect of each, the purported 'crisis' will be linked to shifting understandings of heterosexual social practices, an expanded surveillance of childhood and, in particular, to changes in the ways in which the concept of the child is itself presently being refigured. In short, through re-reading the 'trouble with boys', this chapter seeks to reframe, fracture and reform notions of innocence and otherness through which, I shall suggest, shifting discourses around both heterosexuality *and* masculinity have together constituted, and continue to construct, 'dangerous' or 'wild' male youth in particular ways. In the fifth section I set out the implications of this argument for seeking to respond to the offending of male youth in ways which might transcend the – increasingly prevalent – representation of boy-children as embodiments of either (dis)order or innocence; as either 'devils' or 'little angels'.

Boys, (dis)order and the crisis of youth

In her book *The Trouble With Boys: Parenting the Men of the Future* Angela Phillips (1993) asks a question which has come to encapsulate the debate presently taking place in Britain around 'what is happening' to boys and boyhood. Why, she asks, 'do so many lovely boys turn into such unlovely men?' Phillips' book is just one of a multitude of sources – newspaper and magazine articles, radio and television programmes – which have, during the 1990s, sought to address and tackle the 'problem' of boys and young men in contemporary society. Traditionally, feminism has tended to depict boys as being empowered and privileged in a variety of ways relative to girls (Askew and Ross, 1988; Lees, 1986; Weiner, 1985). In recent years, however, it has been increasingly suggested, from different quarters, that it is girls who are now advantaged in a number of respects relative to boys. When allied to the broader notion that contemporary advanced capitalist societies are experiencing no less than a crisis of masculinity, this (purported) power-shift between boys and girls has been linked to the making of an explicit association between masculinity, crime and social disorder. A change is taking place in gender relations, it has been argued, which is resulting in (hitherto) 'lovely' boys turning into 'unlovely' men. It is these men who have become, in the words of Phillips' book, 'the rogue elephants of society, roving around the family unit and allowed access only for the process of mating'. The general thesis, captured in numerous newspaper headlines along the lines of 'Is the male redundant now?' and 'Does our society have any need for young men'?, can be simply put: men and boys, and in particular their masculinities, are in – or are approaching – a state of crisis.

This 'trouble with boys' thesis has, in fact, come to embrace a complex range of themes and issues around questions of social, economic, cultural and political change at the end of the twentieth century. Of particular prominence within recent debates in Britain has been a series of events which have been taken as exemplifying the growing problem of youth and masculinity (this list is by no means exclusive or in order of priority):

- There is a growing concern about what is seen to be boys' widespread educational failure relative to girls' (Browne, 1995; Mac an Ghaill, 1996), a concern encapsulated in the British tabloid newspaper *The Sun*'s headline 'Great White Dopes: Working-Class White Boys are the Big Failures in Britain's Schools' (7 March 1996). In July 1996 schools inspectors in England and Wales, picking up this theme, called for a programme of 'positive action' in order to combat the 'persistent under achievement' of boys at 'almost every level of the education system' (*The Guardian*, 11 July 1996; see further Jackson and Salisbury, 1996).[1]
- There have been a series of incidents in British schools involving boys considered 'too unruly too teach'. In 1996, and amongst much publicity, a range of schools were closed specifically because of the behaviour of 'unruly pupils' on a scale which had been unprecedented in recent educational history.[2]

- There is an increasing recognition that boys and young men are lacking the kinds of interpersonal and employment skills necessary for integration into the post-industrial, and increasingly service-based, labour markets of the new millennium (Ashton and Lowe, 1991).
- Related to the above, there is a growing perception that significant numbers of young men are, within a context of changing household and family structures, becoming 'unmarriageable';[3] or, conversely, that these young men are turning away from and rejecting marriage and the family in order to pursue their own hedonistic and selfish ends (see Chapter 5, pp. 129–31).
- Boys and young men have participated in a series of incidents involving horrific crimes of violence. Of particular significance in Britain has been the murder of the London head teacher Philip Lawrence and a series of cases in which boys have been charged with rape and other violent sexual offences. However, perhaps the most symbolically significant of all in shaping the contours of present debates around boys and crime has been the murder of the two-year-old James Bulger by two ten-year-old boys, Robert Thompson and Jon Venables, in February 1993 (King, 1995; Moore, 1996: 78–81; Morrison, 1997; Young, 1996: Ch. 5).[4]
- Finally, and more generally, there has occurred a series of concerns around questions relating to youth crime involving issues such as a perceived growing problem of persistent offending by male youth, increased incidents of 'bail bandits' (offending whilst on bail) and a laxity around issues of morality, authority and discipline. In these debates the figure of the persistent offender, variously termed 'predator', 'yob' and 'vermin' by both the media and politicians in Britain, has throughout the 1990s become the focus of considerable discussion, analysis and vilification.

If the above denote specific events which have recently been taken to be indicative of the crisis of masculinity in Britain, it is also possible to identify a number of more general recurring concerns and/or themes. Within both media texts and the pronouncements of politicians, church leaders and social commentators, as well as in the statements of various policy and pressure groups, the 'trouble with boys' thesis has been constituted at a nexus of broader debates and conversations around the following issues:

- Changes in social values, morality and the perceived need for a 'moral' discourse to meet changing times.[5]
- An apparent rise in incidences of 'family breakdown' and increasing uncertainties around men's 'role' in the family, in particular in the context of widespread divorce and cohabitation. An increase in the number of births outside marriage (Collier, 1995a) alongside technological changes which have transformed 'natural' reproductive practices (Stanworth, 1987) have further undermined traditional ideas of fatherhood and paternity.

- Changing structures of employment which have been seen by some to have resulted in the emergence of a 'new British underclass'. The underclass is a concept which, cutting across the political spectrum, has been used to explain and account for a range of attributes relating to the social, economic and cultural experiences of specific (largely urban) populations (see Chapter 5, p. 129). Any 'gendering' of this underclass debate has, however, tended to be the exception rather than the rule.
- Finally, and more generally, a number of concerns have been expressed about a range of cultural phenomena which have been associated with the 'loutish' behaviour of men and boys in the 1990s, notably the rise of what has been termed new 'laddish' culture.[6] The phrase 'men behaving badly' has recently been applied in Britain to a variety of discussions of men's behaviour. At times these cultural shifts have been interpreted as reinforcing a traditional 'boys will be boys' misogyny. In other contexts, and in some accounts at least, 'laddism' has been taken as indicating and celebrating a post-feminist, postmodern 'ironic' heterosexual performative practice on the part of men. In each case, however, questions of masculinity have been seen as central to these attempts to understand the nature of social change.

It is important to note at the outset the historical centrality of male youth to 'law and order' debates more generally. On one level a concern with male youth has been a familiar, if not the principal, subject matter of criminology.[7] As such, it might be argued that there is in fact little new to these recent debates. What has been central to the *contemporary* 'trouble with boys' thesis is, however, a belief that there is in fact something different to what is presently taking place, something which might then usefully be conceptualised through the language of changing 'gender' relations (that is, through changes in masculinity). This is in marked contrast to those previous, and well-documented, 'moral panics' around youth, crime and disorder where changes in the circumstances of youth tended to be accounted for in terms of shifting class relations (Pearson, 1983). The 'hooligan', such an iconic figure within both criminology and 'law and order' rhetoric, is in a sense mutating into something else: a 'new breed of man', a man who, crucially, can no longer be accounted for, explained and assessed solely within the terms of the familiar criminological concepts of class, poverty and disadvantage. What explanation of *this* figure seems to require, it is being suggested, is a new language and new concepts, a language which might speak to, and reflect, a new configuration of concerns around crime within a rapidly shifting economic, social and, importantly, *gender* order; that is, the language of masculinity/ies and, in particular, the idea that what is presently taking place is no less than a contemporary crisis in gender relations. The political appeal of the concept of masculinity, we have seen in Chapter 1, can be considerable. Both feminist and underclass variations on this 'trouble with boys' theme have each articulated a crisis of masculinity idea which,

though coming from very different political positions, nonetheless shares –
as we shall see – certain key themes.

Representing male youth: masculinities, subcultures and delinquency

In order to unpack and understand the specific ways in which masculinity is
being made to signify in these recent debates around youth crime, it is useful
to consider first the ways in which historically this association between boys,
young men and crime has itself been rendered inseparable from the
interrelated histories of the criminal justice system, penal policy and
criminological theory. The development of a separate system for dealing
with young offenders (for the purposes of the British penal system, now
understood as a category under the age of twenty-one) has been based on the
assumption that both the reasons for youth law-breaking and the optimum
response to the problem in terms of procedures, penal and corrective
measures require a differentiation to be made between the 'adult' and the
'juvenile'. Notwithstanding the many policy changes which have taken place
in the post-war period, this division continues, broadly, to structure the legal
framework which provides instructions, measures and procedures for dealing
with young people 'in trouble' (Harding and Koffman, 1995: 349). Within
penal policy the balance of the relation between welfare and punishment in
the context of youth offending has shifted depending on the government
(and, indeed, Home Secretary) of the day. Within criminology, however, it
has tended to be a constant theme that the primary focus of investigation has
been the crimes of lower/working-class young men and, in particular, the
offences of this group relating to property (Box, 1983). Although mediated
in important ways by questions of race/ethnicity, in other words, it has been
a concern with an 'unruly' male youth and their association with dangerous
populations, 'no-go' urban areas and general moral laxity which has
constituted a significant proportion of criminological knowledge and
endeavour. Youth/adolescence has been, and remains, a powerful cultural
and ideological category through which adult society has constructed a
specific age stage as, simultaneously, strange and familiar; and youth/
adolescence, as recent debates in Britain make all too clear, remains the
focus of adult fears and pity, of voyeurism and longing (Griffin, 1993).

It is difficult to overestimate the centrality of male youth to sociogenic
criminology. Inter-war and post-war criminologists, in seeking to place the
discipline firmly within the sociological framework, had embraced a general
(though not total) rejection of earlier wholly biogenic and psychogenic
theories of crime causation. Building on the groundwork laid by the Chicago
School (Burgess, 1928; Park, 1952; Shaw and McKay, 1942), a series of
subcultural studies emerged which focused on what was perceived at the
time to be the growing problem of urban male street gangs. Studies such as
Thrasher's (1936) *The Gang*, Whyte's (1943) *Street Corner Society*, Cohen's

Delinquent Boys: The Culture of the Gang (1955) and Miller's work on 'lower class culture' (1958) arose in the context of a widescale post-war alarm about youth and, in particular, a concern that urban young (men) were increasingly engaging in 'non-utilitarian' activities, stealing 'for kicks' and taking part in various 'negativistic' and 'malicious' forms of deviance. The studies of youth crime which emerged during this period reflect the intellectual and political context of the day. They are, broadly, positivist, have an individualist focus and embrace a functionalist account of masculinity couched, most often, in terms of the once ubiquitous 'sex role' framework (Parsons, 1954; see further Allen, 1989; Naffine, 1987: Ch. 4, 1985). Following the criminological 'big bang' of the 1960s and 1970s, later accounts of youth crime forged from within the agendas of 'radical' and 'new' criminology' sought, in contrast to these earlier (and predominantly North American) subcultural studies, to bring social, cultural and structural elements to bear in such a way that might challenge the individualist focus, and victim-blaming tendencies, of the earlier accounts (Brake, 1984; Corrigan, 1979; Hall and Jefferson, 1976). Moving from the authoritarian, correctionalist and empiricist criminology of these studies, which had considered the criminal essentially to be other, within British criminology's marxist turn a more 'fraternal' criminology emerged in which the criminal was to be constructed more as akin to a 'bad younger brother' (McRobbie, 1980; Naffine, 1997). And yet, notwithstanding the diversity of these later studies in terms of their underlying methodology, theoretical and political standpoints, there remained a certain continuity with the earlier subcultural studies in one crucial respect. Each, whilst producing texts rich in representations of masculinities and male subjectivities, systematically effaced the sex specificity of crime itself. What was taken for granted, considered to be so obvious that it was not in need of explanation, was that the subject under discussion should be, not youth in general, but (largely) lower/working-class men. Men, *as men*, remained invisible. In so doing, as Groombridge (1997) has suggested, this tradition was to say as much about men and criminology as it did about 'criminals'.

Unpacking masculinity: the 'macho', the 'cool' and the dissociation from the familial

Re-reading these 'classic' texts, it becomes clear that sociogenic criminology has produced a distinctive, and at times rich, model of urban youth and lower-class masculinity. Though there exist differences between specific accounts, mediated by culture, ethnicity and generation, it is possible to identify a number of key or recurring concerns in this work. The dominant masculinity of the North American gang studies embodied, perhaps above all, a 'cool', in control and authoritative ethos. What emerges from the work of Cohen (1955), Miller (1958), Cloward and Ohlin (1961) and others is a model of masculinity which corresponds well to, and in some ways can be seen as the apotheosis of, the attributes which are presently being associated with masculinity's 'hegemonic' form (see Chapter 1, pp. 18–23). The qualities of toughness, smartness, excitement, fate and autonomy, Miller's influential 'focal concerns', mesh well with what contemporary men are said to 'do' in accounts of masculinities which are 'accomplished' through crime (Messerschmidt, 1993, 1997). This is akin to the delinquent as, in Cohen's now infamous phrase, 'rogue male' (Cohen, 1955: 14). Young men drink, fight, get into (and stay out of) trouble (Canaan, 1996), young men 'do nothing' (Canaan, 1991), are physically and spiritually 'tough' (albeit at the cost of 'repressing' their more feminine sides), they 'have a laff' (Messerschmidt, 1993: 98; Willis, 1977: 13); young men demand recognition, excitement and the 'rush' of adrenalin. The contexts, cultural styles and language through which these traits are articulated differ. However, the general qualities of 'the masculine' in this context have remained broadly constant and subsequent accounts of male youth and subcultures have, to the present day, followed through this model of a tough, aggressive, 'in control' masculinity. The attributes deemed 'masculine' in Campbell's (1993) account of urban disorder in Britain, for example, and the 'machismo' depicted by Young (1986) as 'haunting' contemporary British streets would each, in all likelihood, be familiar to the earlier subcultural theorists. Boys, it could be argued, on one level continue to be boys in much the same ways as they have in previous generations: '. . . it is important to recognise the ismorphism of certain forms of masculine desire and crime: the near perfect fit between the mortice of masculinity, and the tenon of crime' (Jefferson, 1994b: 80). The pleasures of crime and the pleasures of 'the masculine', it appears, continue to fused.[8]

Or so it would seem. It is necessary at this stage to unpack some of the assumptions which are being made here about the relationship between masculinity and male youth. Or, to be more accurate, it is necessary to investigate the ways in which the concept of masculinity is here being made to signify certain features of the men/crime relationship at particular moments and in certain contexts. What is revealed, I now wish to argue, are some interesting continuities and differences between cultural mappings of the relationship between 'dangerous' male youth and the constitution of the specific subjects of criminological knowledge. What assumptions are being made here about men, youth and crime? And how does this relate to understandings of the 'masculinity' of sociogenic criminology, as discussed in Chapter 2? It is possible to make a number of observations.

Work   Firstly, the 'problems of adjustment', 'status frustration' (Cohen, 1955), 'blocked opportunity structure' (Cloward and Ohlin, 1961) and lack of 'legitimate means' (Merton, 1957) faced by young men rest on a particular correlation being made between men and work. Put simply, work is (or should be) the key reference point through which men's subjectivities are understood. Without work, and in particular without an appropriate *initiation into* work, the transition from childhood/youth to male adulthood is rendered problematic. Boys 'remain' boys and full adulthood is then deferred, achieved precariously or ultimately not achieved at all. Within the contemporary underclass theory variant of this argument, the link is made explicit in the suggestion that it is work which, alongside marriage, civilises the otherwise 'uncivilised' male youth (this issue is considered in more depth in Chapter 5). No such association between work and 'delinquency' is made for women and girls, whose subjectivities, we have seen, have been constituted in rather different ways. Within such an engagement, 'the idea of the masculine role per se . . . the priorities that have traditionally been given in lower-class neighbourhoods . . . to young men getting jobs, are never problematized' (Taylor, 1994: 480). It is taken as axiomatic that the central activity of the men under scrutiny is, or should be, paid employment, although such notions about the effect of unemployment on crime cannot be sustained when it is female, and not male, crime which is the object of study (Naffine and Gale, 1989).

Class   Secondly, and relating to the above depiction of an initiation into 'responsible' adulthood, the masculinities of male youth appear as precarious, fragile, ever fluid. The measurement of what is 'truly' masculine is, at once, normative and yet it is also indefinite, relative, an 'accomplishment' which is without a stable resting point, or, rather, with a point which always manages to be 'just ahead' (Merton, 1957). Crucially, this is a masculinity the affirmation, accomplishment or 'doing' of which is seen to take place via the involvement of young men in delinquent activity. It is, however, a masculinity accomplished in ways which are mediated, above all, by the *class* location of the youth in question. Within sociogenic criminology generally a range of masculinities have been constituted through, and differentiated from each other in terms of, a core division between lower/ working- and middle-class youth. It is working-class young men and boys who are depicted as experiencing a series of 'absences', not just of monetary resources but also the (related) impoverishments of (a lack of) educational credentials, rewarding employment, self-respect, interpersonal skills and 'appropriate' cultural values – caution, delayed gratification, and so forth. Judged against a middle-class cultural norm, working-class youth cultures appear as 'delinquent solutions' (Downs, 1966), serving the function of affirming class-based identities which are formed in subcultural identification and in leisure consumption (Hall and Jefferson, 1976; Hebdige, 1979). It is in its obedience to the norms of the lower-class culture that a working-class masculinity is here being constituted as inherently crimogenic: class and criminality are thus rendered inseparable at the very moment a notion of *individual* masculine crisis – that ever-present struggle to 'be masculine' – is seen as resulting from the *structural* location of the youth in question. Their fragile, fluid masculine gender identity is bound up with a class-specific response. What we have in such criminological studies is, in effect, a sex-specific engagement with the 'delinquent' values of working-class young men, central to which is a particular model of masculinity which has been

seen as having evolved to fit the conditions of working-class neighbourhoods and communities as a whole (which, depending on the study in
question, appear as the slum area, the inner city or the council estate, and so
forth). Yet the central question has been, and remains, how do these young
men cope with the social circumstances which they face? The answer is
organised as a class-specific, as opposed to sex-specific, response. It is not
simply that, as feminism has pointed out, young women and girls have been
invisible in these accounts. It is also not so much that the 'sex question' is
not, in a sense, being asked at all – these are texts which are clearly rich in
representations of masculinities; rather, it is asked in such a way that many
questions about the sexed specificity of the relationship between men and
crime more generally remain, as we shall see, unanswered.

Family   It is at this point that we come to a dimension which, though present
within criminological accounts, has traditionally been associated with the
worlds of women and girls and not men and boys: the family. Implicit in the
above correlation between (fragile) masculinity, lack of (or limited) employment opportunity and crime/delinquency is a presumed *dissociation* of
young men from the domain of the familial alongside, revealingly, a
simultaneous analytic privileging of relationships *between* men. In marked
contrast to women and girls, who appear peripherally as wives, mothers and
girlfriends (Smart, 1977) – as, that is, coded familial(ised) individuals – the
masculine subject is constituted through reference to other (non-familial/
affective) associations. At times he appears literally of no family, somehow
beyond dependencies and responsibilities apart from those of his 'higher'
loyalties to the gang, the group, his 'mates'. Indeed, it is the very *lack* of
familial ties which becomes, at times, the mark of the 'truly' masculine man
(Ehrenreich, 1983; cf. Becker, 1973). Yet the familial does, however, cast its
shadow of vulnerability and inevitable dependencies over the outward
'machismo' of the youth subculture. The mother, the girlfriend and the sister
may know what a young man is 'really' like 'at home', in another world far
removed from the street corner. When such dependency *is* revealed, the
'tough' lad can appear to be not so 'tough' after all, displaying a vulnerability and fragility at odds with the otherwise 'macho' masculinity. Crucially,
however, whereas working-class women have been spoken about in discourses of developmental psychology, education and social work, and
whereas women have systematically appeared as 'bad' or potentially bad
mothers (Walkerdine, 1995: 321), it has been primarily from *within a
discourse of crime – and not the family –* that men have been understood to
be constituted as masculine in the first place. The assessment to be made is
not one of bad (or potentially bad) 'fathers', not one of men who are 'sons',
'brothers' or 'husbands', but one of men who are (at least) potentially and
(more usually) essentially crimogenic. In other words a masculinity–crime
correlation is established at the very moment an understanding of the gender
of men is being dissociated from the sphere of the familial, from the domain
of private, affective relationships which have been coded 'feminine' – apart

from, crucially, questions of (hetero)sexuality. Ironically, it is through relations encoded *as* masculine/familial that the historical shift from the empiricist, positivist criminology (of criminology as correcting Father) to the appreciative studies of the British tradition (of criminology as empathetic Brother) has itself been subsequently understood.

If this masculine subject is dissociated from the world of women and children, therefore, it is also clear that relations with other men have assumed a central place in the constructing of this dominant masculinity. The inter-subjective processes of peer pressure, being 'seen' to be 'tough' and so forth, is far from straightforward and can usefully be seen in terms of the complex, contested and always negotiated dynamics of intra-male relationships. The psycho-social contours of these relationships, however, do not stand apart from questions of heterosexuality. They are played out in terms of hierarchies between men which mediate a performativity ('looking hard') which has been structured around the avoidance of 'being seen' as that which is the apotheosis of the 'not masculine': being, that is, 'homo-sexual', being 'womanly' (being a girl, a 'puff', a 'fag', and so forth, the routine and pervasive derogations of hetero-masculine culture). Whilst much of the subcultural tradition in criminology focused on such issues as class and 'style' (Hall and Jefferson, 1976; Hebdige, 1979), that which was being reacted *to* in the formation of the particular subculture was understood through drawing largely on marxist and semiotic frames of analysis. That a particular male *heterosexuality* was here being constituted tended not to be addressed, even though the 'lads' ' masculinities were clearly being defined in relation to and against the other of women, femininity (effeminacy) and homosexuality. These are the unspoken associations, the taken-for-granted within these accounts of youth subcultures. And yet it is these very features – questions of class, family and the construction of sexual/sexed 'others' – which, I shall argue in the remainder of this chapter, are of central significance when seeking to understand the symbolic and emblematic significance of youth crime within the contemporary debates around 'the trouble with boys' discussed above.

In order to illustrate this argument, the following two sections seek to explore areas in which, in marked contrast to traditional criminological studies, questions of sex/gender have recently come to the fore in a number of accounts of the offending of boys and male youth. In what follows I wish to explore further the discursive construction of offending male youth by focusing on the complex ways in which, I shall argue, a range of discourses have recently interweaved to bring into being a problematic subject – the offending boy – who is constantly in need of surveillance and regulation. The areas to be discussed are, firstly, that of boys, schooling and gender and, secondly, the issue of male youth and urban disorder. Each is an area in which the 'trouble with boys' thesis has been articulated in a particularly high-profile way in Britain via the making of explicit links to the more general 'crisis of masculinity' idea. What is taking place, in other words, is not simply about questions of male youth. It has also been interpreted as saying something about 'what is happening' to men and masculinity per se in today's society.

Schooling: boys, delinquency and the 'making' of masculinities

Given the symbolic significance of the category of youth, it is perhaps unsurprising that analyses of the institutions in which young people spend so much of their time – schools – should have been the subject of considerable attention and scrutiny within post-war criminology. The history of the relationship between schooling and offending has a long and well-documented history (Power et al., 1967) and recent studies continue to confirm the centrality of the school experience and adolescent peer relations in influencing offending (Graham and Bowling, 1996). The form which such studies of schools have tended to take has been that of an empirical investigation in which the progress of boys has been charted and the effects of schooling processes on offending assessed. Thus, it has been found, the prevalence of offending can vary dramatically among different secondary schools (Farrington, 1972). Whilst some accounts have linked such variation in delinquency rates among schools to differences 'in their intake of troublesome boys' (Farrington, 1994: 551), others, in contrast, have found clear correlations between the presence of high delinquency and truancy rates, low-ability pupils and parents of lower social class which, importantly, could *not* be explained entirely by the pupil intake (Rutter et al., 1979). In other words, it has been the school climate itself, its cultures, structures and educational ethos, which has been seen as promoting, or inhibiting, offending by boys. Within these 'traditional' studies of schooling and offending generally, however, the question of the sex specificity of crime tended not to be addressed. It has been presumed, in much the same way as we have seen above in relation to the subcultural accounts, that it is boys who constitute the object of study. Questions relating to the sexed specificity of the ways in which boys and girls themselves experience school processes, which might then promote or inhibit offending, are not addressed. It has, in short, been taken for granted in accounts of youth and schooling that it should be 'the most troublesome *boys*' who 'tended to go to the high-delinquency schools, while the least troublesome *boys* tended to go to the low-delinquency schools' (Farrington, 1994: 551; my emphasis).

In contrast to this approach, it has been from within a somewhat different strand of writing on schooling, the series of 'anti-school' studies which emerged during the 1970s and 1980s, that a more theoretically sophisticated attempt to tackle issues of youth, crime and delinquency has been made. Coming from something of a mid-point between the fields of cultural studies and criminology, there is to be found in this work a conceptualisation of 'masculinity' which in many ways embodies both the strengths and weaknesses of the kinds of subcultural engagements with male youth discussed above. The over-riding conceptual distinction in this work, the core division, as it were, around which the subsequent analyses of school dynamics have been built, has been that of a bifurcation of groups of boys based primarily on class identification. Specifically, and as in the subcultural studies, this has been a division between middle- and working-class youth. Once again, the principal focus of analysis has been working-class male youth activities, only this time in the specific context of schools. In this work the school is itself conceptualised, and problematised, in terms of its dominant structural and cultural location within capitalist society as a 'middle-class' institution. Earlier work thus focused, above all, on the school as a site for the 'reproduction of labour' (Corrigan, 1979; Willis, 1976, 1977). Studies of girls remained rare. In seeking to understand the dynamic relationship between the school and 'the lads' the researcher then sought to separate out, for heuristic purposes, the (largely) boys into particular categories: thus we find accounts of 'the Saints' and 'the Roughnecks' (Chambliss, 1973), 'the Socialites' (Socs) and 'the Street Corner Youth' (Eses) (Schwendinger and Schwendinger, 1985), and (perhaps most famously) 'the Ear'Oles' and 'the Lads' (Willis, 1977). Within each of these binaries the former is taken to refer to middle-class youth; those who engage in 'pranks' and vandalism outside school but, importantly, conform inside the school. The latter encompasses the more serious crimes, the machismo, the aggression and fighting (the familiar 'focal concerns') and complex anti-school cultural resistances of working-class youth. In effect, these studies modified, but broadly supported in the school setting, the general points arising from the conceptualisation of masculinity within the subcultural theory discussed above. The over-arching frame is, like subcultural theory generally, one of sex role socialisation in which 'gender' is understood as the expression of behaviour learned through various socialisation processes.

It is possible to identify in these 'anti-school' studies at least the (tentative) beginnings of a critical engagement with the concept of masculinity (notably in the work of Willis, 1977). However, the beginnings of a more explicit focus on the subject of masculinities, Nayak and Kehily (1996: 211) have suggested, emerged first not from within the accounts of school subcultures written predominantly by men but from within the context of feminist concerns to 'make visible' girls within the schooling process. Thus, and in much the same way as feminist studies of girls and subcultures had sought to redress the shortcomings of the earlier 'classic' studies in criminology (Campbell, 1984; McRobbie, 1991, 1993; McRobbie and Garber, 1976), the 'masculinist' assumptions of the earlier work on education were here identified and challenged. Feminist research on schooling highlighted the need to account for, and challenge, the pervasive 'sexism' and the systematic inequalities which were identified as existing between young men and women in schools (Askew and Ross, 1988). This work offered a perspective that sought to place gender alongside class in terms of significance; it 'called for a reformulation of class based analyses in relation to the structure of schooling' (Nayak and Kehily, 1996: 211). However, importantly, it also continued to presume the analytic purchase of the sex/ gender distinction itself. The focus, moreover, remained one of inter-gender differences and power relations between young men and women. As a result, Nayak and Kehily (1996) suggest, these feminist studies produced an over-emphasis on the categories 'boys' and 'girls' which, ultimately, served to conceal differences *within* these groups (for example, in the dynamically contested interconnections of 'race', ethnicity, class and sexuality). Whilst the complexities of gender relations within the school were identified and interrogated, 'masculinity' nonetheless remained monolithic, conceptualised in terms of a unified gender/ed role ascribed to boys and men.

It has only been in more recent scholarship on gender and education, increasingly influenced, significantly, by developments around postmodernism, gay and lesbian studies and queer theory, that an engagement with masculinity has been coupled with analyses of sexual difference and an awareness of the complexity of what it means to speak of the category 'boys' in the first place. Much of this work has come from within a framework of pro-feminist scholarship within the field of gender and education; and in seeking to (re-)read the relationship between boys and schooling, so central as we have seen to present reconfigurations of the 'trouble with boys' thesis, it has considerable implications for criminology.

This work has drawn on, but developed and extended, the insights of earlier research by foregrounding an analysis of the discursive production of heterosexuality/ies, identity and men's subjectivities (Haywood and Mac an Ghaill, 1996). If there has been one central theme to this work it is that schools are not gender-neutral, pre-given institutions but are themselves sites for the active *production* of gendered/sexualised identities, and not simply agencies which reflect dominant power relations (Browne, 1995; Connell, 1989; Kehily and Nayak, 1997; Mac an Ghaill, 1996; Nayak and Kehily, 1996). The school is thus conceptualised as being a 'masculinizing agency' (Jordan, 1995; Mac an Ghaill, 1994) and, working on the premise that sexual identities are not biologically given but interdiscursively constituted, boys' identities are themselves seen as being created through a series of institutional and lived practices in which, importantly, the experience of school is accorded a central significance. Boys are located as sexed subjects engaged in a 'struggle for masculine identities within schools' (Nayak and Kehily, 1996: 212). The key concern, and object of analysis, becomes understanding the nature of the complex process whereby this constitution of sexed subjectivity takes place. Crucially, and in marked contrast to both the subcultural and anti-school studies discussed above, this has entailed an analysis of the production not only of the 'usual suspects' of criminological thought; that is, marginal and/or oppressed identities conceptualised in terms of class. Increasingly, attention has turned to those subjects constituted as dominant groups. What marks this recent scholarship as different from what has gone before, therefore, is an engagement with the (sexed) specificities of the experiences of white, middle-class youth (Connell, 1989; Kehily and Nayak, 1997; Messerschmidt, 1994: 87). And, in so doing, what has occurred is, in effect, a shift in the gaze of the researcher away from analysing sexualities/youth groups hitherto deemed subordinate and towards a questioning of the assumptions, practices and identities of dominant groups themselves. In so doing, and in 'sexing' subjectivities, the school itself has been reconfigured as a complex gendered and heterosexual arena (Mac an Ghaill, 1994: 3–4; also Mac an Ghaill, 1996; Skeggs, 1991). Such explorations of the interrelationship between schooling, masculinities and sexualities have turned to analyses of such issues as the gendered dimensions of student selection, subject allocation and stratification, disciplinary modes of authority, instruments of surveillance and control, and gendered student–teacher and student–student social relations.

This recent research on boys and education has, in short, sought to explore the complex relationship between schooling and gender through valorising the positive, productive role of the school as a *discursive site* within which particular subject positions (be it of boys, young men or, indeed, the teaching staff themselves) are constituted (Connell, 1989; Mac an Ghaill, 1994). In so doing, this theoretical approach has not simply opened out the area to further analysis, lending itself particularly well to small-scale intensive fieldwork projects. It has also fragmented 'masculinity' in surfacing the (hetero)sexed framework within which understandings of men's subjectivities have been constituted in the first place. The analysis has been of the reproduction of ideas about men's subjectivities within specific local contexts and social settings. However, tapping into and directly addressing the range of concerns which make up the 'trouble with boys' thesis, this theoretical frame, and the questions it raises, also opens up an analysis of masculinity and crime to a consideration of the mutual constitution of class *and* heterosexuality which is very different from that of the earlier criminological studies. In relation to recent feminist accounts of masculinity and urban disorder this approach has been carried forward in such a way as to raise some very different questions about men, heterosexuality, the family and crime.

Urban disorder: 'maverick masculinities', 'wild boys' and the combustible city

At the same time as these questions around sex, gender and masculinity have been raised within the field of education it has been, perhaps ironically, in relation to one of the most familiar and researched areas of criminology – the relationship between youth and urban disorder – that the 'masculinity question' has recently surfaced most visibly as an important variable in its own right in seeking to explain crime. For some, the emergence of the 'masculinity question' within this context has been seen as constituting no less than a conceptual breakthrough in the relationship between gender and crime more generally. Within two major texts aimed primarily at students of criminology, Walklate's *Gender and Crime* (1995) and McLaughlin and Muncie's (1996) *Controlling Crime* (see Pitts, 1996), the question of masculinity has been addressed specifically within this context of urban disorder and, in particular, via an engagement with the journalist and broadcaster Bea Campbell's (1993) book *Goliath: Britain's Dangerous Places*. These discussions of masculinity are significant, and deserving of further exploration here, not just because of their general rarity within criminology. On one level these texts provide further evidence that 'masculinity and crime' is emerging as, in Walklate's words, a 'new equation for criminology' (Walklate, 1995: 160). However, the fact that the discussion should be raised via an engagement with urban disorder and, in particular, with Campbell's *Goliath*, is not only in part testament to the power and force of the book's argument (described by Walklate as 'one of the most readily available and thoroughgoing accounts and analyses' of masculinity and crime: 1995: 174). Each of these engagements, importantly, also provides an opportunity to explore and reassess, via Campbell's account, some of the ways in which this 'new equation for criminology' is presently being addressed.

Dangerous male youth, as we have seen, has long been emblematic of wider social concerns and anxieties. Indeed, from the beginnings of both the Lombrosian and governmental criminological projects, those 'first soundings of a modernist discourse about crime' (Garland, 1994: 32), a historical encoding of 'dangerous' populations has been inseparable from a concern with the combustible mix of young men, disorder and the city. The 'riot', 'public disorder' and the 'poor city' can be seen to have been the 'very stuff' of sociogenic criminology (Cohen, 1972; Pearson, 1983). From accounts of the netherworld of the Victorian chronically poor, yet to be civilised into the norms of a new 'respectable' economic and familial order (Booth, 1976; Cohen, 1981; Stedman-Jones, 1976), through to the various interpretations of the riots which took place in Britain during the 1980s (Field and Southgate, 1982; Lea and Young, 1984) and contemporary discussions of the 'no go' *fin de siècle* postmodern city, an association between male youth, poverty and disorder has been a recurring theme within criminology. What is different about Campbell's account, and what links it with the broader concerns around the 'trouble with boys' thesis discussed above, is the way in which it seeks to explicitly foreground an engagement with the concept of masculinity in its analysis of urban disorder. It also, importantly, seeks to address the criminality of young men not through reference to a familiar pathologised working class but in terms of a more general, and cross-class, 'crisis of masculinity'. At issue is the question of what 'men do', and not *just* the 'wild' or 'delinquent' pursuits of a particular section of the population. In so doing the analysis seeks to disturb at the outset the perceptual grid which has rendered the 'masculinity of crime' invisible within criminology. In seeking to 'recognize the extent of the complex mutually reinforcing nature of men's power as a class, and the diversity of men and men's power' (Hearn, 1992: 96), the argument *begins* from the identification of an absence: the absence of masculinity and the poverty of existing public debates around the subject of men, urban disorder and crime.

Bea Campbell's book *Goliath* (1993) is about the rioting which took place on mainland Britain during 1991 in the urban conurbations of Tyneside, Oxford, Coventry, Bristol and Cardiff. The analysis of urban disorder which is presented is framed by an understanding of a gender regime which, Campbell argues, connects the young men who live on these poor, impoverished housing estates with the men who police such estates in what she terms a shared 'culture of masculinity'. Central to Campbell's argument is the belief that women and men have very different experiences of life in such economically and socially marginal communities and, it is inferred, more generally. Sex difference is thus, in a sense, integrated into the conceptualisation of gender relations at the beginning. Men and women 'do' things differently. Far from addressing the 'routine' crimes of young men solely in terms of their class location, Campbell seeks to explore the reproduction of various value systems, motivational imperatives and differential access to public space which is, she argues, common to men of all classes. The argument does not seek to negate the fact that the attentions of the criminal justice system remain largely directed towards the property crimes of the 'lower' classes. It is concerned to identify, however, within this broader masculine culture something which cannot be confined to just one class. In a sense, therefore, Campbell's text can be seen as overlapping in certain respects with the Left Realist rejections during the 1980s of the idea that property crime somehow constitutes a 'proto-revolutionary' event (cf. Lea and Young, 1984). Central to Campbell's account of the 1991 riots is the recognition that these young men, and their 'wild' masculinities, *do* terrorise their own communities. What emerges, in a series of powerful and moving testimonies (of the mothers, of the 'others', of the 'lads' themselves), is the very real pain and suffering experienced by those who have to share the community, or otherwise share their lives, with these boys and young (and not so young) men. The question which ultimately frames *Goliath*'s account of masculinity and crime can, therefore, be simply put. Why do men respond differently from women to the circumstances of local economic crisis? More specifically, why do the 'modes of masculinity' which Campbell argues are 'revealed' at such moments of 'crisis' then take such destructive forms?

In order to address the possible implications of this work for developing an understanding of the relationship between men and crime more generally, and in particular why it should have impacted on criminology in the way it so clearly has,[9] it is first necessary to unpack further the kinds of associations which are being made here between male youth, masculinity and urban disorder.

An escape from women? Sex difference and the diverse meanings of 'masculinity'

Masculinity is in fact conceptualised in *Goliath* in a number of different ways and to a number of argumentative ends. On the one hand there is the distinctive 'culture of masculinity' which is, we have seen, identified as connecting the 'lads' with the police (especially in their shared relationship to cars: on joyriding and car culture see further Groombridge, 1993; Jackson, 1992; Jefferson, 1992). Other connections include the significance attached to homosocial bonding and masculine solidarity and the familiar 'focal concerns' of youth, fun, excitement, the adrenalin rush of 'trouble' and the 'thrill of the chase'. This is a dominant masculine culture which, once again, maps well onto the traits of hegemonic masculinity depicted elsewhere in the literature on masculinity and crime during the 1990s. Thus, masculinity is on one level used as a *description* of a culture and a range of activities which are ideologically and empirically associated with men.

Masculinity is also, simultaneously, evoked by way of an *explanation* of the various criminal activities of young men. The actions of both the lads and the police are described as 'assertions' of masculinity (Campbell, 1993: 319). In contrast to the earlier subcultural studies, unemployment, importantly, is not seen as leading unproblematically to an individual crisis of masculinity. Rather, masculinity generally is seen as being 'accomplished', in much the same way Messerschmidt (1993) suggests, through an engagement in rioting, violence and a variety of displays of machismo (for example, 'joy riding' and 'ram raiding') by young men (cf. Chapman, 1993; Lea and Young, 1993: xxviii). It is Campbell's argument that, faced with the problem of reconstructing a male identity in circumstances of social immobility and protracted adolescence in which, crucially, traditional (empowered) masculine identities are not available, these young, lower/working-class men then seek other, more destructive forms of masculine expression. The resulting mode of masculinity is, in some respects, not dissimilar from that of the subcultural accounts seen above. In the face of 'blocked' legitimate opportunities, a means to being successful 'as a man' is linked to an engagement with crime and/or delinquency. However, what is different in Campbell's account is the integration of questions of sexual difference and a conceptualisation of masculinity which, transcending the individual, is constructed through structural and interpersonal relations of power. Men and women, she argues, have very different experiences of life in these economically and socially marginal communities; they inhabit different 'gender traditions'. Whilst women engage in self-help, caring, constructive activities, Phillips argues in *The Trouble With Boys*, echoing Campbell's argument:

> In the barren estates of de-industrialized Britain few men have power for anything other than destruction. . . . it is nearly always a group of women who are using their interpersonal skills, their ability to work co-operatively, and without

hierarchies, to make and mend, keep each other together, campaign to keep their communities afloat, and occasionally to perform real miracles to ensure that life doesn't go on getting worse. (Phillips, 1993: 251)

This 'assertion' or 'accomplishment' of masculinity cannot just be seen in relation to the familiar 'public' contexts of the usual terrains of crime: the street, the pub, the 'public' space, those various domains associated with men. It is also, crucially, formed in a relation to – or, to be more accurate, through the *dissociation from* – the familial; that is, that which has been traditionally associated with the 'world of' women. Campbell's argument thus engages with that which had been implicit, unspoken, in the earlier criminological work: that these young men appear incapable of sharing a space, a community, with the women and children in their lives. And yet in so doing, and as we have seen from the representations of masculinity within the criminological accounts discussed above, in this respect they do not appear to be so different from previous generations. If this behaviour is indicative of a 'crisis' of masculinity, then it could be argued that it is a crisis which has been underway for some time now.

The point bears repeating: the various dualisms through which men and women's experiences of work and home have been constituted within modernity – dualisms such as breadwinner (man) and homemaker (woman), of public (work) and private (family) – are not simply revealed in this argument as having been 'gendered' myths all along. Men of *all* classes have historically sought escape from the world of women and into the company of other men (Collier 1996a; Ehrenreich, 1983). It is at the present moment, however, and in the context of the economic, social and cultural reconfigurations of the domains of 'work' and 'family' taking place within late modernity, that a range of lower/working-class subjectivities of dispossessed, marginalised young men are being presented as being in 'crisis' because, it is presumed, they somehow remain committed to these 'outdated' divisions and heterosexual expectations. In a sense these men appear as a 'throwback' to an earlier time, albeit in a rather different way than Lombroso may have imagined; far from it being biologistic reasons, it is in terms of their *gender* expectations – their *masculinities* – that they appear as having not 'moved on', having not recognised and adjusted accordingly to the fact that the sociality of modernity which had bound them to community, to paid employment, to wife, child and culture, has itself fragmented. That is, that the economic, cultural and structural supports of 'traditional' gender relations have themselves, quite simply, disappeared (or are disappearing) in the areas of cross-generational unemployment which were the locale for the 1991 riots.

Crucially, these masculinities are depicted as being 'in crisis' in ways very different from the masculine subjects of the middle-class urban, men who might equally be interpreted as being engaged in a set of practices which involve seeking out, or seeking to express, a 'deep masculine' security at a moment of ontological *in*security (albeit that middle-class men appear to do so in some very different forms: see Chapter 5). As Walklate summarises the sexed specificity of the response to this new gender order:

> ... what the lads do is create a sense of themselves in the space available to them, not between home, work and the public house, ... but between home (meaning their mother's or sometimes their girlfriend's home) and the street (where they hang out and do business). (Walklate, 1995: 176)

These are spaces, crucially, which are – no less than in the case of schooling and education discussed above – experienced through codes of heterosexuality which are themselves class-, 'race'- and ethnically mediated.

There are certain problems, or unresolved issues, within Campbell's analysis. It is possible to read her account of sex difference, for example, as at times residing in, or at least hinting at, certain ontological assumptions about the essential nature of men and women: 'Crime and coercion are sustained by men. Solidarity and self-help are sustained by women. It is as stark as that' (Campbell, 1993: 319). Are all men actual or potential 'yobs', in much the same way, Walklate (1995: 178) has asked, that all men have been seen as potential rapists? Or is what is taking place here, in effect, a 'feminising' of a 'respectable' *middle-class* culture in the depiction of the 'brutish machoism' of working-class communities (cf. Hume, 1996)? Moreover, the suggestion that 'unemployment *reveals* a mode of masculinity whereas the common-sense has been that it causes a crisis of masculinity' (Campbell, 1993: 202; my emphasis) appears to presume the existence of an a priori, pre-discursive masculine form which is then 'revealed' at certain moments (be it times of stress, economic crisis or blocked opportunity). On the one hand, masculinity functions as an explanation of an individual man's desire to commit crime. Yet, on the other hand, it is also evoked by way of a more general explanation of criminal behaviour (Walklate, 1995: 179); that is, as the 'cause' of a range of (diverse) behaviour on the part of men. Absence from child care, youth joy riding, burglary, domestic violence, general aggression, men's homosociality and economic self-interest – each appears as a manifestation of 'masculine' behaviour. The conceptualisation of masculinity as both description and explanation of the causes of crime does not only 'reflect a failure to resolve fully the tendency towards universalism, it can also be read as tautological' (Walklate, 1995: 181). As we have seen in Chapter 1, in such accounts of men 'expressing', 'asserting' or 'reinforcing' masculinity, the question remains as to precisely *what* it is that is being lost, asserted, expressed, and so forth. Is this masculinity an expression of a 'gendered' learned behaviour, as in the earlier sex role socialisation accounts? Or is it something negotiated in different social-structural locations in which individual men are presented with a series of structured choices (cf. Messerschmidt, 1993)?

There are elements of each of these conceptualisations of masculinity in Campbell's argument. In associating 'being a lad' with the cultivation of a hyper-heterosexualised identity, something is, as Walklate recognises, 'left untouched by this way of thinking about the relationship between masculinity and crime' (1995: 179). What does not tend to appear in such an account is that which is, arguably, present in the more recent work on boys and schooling – an appreciation of the contradictory and fragile nature of this hyper-heterosexual masculinity, the complex ambiguities of lived experience and, importantly, the contradictory dynamics of power. Campbell's construction of criminal male youth, on one level, overlaps in several respects with that to be found in neo-conservative and underclass imaginings of intellectually and biologically deficient male 'barbarians' at the gate of middle-class respectable society (Murray, 1984, 1990; see below pp. 129–31). Such 'strong parallels' between Campbell's 'wild masculinities' and the 'yob culture' evoked in neo-conservative 'law and order' rhetoric has been seen as a further cause for concern (Walklate, 1995: 177). In fusing the idea of the 'yob' with a critique of masculinity, Coward (1994) suggests, one result has been to further attack some of the least powerful men in society.

Notwithstanding these points, Campbell's analysis of urban disorder does raise important questions about the ways in which the relationship between masculinity and crime has been conceptualised in criminology. What it does, in particular, is integrate and render problematic issues of men's historical dissociation from the *familial*, the dynamics of *homosociality* and, crucially, questions of *sex difference*. Each, I have suggested, in different though interlocking ways, problematises the relationship between men, *heterosexuality* and crime. Taken together, the work discussed in this section in the areas of both schooling and urban disorder has made a valuable contribution to the study of the relationship between men and crime. In rejecting a conceptualisation of sexuality as seen through a straight/gay dualism, the recent work on boys and education has sought to engage with the complex interrelationships of gendered processes in the lives of young men. In so doing the 'everydayness' of homophobia in schools, for example, has been seen as bound up with, indeed as integral to, the constitution of heterosexual normativity. The kinds of homophobic practices identified by Nayak and Kehily (1996: 212) as ' "natural", routine activities in the developing lives of young men' in schools have assumed a naturalised status within prisons, the police force, the criminal justice system more generally and, of course, the urban areas which are depicted as the territory of 'maverick masculinities' (Pitts, 1996: 280) in the accounts of urban disorder discussed above. In relation to each, physical manifestations of homophobia are manifest in extrovert displays of heterosexuality and in the enacting of a supposedly 'natural' masculinity. In the school, diverse pupil sexual cultures, verbal and visual displays and psychic investments in these processes themselves emerge as being active in the shaping of gender relations (Kehily and Nayak, 1997; Mac an Ghaill, 1994). In relation to urban disorder what surfaces is the diversity of the alternative performative routes which young men may pursue whilst remaining within a broader heterosexual matrix, a matrix which frames the gender relations not just of the 'lads' (on both sides of any class-divide) but also, I have argued, of the police and those criminologists whose own subjectivities have been historically effaced from their considerations of such 'maverick' youth and 'wild' masculinities.

What recent work on masculinity and urban disorder has done is highlight this crucial, but under-explored, dimension to the men and crime debate: the complexity and contested nature of the relationship between men, heterosexuality and changing ideas of family in terms of sexual difference. Bea Campbell's *Goliath* is at its most powerful as a critique of the particular form of normative (hetero)sexuality which underpins the location of young men's subjectivities within different contexts. What the police and the 'lads' can be seen to 'share', for example, is a heterosexual culture steeped in homophobia (Fielding, 1994; Westmarland, 1997) and in which routine derogation of the 'other' (women, the homosexual) serves to naturalise and enforce the power of that norm. In the negotiation of or straining towards a coherent 'masculine' identity the activation of psychic investments is played out both internally and externally. The other to this heterosexual norm is always an (absent) present, ready to surface, to reappear, to speak of its existence. It is at this stage, therefore, that my analysis shifts to how such fantasies around the nature of this other – fantasies about class, heterosexuality and the criminal(ised) body – are themselves (re)produced in specific instances. In the next section I wish to explore further the ways in which this other has been constituted in the first place *through*, I shall argue, the making of a particular construction of the relationship between *men* and *crime*.

'Rat boys and little angels': corporeality, male youth and the bodies of disorder

The central binary at the heart of the literature on youth, schooling and urban disorder has been, we have seen above, a division between a (normalised) middle-class and a (pathologised) working-class culture. Earlier economistic models of subcultural theory conceptualised a male subject as being engaged in a process whereby his perception of the 'truth' of his experience was being somehow distorted. A working-class consciousness was seen as having been produced out of a shared experience of oppression; but the way in which that working-class subject was himself constituted *as* problematic tended to be taken for granted. The 'delinquent solutions' he reached, the 'communities' he formed, involved 'imaginary' and not 'real' (structural) solutions/change. Underlying such accounts was an inherently empiricist notion of 'shared experience' in which a distinctive working-class 'identity' was depicted as being produced in specific contexts (the 'slum' area, post-war economic restructuring, the domain of leisure, and so forth). It was this identity which was then to be observed, judged and assessed by the (usually male) criminological researcher. Implicit was the idea of a (normative) masculinity somehow waiting to be 'expressed' in these particular scenarios.

The subject which was being constituted in this work was certainly, in one sense, 'active': 'reaction formation', 'status frustration' and the construction of 'imaginary solutions' each envisage an agent working on, and responding to, the world in which he lives. Yet the subject *him*self was, throughout, prefigured within a particular theoretical frame in which his 'sociality' was constituted, a priori, through the making of certain (problematic) assumptions about various processes of socialisation which, crucially, were themselves experienced and mediated by sexual difference. Importantly, there was a systematic failure to engage with the *production* of the idea of the subject per se. What was unspoken in such accounts of youth and crime was, in short, the way in which a particular gendered social subject was itself being conceptualised.

The subject, the 'social' and sexual difference

At this stage, and in the light of the above, I wish to investigate the ways in which the male subject of criminology has been configured in this context. In particular, I shall address how (his) corporeality has been 'sexed' as male in frequently contradictory ways. In 'making social' this subject what is needed – and what has been absent – is a theory of a psychologically complex subject, a subject which might then be conceptualised as central to developing analyses of the social world (Henriques et al., 1984; Hollway, 1989). In the context of an engagement with social change, masculine crisis and the 'trouble with boys', my concerns in this chapter, what this approach requires is an investigation of the connections which exist between this subject and the specific ways in which ideas of the 'social' per se are produced at particular moments.

The dualism between the individual and the social, the split between psychology and sociology, remains central to sociogenic criminology. Yet the problem with criminology, as feminists have pointed out, has not simply been that a range of experiences have been unified, with the result being an effacing of the ways in which men and women may exist in differential relations to notions of 'community', urban space, and so forth (cf. Massey, 1994; Rose, 1993). Criminology has also failed to engage with the ways in which the subjects under scrutiny have themselves been produced within certain discursive practices. Far from identifying categories such as 'the child', 'masculinity', 'disorder' or, indeed, 'man' and 'woman' as being pre-discursive – as universalist, essentialist and 'given' –, what becomes necessary is to investigate the discursive production of such categories themselves within 'specifically historically and culturally located practices in which subject positions are produced through the interchange of signs' (Walkerdine, 1995: 312). In conceptualising the individual as a historically specific form of the subject, this approach opens out to analysis the various ways in which criminal boys and men have themselves been produced by a set of apparatuses of social regulation and management. In so doing, crucially, certain knowledges – such as criminology – which have made claims as to the 'truth' of the social and subjective themselves appear as fictions, as stories. The subject of criminal youth is thus not a pre-given entity. It is something produced in a series of the fictions and fantasies which make up the social world. This is *not* to claim that the criminological stories of youth crime discussed in this chapter and elsewhere in this book, be they sociological or psychologically focused, are 'false', in the sense that they are 'pseudo-science' or evasions of some (yet to be discovered but ultimately obtainable) 'truth' of crime. It is to state that they are, as Walkerdine has argued, 'fictions which function *in* truth, scientific stories whose truth-value [has] a central place in the government and regulation of the modern and postmodern order' (1995: 312; my emphasis). The 'truth value' of these fictions in constituting contemporary imaginings of men and crime can be illustrated by further consideration of two of the main elements through which, as we have seen throughout this chapter, contemporary representations of the dangerous male child have been constructed: fantasies, and changing configurations, of the *working class* and *childhood*.

Fantasy, fear and the body of the other: (re)constructing the working class

In focusing on a pathologised working-class other, that which the term 'middle class' has been made to signify within criminology has been systematically normalised. As a result attention has not simply been diverted from the ways in which subjectivities constituted as 'masculine' may in fact cut across class and/or other positionings based on 'race'/ethnicity and sexual orientation. What has resulted is the production of a working-class male subject who, depending on the political perspective of the criminological researcher, appears variously as the 'victim' of socio-economic change, the 'inert' consumer of a pathologising media or, perhaps and in other contexts, the ever-constant repository of the revolutionary vanguard. What unites each of these perspectives is, however, a construction of the working class as a category which always exists as a *problem*, something to be solved or transformed one way or another, to be 'endlessly described and monitored in every detail' (Walkerdine, 1995: 318). To depict this working class as not a 'fact' of modernity, but itself a fiction, a fantasy, is not to argue that poverty, oppression and exploitation do not exist or, importantly, that class is not an important designation through which we recognise ourselves. Rather, this 'working class' is itself, Walkerdine has argued, 'a fiction, in Foucault's terms, functioning in . . . very powerful truths that constitute and regulate modern forms of government' (1995: 316):

> . . . the way the working-class is created as an object of knowledge is central to the strategies which are used for its creation as a mode of classification. . . . These strategies tell us about the fears and fantasies of the regulators . . . for whom the proletariat forms an Other, to be feared, desired, directed, manipulated . . . this truth is constructed inside the fertile bourgeois imagination, an imagination that sees threat and annihilation around every corner . . . . (Walkerdine, 1995: 316–17)

This is a working-class subject which, Walkerdine suggests, has itself been placed in a hopelessly contradictory position; for at the very moment the white working class have disappeared from the political and intellectual agendas of the Left, to be replaced by questions of gender, race, sexuality, ethnicity (and now masculinity?), 'the proletariat, the mass, has been an obsession, a central if sometimes silent figure during all the debates from modernity through to postmodernity' (Walkerdine, 1995: 315; see also Morris, 1994). This is an obsession which is all too clear within the contemporary crimino-legal constructions of youth crime discussed above, and in relation to the representation of the dangerous male body within these debates the sexed corporealising of the proletarian mass or mob has itself been central to conversations around 'the trouble with boys'. It is in these debates that the contours of a 'fertile bourgeois imagination, an imagination that sees threat and annihilation around every corner', has manifested itself in a particularly striking way. In short, that which has in recent years become the object of such fears has been the corporealising of the body of dangerous male youth and, within it, the 'crisis of masculinity' with which this 'trouble with boys' is now being associated.

The case of the 'Rat Boy': de-humanising the (dangerous) bodies of youth   To illustrate this point with an example: the de-humanising of the young offender is, in one sense, a familiar strategy. The delinquent as 'yob' and 'hooligan' has a long and well-documented history in criminology (Pearson, 1983). In recent years, however, such a 'rendering animal' of the body of the offender has been particularly marked within constructions of and debates around youth crime and criminality. Both in Home Office crime prevention literature in Britain and in a succession of government ministerial statements, young male offenders have been routinely characterised as 'animals', 'monsters', 'vermin', as beyond the social, outside society, as feral. The sentiment may be afforded some sympathetic understanding if it is taken as indicative of the depth of 'official' and public frustration and anger in the face of persistent offending. It is, however, revealing of the broader process whereby youth offending is simultaneously sexed (as masculine) at the very moment that any consideration of the sexed specificity of youth crime itself – the fact these are overwhelmingly the activities of boys and young men – is being effaced through the making of this association with the 'non-human' (the criminal, the feral, and so forth). In the controversy surrounding the case of the 'Rat Boy' in Britain during 1993 the characterisation of the body of the young offender as monster/animal reached perhaps its apotheosis. Here was a figure who was simultaneously constituted as being like other boys and yet who also appeared as other, as less than human, as *different* from other boys, as telling something about the 'trouble with boys' more generally.

   Throughout the 1990s persistent youth offending has been seen as creating an increasing problem in particular localities in Britain, to such a degree that the normal policing of many city areas has been said to have suffered (for example in the taking up of many hours of police and forensic officers' time and related court costs involved in dealing with such offenders 'Bill for Rat Boy is Put at £200,000', *The Glasgow Herald*, 8 October 1993). Singled out as a matter of particular concern has been not just the increasing *number* of children coming before the courts but also the *age* of these offenders, with widespread media coverage being given to police claims that it has become commonplace for youngsters in the ten–fifteen age group to now have multiple arrests for a range of serious offences including theft, car-taking, burglary, shoplifting, criminal damage, arson, robbery and aggravated burglary.

From the perspective of the administration of criminal justice, the case of the Rat Boy in 1993 arose in the context of a growing public concern about 'what to do' with the problem of these persistent young offenders who were known to the police. These are boys who go on 'crime sprees', many it appeared after absconding from council care community homes.[10] It is these boys who, in Campbell's (1993) terms, terrorise their own communities by their actions. The Rat Boy was so named because of the habit he had developed of hiding in a maze of ventilation shafts, tunnels and roof spaces in the Byker Wall Estate in the city of Newcastle upon Tyne, England, while trying to evade capture by the police. The facts of the case, which emerged from intensive media reporting of his 'life and times', are on one level not dissimilar to those of many other persistent young offenders in Britain.[11] A teenager, he admitted committing fifty-five offences in three years and a special police squad had been formed, following his thirty-sixth escape from the custody, to get 'to him before angry vigilantes' (*Daily Mail*, 5 October 1993). Described by police as 'a miniature crime wave', the Rat Boy soon became emblematic within media reporting of some broader practical and philosophical concerns around the problem of boys and crime. Before long the term 'Rat Boy' itself became generic within accounts of prolific youth offending more generally, not just in the context of this specific case from the north-east of England but nationally.[12] It is, on one level, important not to overestimate the significance of the phenomenon of the Rat Boy. The various depictions of 'Blip Boy', 'Rat Boy' and 'Safari Boy' which surfaced during 1993 all captured the headlines at a time when the then British Prime Minister, John Major, had cautioned the judiciary to 'condemn a little more and understand a little less' in the aftermath of the murder of James Bulger. In such a context the Rat Boy emerged as 'a monster figure straight out of the steamy New York tenement blocks' (*The Sunday Times*, 28 February 1993), something very 'UnBritish', once alien but now increasingly familiar. In relation to the ways in which the Rat Boy was constructed as an object of knowledge about crime, however, it is possible to make a number of points.

Firstly, the very language of the Rat Boy promoted an extreme hostility to young offenders generally. This fed into, and can itself be seen as a consequence of, the dominant punishment/retributivist penal agenda which has marked much of British criminal justice policy throughout the 1990s. In so doing such language has had real effects in legitimising the call for 'tougher' penalties and in influencing debates around substantive legal change, notably in relation to the question of whether children under the age of fourteen are capable of knowing they have committed a crime.[13] Secondly, it has been a function of the 'fiction' of the Rat Boy to police boundaries in relation to ideas of dangerous male youth. Class-mediated fears of the criminal Other have been encouraged in the notion that there may be hundreds of 'wild' (working-class) city children terrorising the population. The working-class city itself has, of course, like the working-class body, long been seen as a site of fear, desire, disgust and fascination from the perspective of the middle-class gaze. In a sense, the Rat Boy embodied some familiar fantasies around the corporeality of the working-class urban poor. In contrast to 'cleaned up', fed and educated bourgeois children, proletariat youth appear as 'savages', their undisciplined bodies to be censured, disciplined and controlled, their very presence a 'plague' on the respectable streets. Crucially, the proximity of these dangerous bodies relates directly to the intensity of the fear their presence generates. No longer expunged from civility (in the slum, the ghetto, the council estate), within the postmodern city the perceived (if not the actual) threat of this body appears mobile, associated with disease, contagion and the 'plague' (of the 'rat boys'). The fact that the number of persistent offenders is relatively low, accounting for around 10 per cent of all juvenile crime, does not detract from the discursive power: the Rat Boy speaks of other fears, other anxieties.

Thirdly, and importantly, the designation 'Rat Boy' ultimately questions the status of the child itself by dehumanising certain children and suggesting a division between boy children more generally. These are boys who are not like other boys and in so doing the ontology of the boy 'child' is itself thrown into question. Are they 'bad'? Or are they just another manifestation of what is considered to be 'normal' male behaviour? Thus, *The Times* noted:

> Hyperactive and wantonly destructive, apparently living only to smash and grab, such little boys dog the daily life. .... They are hell to deal with, but their behaviour falls within the range of the normal. That is, they are not monsters, nor are they in the technical sense mentally disturbed. (11 August 1994)

It is at this point, and in relation to the suggestion of there being a transformation in the boundaries of childhood itself, that the Rat Boy emerges at the nexus of the crisis of masculinity and broader changes within conceptions of sociality. The crisis of masculinity idea has, I have argued, been constituted through some complex reconfigurations presently taking place around the ways in which the categories of class and sex/gender are reforming in late modernity/postmodernity. In order to address how this is being played out in relation to the 'trouble with boys' thesis, it is necessary to explore in more depth the second strand to contemporary representations of the dangerous male child; that is, the category of 'childhood'. What is at issue here, I shall now argue, are the very systems of thought through which this criminal male subject has been understood as other at the same time that his (hegemonic, class-based) masculinity has itself been constructed as inherently, normatively crimogenic.

Nostalgia, futurity and the 'death' of childhood

It is a familiar story that the distinction between 'adult' and 'child' is of relatively modern origin. The construction of the category of childhood, in particular during the period from the nineteenth century to the present day, has been well documented as various factors have been identified as 'producing' the modern child (James, 1993; James and Prout, 1990; Jenks, 1982). Far from seeing this development as reflecting a benign, phil- anthropic and humanitarian concern with the welfare of children, the 'welfare justification' which has informed changing conceptions of child- hood has itself been treated with increasing scepticism, a cloak for more insidious motives of societal control and regulation. Within this revised history of childhood the juvenile justice system has been identified as one of the central institutions through which the control of children, and particu- larly lower-class city children, has taken place. It is in the context of such a 'class-inspired manipulation of developing personalities' (Parsloe, 1978: 3, quoted in Harding and Koffman, 1995: 251) that the language of the 'yob', the 'hooligan' and, more recently, the 'Rat Boy' has served to echo some familiar and recurring anxieties (Coward, 1994; Walklate, 1995: 177).

In seeking to make sense of such changing conceptions of childhood, Jenks (1996) has argued that there have been two models, or 'visions', of childhood – 'futurity' and 'nostalgia' – which have corresponded to the structural transition which has taken place from a state of modernity to that of postmodernity. Modernity, according to Jenks, is marked by a commit- ment to childhood, a promise of the future and a conception of children as central to the construction of adulthood itself. That is, as adults are the protectors and nurturers of the child, so children have become 'our primary love objects, our human capital and our future'. The 'child' of modernity – 'futurity' – is 'an ideal being . . . a stranger to avarice and is imbued with a natural altruism and kindness' (Jenks, 1996: 13-14). Within modernity, Jenks argues, the relationship between adults and children has been gov- erned by the dominant welfarist principle of 'care' whereby childhood has gradually claimed a greater duration within the total life experience, usurp- ing and assuming greater segments of the collective labour (both cognitive, affective and manual) of adults. In short, the child of modernity, Jenks argues, was a child dedicated to the *future*. Thus, a range of crimino-legal interventions premised on a belief in welfarism have rested on this concep- tion of the child as being essentially different from adults, a child as someone to be protected, secured and nurtured (Dingwall et al., 1986).

The child within the conditions of postmodernity (Bauman, 1992; Lyotard, 1986) is, in contrast, very different. It is Jenks' argument that the concept of the child within postmodern cultural configurations has become the site for the relocation of a variety of discourses concerned not so much with futurity as with questions of stability, integration and the maintenance of the social bond itself. Here, far from embodying the promise of a better future, a promise captured by the emblematic nature of childhood 'innocence', within recent debates the postmodern child appears as the guarantor of the sociality of the present as well as, given the heavy investment which has been made in this child, a potential threat to that social bond. The child thus constitutes sociality at the very moment the child itself appears as being no longer in control, as somehow beyond society (see also Probyn, 1996: 93–125). The child of postmodernity

> is now envisioned as a form of 'nostalgia', a longing for times past, not as 'futurity'. Children are now seen not so much as 'promise' ... as primary and unequivocal source of love, but also as partners in the most fundamental, unchosen, unnegotiated form of relationship. *The trust that was previously anticipated from marriage, partnership, friendship, class solidarity and so on is now invested more generally in the child.* (Jenks, 1996: 19; my emphasis)

It is in the light of these adult investments that the betrayal of the child is so keenly felt and, in the context of youth crime, that the consequences of this betrayal have become enmeshed within the crisis of masculinity discourse. What is taking place at present is no less than a fracturing and reforming of the socially constructed 'childhood' of modernity. Whereas children used to cling to us through modernity, for guidance into their/our futures, now we

> cling to them for 'nostalgic' groundings because such change is both intolerable and disorienting for us. They are lover, spouse, friend, workmate and, at a different level, symbolic representations for society itself. (Jenks 1996: 20)

Within postmodernity, between an ontological security and existential anxiety (Giddens, 1991) in which the previously centred, continuous self of modernity has become a 'reflexive project involving disparate interactional planes rendered coherent through a revisable narrative of self-identity' (Jenks, 1996: 17), the relationship between adults and children has itself become as contested a terrain as the breach of the social itself. What appear as contestations around childhood are thus reformed as questions about the (re)constitution of social within postmodernity; what appear as questions about childhood and children emerge as being, in fact, questions about adults and the adult world (see, for example, on the Bulger trial, King, 1995; Morrison, 1997):

> We need children as the sustainable, reliable, trustworthy, now outmoded treasury of social sentiments that they have come to represent. Our 'nostalgia' for their essence is part of a complex, late-modern rearguard attempt at the resolution of the contradictory demands of the constant re-evaluation of value with the pronouncement of social identity. (Jenks, 1996: 21)

Thus, on the one hand the child appears as the 'little angel', the embodiment of innocence, the victim incarnate. On the other, the child is constituted as 'evil', beyond order, as something *other than* what is truly the (modern) innocent child. Yet both, I have suggested, can be seen as class-mediated fantasies in which, crucially, a particular relationship between the sexing of this dangerous child and the reconfiguration of the social itself is being fused within the present 'trouble with boys' debate. It is at this point that a number of interrelated elements, each of which has run through the discussion presented thus far in this chapter, now surface as having been the hitherto 'unspoken' other of what I have suggested has been the fused, mutually constituted crises of masculinity and the 'trouble with boys'. We return, once again, to that which we have seen was implicit within traditional criminological accounts all along: the problematic nature of men's relationship to the family and, inter alia, the 'worlds' associated with women and children.

Sexual difference and the changing boundaries of 'family'

Within the refiguring of the socially constructed 'childhood' of modernity the very idea of the heterosexual 'family' is being reconstituted as relationships between adults and children, women and men are transformed. This is, on one level, unsurprising considering the way in which the modern family 'has become the locus for the confluence of politics and individual psychology . . . the primary unit for, and also the site of, governmentality; that is, it both absorbs and, in turn, distributes social control' (Jenks, 1996: 14; see also Collier, 1995a: 77–80; Donzelot, 1980; Rose, 1989). It is, by itself, 'no great leap to see the absolute necessity and centrality of the modern nuclear family as the pivotal social space in this system of socialisation' (Jenks 1996: 14). In seeking to 'gender' or 'sex' the nature of this transformation, however, what becomes necessary at this point is to integrate the force of feminist arguments and, in particular, to recognise the importance of sexual difference (as conceptualised in Chapter 1) within an account of the ways in which the ideology of 'care', so central to the transition from 'futurity' to 'nostalgia', has itself played out differently for men and women. It is not 'adults' but, primarily, mothers who have been depicted as 'sacrificing everything' for their children. Men, and in particular paternal subjectivities, have been constituted in other ways through an assumed or implicit dissociation from the familial (Collier, 1995a; see also Chapter 5). Criminal male youth, we have seen in this chapter, have been constructed as 'Other' to the family, as being separate, apart from the worlds of women and children. Seen in this way the 'trouble with boys' becomes not so much a question of 'family' breakdown or reconstitution (though this has been the traditional framework for analysis of both political Left and Right), but more a matter of the ways in which particular constructions of sex specificity have themselves been grounded within specific crimino-legal discourses. It was, for example, the mothers and not the fathers of Robert Thompson and Jon

Venables who were singled out for opprobrium in the aftermath of the Bulger murder (Young, 1996: 117–25). It is the mothers, and not the fathers, of the Rat Boy and his contemporaries who feel the finger of condemnation being pointed by police, politicians, child psychiatrists and the media. As the mother of the Rat Boy commented:

> 'Everyone has some thing to say,' she says. 'You hear them, "If it was my boy I'd do this, or that." Don't you think we have tried everything? I must have gone wrong somewhere, but I don't know where,' she adds, twisting her wedding ring round and round on her finger. (*Mail on Sunday*, 2 May 1993)

> Do you know what it's like ... when people are talking about the Rat Boy, unaware that I'm his mother? ... Who's going to trust me, who's going to want the mother of Rat Boy working for them? (*The Sunday Times*, 6 April 1997)

It is, consistently, the mothers who are judged, held responsible and who are seen as having failed in this duty of care. It is the mothers of persistent offenders who are routinely paraded in the media, asked to explain, account for the crimes of 'their' boys ('The school says he's violent. His mother says he's not': *The Independent*, 18 August 1996). Meanwhile the paternal relation is, in contrast, both simultaneously hidden and unspoken whilst it is also constituted as central – through the concept of father-absence – to this particular story of crime. Far from men being the main players in this crimino-familial narrative, it is the men who fade into the background, setting the scene for the women to care, to fail and to be judged. It is their very *absence* from the family which is, as we shall see in Chapter 5, then deemed to be the source of the criminality of young men.

Given the profound changes presently taking place within household and familial structures it is unsurprising that an acceleration in the intensity, purchase and currency of emotions centred on the changing family should have assumed an increasing significance in grounding both men's and women's experiences of the 'social'. In this reconfiguration of the familial, however, that which has surfaced as problematic is also that which had hitherto been unspoken, natural, inviolable and unquestioned: *the relationship between men and children*. In short, the reorganisation of the patterning of relationships deemed 'familial' within postmodernity has been inextricably bound up with the nature of the crisis of the social as signified by the 'trouble with boys' (equals) 'trouble with masculinity' thesis. In effect, an ideology of care which had itself been premised on a rigid sexual division of labour which 'lubricated and legitimised the investment of economic and cultural capital in the 'promise' of childhood' (Jenks, 1996: 15) has itself been reconstituted in the face of changing sexual subjectivities, employment structures, cultural formations and political changes. The problem of 'youth' within modernist criminology was, we have seen, understood in terms of 'broken' families, broken communities, broken solidarities. In highlighting and undermining the dualisms through which the idea of the 'unbroken' 'family' had been constituted in the first place, and in surfacing the sexed (as different) experiences of community, solidarity, 'family life', and so forth, the taken-for-granted nature of men's location within this social has been disturbed. And this is a disturbance which has been felt particularly acutely with regard to men's relationships to/with children. Thus, as 'the enhanced interest in men's relationship to children and of men in children' grows (Jenks, 1996: 20), as the mutual constitution of fatherhood and (hetero-) masculinities are subjected to increasing critical scrutiny (see Chapter 5), the iconic status of the postmodern child has become the disputed territory in which an assessment of the contribution of men to the social per se is taking place. It should not surprise that what this has led to should be interpreted as a 'crisis of masculinity'. For, if masculinity itself is to be seen as dangerous and/or problematic when so close to home (in the form, for example, of the abusing or dangerous father), what does this say about the family? What does this say about the social? What does this say about men?

Concluding remarks: reconstructing the 'crisis' of male youth

> Class domination does not just touch the working class ... [it] is central to the fantasy structures and defences of the bourgeoisie. ... Middle-class people often only see the working class in relations of service or as frightening others in areas of town that they do not want to enter. Their defences are cross-cut by the way in which the Other is made to signify and the fictions in which they are inscribed. (Walkerdine, 1995: 325–6)

A story has been told. From nineteenth-century Lombrosian conceptions of the criminal as a naturally occurring entity – a fact of nature rather than a social or legal product – through to twentieth-century sociogenic accounts, criminology has offered a scientific respectability to some deep-rooted cultural prejudices around middle-class perceptions of the 'criminal classes'. It has been through an association with the lower/working classes that images of 'wild' and 'dangerous' masculinities, masculine crisis and social disorder have been primarily (if not exclusively) constituted.[14] In the form of contemporary underclass theory, as we shall see in the following chapter, a range of attempts have been made to divert the reconfiguration of the social in modernity from the global level, to the national and then to the local – to the identification of particular 'communities' of crime, to urban wastelands, to 'no-go' areas and to the personal immorality and 'lifestyle choices' of a new urban 'underclass'. This 'mass' continues to be set in opposition to civility, to be associated with the corporeal, with the pleasures of animality. It continues to *be* – as in the case of the Rat Boy – that which is ontologically *other*, that which is non-human or beyond humanity.

There has been a certain constancy to the ways in which some familiar ideas of disruption and unruliness have been seen to stem from the biology of the body of the proletariat male youth. The criminal underclass consume, but do so illegitimately, procreate, but do so without order and morality, revolt and resist their 'masculine crisis', but do so in ways beyond democratic means (they do not seek therapy, they do not take to the woods with other men: Harding, 1992; cf. Bonnett, 1996; Kimmell and Kaufman, 1994). This underclass has been brought into being at the very moment that it is subjected to modes of regulation by a set of characteristics 'designated as natural within the discursive act of . . . [their] very construction' (Smart, 1992: 8). Central to these characteristics have been, I have suggested, certain stories about the urban 'mass' which, we have seen in this chapter, circulate endlessly within the contemporary crimino-legal domain. In the aftermath of the murder of James Bulger, for example, the atomised mass appeared as simultaneously active in its retributive calls for vengeance and punishment of the child-killers, and yet passive in its representation as a disorganised community which had 'failed' to 'do something' to prevent a two-year-old boy being led to his death. This mass was seen as being saturated with violence in its inadequate parenting practices, in watching too much television, too many inappropriate videos. The threat or the eruption of violence continues to be blamed on the family that is 'not a family', on consumers who consume 'too much', and, ultimately, on the boys who are, simultaneously, 'not really boys' at the precise moment they are just a little *too* masculine, just a little bit too much like all other 'ordinary' boys.

All of this, ultimately, places the postmodern boy-child in something of an impossible position. There has been one resounding silence, one absence within this story. Something is *not* being said. Young people are vulnerable. They have no ready constituency, economic power and, in reality rather than rhetoric, limited legal rights.[15] What we have seen in this chapter, whether in debates around schooling, education or the crisis of male youth, in the images of 'rat boys', 'yobs' and 'predators' (and, implicitly, 'little angels'), has been the contradictory positionings of the (postmodern) child. The child continues to be the innocent victim, as we shall see in the following chapter. This child is permanent, dependable, the incarnation of the 'child as nostalgia'. Yet, as we have seen above, the child 'who is not really a child', the criminal child, is also a repository of values the adult world itself both falls short of and shares. Such a child

> figures largely as symbolic representation of this welter of uncertainty, both literally and metaphorically. . . . Children have become both the testing ground for the necessity of independence in the constitution of human subjectivity but also the symbolic refuge of the desirability of trust, dependency and care in human relations. . . . 'childhood' sustains the 'meta-narrative' of society itself . . . . (Jenks 1996: 23)

The 'trouble with boys' and the 'crisis of masculinity' are, ultimately, about questions of ontological insecurity, of the search for an 'inside' at a time of instability and flexibility in all forms of relations – especially, as we shall see in Chapter 5, heterosexual relating. The 'masculinity' of modernity, of the 'male role', of clear-cut gendered scripts and identities, has become an unreliable position from which to ground men's emotions. In this chapter I have explored the discursive production of the 'dangerous' male child in relation to two sites – schooling and urban disorder. In respect of each, I suggested, attempts have been made to go beyond the familiar dualisms which have structured crimino-legal accounts of male youth crime. In so doing I have sought to present an account of subjectivity which might recognise the place of the popular in the making of oppressed subjects (Walkerdine, 1995: 324).[16] The joyrider, the rat boy, the predators and unruly pupils, we have seen, have together been made to signify the 'trouble with boys' thesis. Each have assumed iconic status within the broader 'crisis of masculinity' discourse. To state that these subjects are fictions is, I have argued, *not* to claim that boys are not unruly, that joy riding is not a problem, that boys do not terrorise their own communities, and so forth. Rather, it is to highlight the ways in which

> the practices in which subjects are produced are both material and discursive, but the relation is not one of representation but signification. Indeed, if fictions can function in truth then fictions themselves can have real effects. Subjects are created in multiple positionings in material and discursive practices, in specific historical conditions in which certain apparatuses of social regulation become techniques of self-production. *These are imbued with fantasy.* We cannot there-fore separate something called 'working class experiences' from the fictions and fantasies in which life is produced and read. (Walkerdine, 1995: 325; my emphasis)

The uncontrollable male child and the reforming of the familial are inseparable because of the ways in which each has been defined through the other. Without this familial sexed (as different) model, however, that which is Other – 'children, women, colonial peoples, the proletariat . . . the mass, the mob' (Walkerdine, 1995: 316) – would be constructed in different ways. Far from addressing such issues, contemporary political responses have legitimated the regulation and further control of already oppressed people and communities. The 'trouble with boys', I have argued in this chapter, is no longer simply one of juvenile delinquency. It embraces the collapse of marriage (or rather a pool of marriageable men), the undermining of the family and, ultimately, a threat to sociality itself, the 'death' of childhood with which we began. The framing of debates around boys, schooling and urban disorder through reference to the crisis of masculinity transcends the sphere of crime and criminality. It draws on wider shifts in cultural configurations of sex/gender through which understandings of the masculine are at present being reconstituted. Underlying such a transition, and the debates around youth which have accompanied it, has been a reluctance to address the sexed specificity of crime and to regard to child as fully human.

Notes

1. In 1997 figures published by the government minister for school standards revealed girls 'outclassing' boys in almost all subjects. In response, teachers'

union leaders called for a government inquiry into the 'chronic under performance of boys in almost all subjects and at all stages of compulsory education'
(*The Guardian*, 26 November 1997). In 1995 it was estimated that, at council-
run schools in Britain, 43.8 per cent of girls and 33.8 per cent of boys passed
at least five GCSEs at Grade C or above. In 1996 45.1 per cent of girls and
34.7 per cent of boys respectively achieved that level. See also 'OFSTED
Urges Schools to "Mentor" Boys', *The Independent*, 11 July 1996; 'The
Problem With Our Wanton Boys', *The Independent*, 7 March 1998.

2. See, for example, 'Defiant Face of Class Yob', *The Express*, 7 November 1996;
'School Shuts as Teachers Run From Menacing Pupils', *The Independent*,
1 November 1996; 'Stand Off at "Trouble Boy" School', *The Guardian*,
4 September 1996. See also *The Guardian*, 29 October 1996. Boys are between
three and four times more likely to be excluded from schools than girls
(NACRO Briefing, 'Exclusion From School', May 1997). Rates of offending
amongst non-attending pupils are estimated as being three times higher than
regular attendance (Graham and Bowling, 1996). There is also evidence that
'pupils see exclusion as "macho" honour' (*The Independent*, 8 June 1995).

3. This issue is discussed in more depth in Chapter 5.

4. The following is not atypical of the tone of much reporting around youth crime
in Britain, in particular during 1993 and in the months following the murder of
James Bulger: 'Last week alone the British public shook its collective head in
sorrow, fear and disgust over reports of an alleged child murder by children,
teenagers prepared to kill for 26p and a man who allegedly butchered a father
and daughter in their home so he could steal a second-hand car' (*The Sunday
Times*, 28 February 1993).

5. Note responses to the murder of the London head teacher Philip Lawrence:
'The world is in chaos . . . something remarkable has to come from his death'
(Frances Lawrence, *The Times*, 19 October 1996). In October 1996 the then
Conservative Government announced that moral instruction was to be included
in every Advanced Level course and a new exam in 'Critical Thinking' would
seek to emphasise the importance of society's 'shared moral values' (*The
Observer*, 27 October 1996).

6. See, for example, 'The Modern Lad Has It Bad', *The Independent*, 8 February
1997; ' "From New Lad to Millennium Man": There's More to Life Than
Football, Beer and Having a Laugh', *The Observer*, 20 October 1997. The
language of 'laddism' has come to pervade public debates around a range of
issues: 'We have to overcome what some call laddism – the belief that it is
cool not to work. Groups of boys are developing a culture of not working, of
thinking it is acceptable to truant and misbehave. Some of these young men
end up carrying knives' (David Blunkett, *The Guardian*, 1 November 1996).
This new generation of feckless 'lads' 'try to cope by acting the goat, by being
the fool. Some boys almost give up on trying to keep up with the girls' (Jack
Straw, *The Guardian*, 3 March 1998). 'Men Adapting Badly Lose in the Job
Race', *The Sunday Times*, 13 April 1997. Compare, for example, 'They Smoke
Too Much and Drink Too Much: Men Really Are Behaving Badly – and Only
Women Can Save Them', *The Independent*, 27 June 1996; 'Lad Mags Defy
Feminists', *The Observer*, 11 August 1996; 'How to Make Men Socially
Acceptable', *The Independent*, 13 June 1996; 'The Rise and Rise of Laddery
from "Loaded" ', *The Independent*, 19 April 1997; 'Rich Rewards for Mags
Behaving Badly', *The Guardian*, 19 February 1997. On the class dynamics of
'laddism' see 'Tycoons of Tomorrow are the Lads Behaving Badly Today',
The Independent on Sunday, 22 March 1998.

7. Forty-three per cent of indictable crime appears to be committed by people
under twenty-one. In 1995, of this group 72,200 men and 11,700 women were
known to have committed an indictable offence (Criminal Statistics for

England and Wales, 1995: Home Office November 1996; NACRO Fact Sheet February 1997).

8. Comparison with representations of 'girl gangs' is revealing (Campbell, 1984): see, for example, 'Rude Girls Rule, but Only at the Periphery', *The Guardian*, 25 November 1994; 'Why Girls Turn to Sickening Violence', *Daily Mail*, 2 May 1996; 'Girls in a New Age of Brutalism', *Daily Express*, 2 May 1996. For an alternative view, 'Modern Myth of Girl Gangs on the Streets', *The Guardian*, 24 July 1997.

9. In July 1997 Bea Campbell was invited to address the 1997 British Criminology Conference at Queen's University, Belfast, as a keynote speaker. Her subject matter was, broadly, that of *Goliath*: the relationship between crime, masculinity and urban disorder. A more general concern with masculinity has been a recurring theme in Campbell's journalism for some time: for example, *The Guardian*, 24 July 1997; *The Guardian*, 3 March 1998.

10. *The Observer*, 10 April 1994. See also 'Dark World of "Rat Boys" ', *The Sunday Times*, 31 October 1993; ' "Rat Boy" Detained by Police', *The Daily Telegraph*, 6 October 1993.

11. For example, 'Lee can rip your car stereo out in 25 seconds flat. He's been charged with 64 offences since Christmas. And he's still only 10. Can anything stop this pocket crime wave?' (*The Observer*, 9 March 1997).

12. The use of the term continues: my local newspaper at the time of writing headlines 'A Plague of 100 Ratboy Crooks is Responsible for 14,000 North East Crimes', *Evening Chronicle*, 8 July 1997. The original Rat Boy himself was later revealed to be Anthony Kennedy ('Spare the Rod, Spoil the Rat', *The Sunday Times*, 6 April 1997).

13. On sentencing post-Bulger, see Justice Report (1996); 'The 10 Year Old Who is Changing the Law', *The Observer*, 9 March 1997.

14. Compare, for example, *The Times*, 3 March 1993: 'Touch of the Whip Reforms Young Delinquent Tories': 'There is glue-sniffing Bill Cash, fixated Euro-bore, eyes glazed with Maastricht's small print; "rat boy" Teddy Taylor, crouching in the ventilation shafts of amendment 443; and ram-raiding, treaty-smashing Tony Marlow.' See also 'Will the Boys Who Can't Read Still End Up As the Men on Top?', *The Independent*, 5 January 1998. Note the (rather different) depictions of public school male youth and disorder: 'Old School, Old Town, Old Scores', *The Independent*, 14 June 1996; 'Townies Declare War on Gordonstoun Toffs', *The Observer*, 9 June 1996.

15. Perhaps exemplified in debates around the age of consent in Britain (see Moran, 1996: 59–60, 191–6).

16. 'We need to look in a new way at our daily lives and recognise that the end of grand metanarratives of "The Working Class" is not to discard oppression. . . . In our understanding of the regulation of the postmodern order, we need to examine the place of that voicing and where it appears, on television, films, the radio, the popular; who is being made to speak, what to and for whom? No, we have to create some other stories, which face the present and confront it, write new songs and begin to sing them' (Walkerdine, 1995: 330).

4 'A Lonely Man with a Passion for Guns': Crime, Community and the Heterosexualised Body

The human mind is the most complex and delicately balanced of all created things. Wisdom cannot foresee all the consequences of its sickness. The most that wisdom can do is shield society from some of the possible consequences. . . .

> (Dr Robert Runcie, Archbishop of Canterbury, speaking at the Memorial Service for the Hungerford victims 1987; quoted in *The Guardian*, Editorial, 14 March 1996)

According to the experts [mass] killers, who are invariably male, are unlikely to be mentally ill but are likely to have achieved very little and, as a result, harbour grudges and resentment that can develop into violent fantasies.

> (*The Guardian*, 29 April 1996, following the murder of thirty-two people in Tasmania by Martin Bryant)

Introduction

This chapter is an exploration of responses to a series of murders which in recent years, in Britain and elsewhere, have become known as 'lone gunman' or 'spree' killings.[1] The particular focus of what follows is the legal, political, criminological and media reception to the events which took place in Dunblane, Scotland, in March 1996 where sixteen children and their teacher were murdered and seventeen others injured by forty-three-year-old Thomas Hamilton.[2] I will argue that the experience of the 'lone gunman' or 'spree killer' is, in both its generic construction and its practice, a gendered and 'masculinised' phenomenon. The central aim of the chapter is to (re-) read the spree killing in such a way as to reposition the sexed male body, as conceptualised in previous chapters, within a range of discourses around crime. It is my intention to seek to illustrate the inadequacy of simply adding 'men' or 'gender' empirically to the study of crime, a central theme of this book thus far, by investigating the epistemological implications of what it might mean to theorise the men/crime relation in the light of recent approaches to masculinity which have sought to dissolve the integrity of the gendered 'identity' of the subject (Gutterman, 1994; Saco, 1992). In so doing, I wish to explore the ways in which the (sexed) bodies of men continue to be constituted as an 'absent presence' within contemporary discourses around crime and criminality; to offer, that is, the significance of sexual difference in engaging with the criminal(ised) bodies of men in cultural and psychical terms (Gatens, 1996; Grosz, 1994; Chapter 1, pp. 23–8).

This chapter explores the content of press discourse constructions of the 'spree killing' and, in particular, representations of the gunman Thomas Hamilton in the aftermath of the Dunblane massacre. I shall argue that a range of dualisms encoded responses to this event in such a way that 'the moment of reception or response' has been 'tied to a rhetoric of visibility and invisibility, of images of the seen and the unseen' (Young, 1996: 112). Crucially, what has been 'unseen' in the press coverage of Dunblane is the question of the bodies (and crimes) of men as men. There has been an *erasure* of men as social and accountable beings. One result of this has been the evacuation of any consideration of the sex of (the) crime secured via reference to a conceptualisation of masculinity understood in terms of the sex/gender distinction. The chapter will explore the genealogy of this silencing of the sexed specificity of the Dunblane murders. In investigating the gender order of the signifying complex which presently surrounds the phenomenon of the spree killing, what follows is, ultimately, an exploration of Thomas Hamilton not as a 'monster', 'pervert' or personification of 'evil', but as a *man*.

Defining the 'spree killing': a note on Dunblane

Over the last few years there has been an increasing fascination with the phenomenon of the 'lone gunman' or 'spree killing', reflected in the rapid spread of the term within diverse cultural artefacts. The spree killing refers to the murder of several victims over a period of minutes, hours or days in one or more different locations 'by an impulsive killer who appears to make little effort to evade detection. . . . At completion of the sequence this type of killer is unlikely to kill again; many commit suicide or are killed in shootouts with the police' (Gresswell and Hollin, 1994: 3). The victims of the spree killing, it has been argued, appear to have some symbolic significance for the offender and are killed in a 'frenzied' attack, whether planned in advance or 'spur of the moment'. Though the details in each case differ, a number of recent murders have been classified as examples of the spree killing. In Britain, prior to Dunblane, the most notorious of these was the case of Michael Ryan, who shot dead sixteen people in August 1987 in Hungerford, England. Within weeks of the Dunblane massacre, in April 1996 twenty-eight-year-old Martin Bryant slaughtered thirty-five people in Port Arthur, Tasmania in the worst spree killing on record ('Slaughter in the Sun', *The Guardian*, 29 April 1996; 'The Misfit Behind the Massacre', *The Sunday Times*, 5 May 1995). Opinion remains divided as to whether the spree killing itself should be considered a separate form of multiple murder (Busch and Cavanaugh, 1986; Rappaport, 1988; Rowlands, 1990). What is agreed, however, is that 'almost all mass and spree murders are male' with a racial composition 'that closely approximates that of the population itself' (Gresswell and Hollin, 1994: 3).

In writing of the murders which took place in Dunblane I feel a word of explanation is necessary for what might appear as 'detachment or even indifference' . . . 'to present the consequences of such a tragic event . . . in the detached terms of sociological theory is not to trivialise the horror felt by the majority of people at [the] destruction of a child's life' (King, 1995: 167). The murders in Dunblane were, perhaps of all the incidents of spree killing in recent years, particularly shocking in their brutality. Writing in the context of the murder of James Bulger by two ten-year-old boys in 1993, others have spoken of their hesitation and unease in discussing 'in the detached terms of sociological theory' events of the recent past.[3] Certainly, 'the following analysis seeks neither to inflame . . . strongly felt emotions nor to hold them up to criticism or ridicule' (King, 1995: 168). It seeks, rather, to develop a deeper understanding of the event by addressing what remains the most obvious, taken-for-granted yet curiously unexplored fact not just about the murders at Dunblane but, as we have seen in this book, crime generally: that it is almost always committed by men. Engaging with this fact is, I shall argue, essential if 'we are ever going to act in a way that loosens that paralysing grip of guilt and helplessness' in the face of men's violences (Jackson, 1995: 3).

Crimino-legal responses to the spree murder: the press discourse in the aftermath of Dunblane

On 13 March 1996 Thomas Hamilton fatally shot sixteen five- and six-year-old children and their teacher in the gymnasium at Dunblane Primary School in Scotland. Seventeen others were injured before Hamilton eventually put one of the guns to his own head. How are we to begin to make sense of the press discourse around such a horrific event? There exists a rich literature concerned with exploring how, as unique cultural products, newspapers and other media outlets tell us much about the social, political and moral order of our culture and, as such, play an important role in the development of an individual's sense of self (McEvoy, 1996: 179–80). However, constructing a reading from something as diffuse and complex as press discourse is notoriously problematic (McRobbie, 1994). The apparently random nature of the spree killing, like the serial murder, runs counter to the general assumption that crimes have 'motives' and can be presented as a deviant form of instrumental rationality. It is, nonetheless, possible to locate a certain homogeneity to the press response. A number of themes emerge and recur within the national and international media coverage of the Dunblane massacre, as a transition takes place from an initial shock and incomprehension at what had happened to a growing demand for answers and explanations.

The vocabulary of evil: Thomas Hamilton as 'inhuman' and 'beyond reason'

The tone of the media reporting in the immediate aftermath of the massacre was encapsulated by the powerful and moving comments of the headmaster of Dunblane Primary School. 'Evil,' he stated, 'visited us yesterday. . . . We don't know why, we don't understand it, and I guess we never will.' This notion that 'only the Vocabulary of Evil could explain what happened at Dunblane' (*Time*, 25 March 1996) set the course for the following press coverage, in which Thomas Hamilton was described as an 'evil freak of nature' (*Daily Express*, 20 March 1996); whilst 'Dunblane returned to God' (*Daily Mirror*, 20 March 1996), he would surely 'Burn in Hell' (*The Sun*, 20 March 1996) – 'His evil is now where it belongs – in the fires of hell.' Notwithstanding differences between tabloid and 'quality' newspapers in their representations of the crimes of men,[4] for each the language of 'good' and 'evil' appeared initially as the only available vocabulary through which the event might be described. Just as Robert Thompson and Jon Venables, the two boys convicted of the murder of James Bulger in 1993, had been described as the embodiment of 'unparalleled evil and barbarity',[5] the good/evil binary here suggested a possibility, if not a firm belief, that there may be no defence to some propensities of the human condition. However, this immediately poses problems for a secularised crimino-legal sphere which demands explanation and account in terms of liberal notions of human nature. As King has noted, 'in modern society, where to be taken seriously communications need to conform with notions of rationality, it is difficult to understand how . . . [the language of] good and evil could still become a prevalent image for making sense of particularly disturbing events' (1995: 167). In the context of Dunblane, it is important to remember what was being constituted at this point as a social problem. Clearly some issues were immediately comprehensible as 'within' understanding. By the end of the day of the massacre two issues – the question of school security and reform of gun laws – had emerged as the dominant 'social problems' raised by the case. Hamilton's *maleness*, in contrast, did not figure in the 'pre-existing categories for rational problem-identification and problem-solution' (King, 1995: 168).

The terms 'evil' and 'human wickedness' promote a construction of Hamilton as a 'monster' or 'grotesque' which is misleading in several respects. Firstly, it rests uneasily with what is now the *familiarity* of the spree killing. If Dunblane was exceptional in terms of the age and vulnerability of the victims, it was nonetheless readily identifiable as a generic crime. The lone gunman, indeed, is a recognisable phenomenon of the late twentieth century and Thomas Hamilton was placed immediately within this established frame of reference. The use of 'evil' has a second, related, consequence. The vast majority of spree killers, like offenders generally, are men. Yet the ontology of Hamilton as 'inhuman' robs both the act of the murders and the body of the murderer of its sexual specificity. Like the 'Rat Boy' discussed in Chapter 3, and like Jon Venables and Robert Thompson, Hamilton is transformed into something 'beyond human', his actions seen as emblematic of an inhumanity beyond comprehension and understanding. The banishing of Hamilton from the social, however, 'erodes . . . responsibility for understanding and challenging the individual and social forces that have produced such an . . . event. To demonise . . . removes the [act] from the realm of social action' (Jackson, 1995: 4). This expunging of the social does not simply individualise crime, however. It also underwrites and legitimates those feelings of despair and helplessness which are common-place responses to particularly horrific crimes: 'We cannot even begin to grasp', it was declared, what could have driven him to act as he did, 'and there is no point pretending we can' (Editorial, *Daily Mirror*, 14 March 1996).

Crimes, even the worst and most seemingly inexplicable, do not happen in a vacuum. In order to reconfigure Thomas Hamilton as a man, it is necessary to relocate his actions by contextualising the atrocity within the social framework in which he lived and died. It is necessary, that is, to reframe the relationship between (the bodies of) men, women and children in such a way as to problematise certain ideas of hetero-masculinity which were, I now wish to suggest, central to, and the sub-text of, press reporting of the Dunblane massacre.

Sexing the social: configurations of community, class and 'otherness'

The ontological importance accorded to the 'family' as the institutional source for the preservation and reproduction of moral order has been central to the discursive construction of the social within modernity (Stratton, 1996: 78; Chapter 3, pp. 96–8). It is in the context of this social/familial frame that Thomas Hamilton was systematically represented as a 'loner'. On the one hand, he appeared to have few friends. No person, no locale appeared willing to claim him as one of their own. He was, on one level, 'not one of us'. Yet his place as an outsider to this social is ambiguous. It is also clear from newspaper reports that Thomas Hamilton was *known* within the community in which he lived. The numerous testimonies to his character, his 'eccentricities' and family background belied the notion that he was a stranger in the midst of an otherwise homogeneous community. There exists a tension therefore between, on the one hand, the (readily accessible) knowledge of Hamilton (who he was, what he was 'like') and, on the other, the desire to expunge him from that community, and from the sociality more generally, through reference to his status as grotesque, as 'inhuman' monster, and so forth. The former places him within a broader community. The latter ensures he is rendered outside the social.

Within this process, of course, something is being said about the community of which Thomas Hamilton was deemed to be not one. In this respect, press representations of the town of Dunblane reveal much about the ways in which the discursive construction of the social has more generally been configured through reference to men's crimes, criminality and the ontological importance of the family. One newspaper declared, '*it would be easier for us* if Thomas Hamilton was simply a madman who came out of nowhere. But what if [he] . . . comes out of a society which itself is showing signs of deranged and violent breakdown?' (*The Guardian*, 15 March 1996; my emphasis). This is, clearly, an engagement with the social. It focuses on such issues as the role of the media in promoting crime, the availability of guns, questions of school security, and so forth. Yet each of these conversations about 'society' stops short of any engagement with the relationship between sex, gender and crime. What results is a 'de-sexing' of Hamilton's maleness by the fusing of two ideas: that of a phantasmatic (non-criminal) *community*, secured as such, I wish to suggest, by reference to a historically specific *iconography of male otherness*.

A space of crime: the (non-)criminal community

To clarify: the town of Dunblane was routinely depicted, almost without exception, as a place to which crime was a stranger. It appeared at the other end of a spectrum from the communities more traditionally associated with high-profile crimes (Young, 1996: 120). It is Britain's 'dangerous places' (Campbell, 1993), as we have seen in Chapter 3, which have come to symbolise social breakdown, moral atrophy and, increasingly, notably in the context of the 'criminal' city, crimes by and against children. Dunblane, in contrast, symbolised something very different. It did not translate into familiar representations of region and place. It was, if anything, a place 'too good to be true'. An editorial in *The Guardian* captured the general assumption being made about this conflation of space and crime. Like Hungerford, the scene of the previous spree killing by Michael Ryan in 1987, Dunblane was

> the last place where one would expect random violence to erupt: small attractive country towns with strong community ties and none of the alienation associated with larger cities. Both killers lived within the communities they devastated. Both are described as lonely, secretive, friendless people. Neither was being treated for any mental disorder. Yet both committed indiscriminate and irrational violence on a massive scale. Why? (*The Guardian*, 14 March 1996)

This image of (non-criminal) community is then fleshed out by accounts of the minutiae of everyday life. Dunblane was a town where 'nothing ever happens', a place where 'if a child fell in the street, three people would rush to pick them up' (Fergurson et al., 1996). Interestingly, even the children who lived in the town appeared at times to be qualitatively different from their counterparts in the criminal(ised) city.[6] *Time* magazine noted:

> ... the names [of the children] ... were as familiar and as evocative of middle-class Scottish family life. ... Ordinary names, pretty names, the names on teachers' attendance lists, on captions of school pictures, on programs for school pageants, on line-ups for school games. (*Time*, 25 March 1996)

On one level such a mythologising of locale, involving a conflation of assumptions about family life and socio-economic privilege, is a familiar phenomenon. What results is a powerful evocation of a (crime-free) world we all, it is implied (and not just the citizens of Dunblane), have lost.

> A generation of professionals – doctors, lawyers, journalists – had dreamed of somewhere the air is so crisp you can actually smell the smoke from a chimney or from a gentle puffing biddy on the street corner; where fearsome things come in picture books; where the water of life is softly reassuring as it falls – or golden, as it washes the back of the throat. Dunblane was that dream incarnate. (*The Observer*, 17 March 1996)

However, it is not simply a (well-documented) association between class, crime and 'respectability' which is being made here. The 'space' of men's crime is itself, on closer examination, bound up with certain assumptions about masculinity which betray the centrality of the family to this particular construction of the social. The dominant image of the community of Dunblane as the embodiment of comfortable, crime-free existence rests upon, and derives from, a heterosexual familial frame signified as such by virtue of the presence of *children*.[7] Dunblane is presented, above all, as a place where 'families moved' and where 'children would be safe'.

Thomas Hamilton as other: the single male outsider

It is against this background that Hamilton appears outside the parameters of the familial. He *appeared* to be of this community. In 'reality' he failed to belong – he was an Outsider, an impostor. Yet the depiction of his otherness involves, simultaneously, the representation of both a familiar and un-familiar figure. Much was made of his 'peculiar' upbringing, a knowledge juxtaposed with the 'normality' of the family life of the Dunblane children, and his sexual status as a single (unpartnered) man. *The Independent*, for example, noted that:

> Loners like Hamilton are where *benign singleness* festers and turn poisonous, where being alone creates the space in which paranoia flourishes to burst out in violence. (My emphasis)[8]

It is estimated that, by the year 2001, lone men will form the largest group of one-person households in Britain (Barker, 1996).[9] Increased social atomisation has brought into focus, and prompted considerable research (notably under the umbrella of the 'crisis of masculinity') into, the ways in which distinctive communities of these 'lone men' are forming. It is men who are increasingly seen to be 'either drifting into despair, illness or break-down, or are aggressively asserting another kind of masculine identity through law-breaking and crime' (Jackson, 1995: 17). *The Guardian* noted how

> The back streets of the shabbier ends of every British town are evidence of the elaborate communities of fantasy that men create as substitutes: martial arts centres, porn shops, tattoo parlours. Plus the erotica, often spiced up with violence, on the top shelf of your neighbourhood newsagent's or video store. Plus the extraordinary ease of buying drink almost everywhere, to help you sit at home and brood on all this. (Barker, 1996)

This, it is implied, was the habitat of Thomas Hamilton, a world sym-bolically far away from, though physically cheek-by-jowl with, the non-criminal and familial community of Dunblane. Quite explicitly it was stated that 'Hamilton *did not belong* to the manicured world of Dunblane. His home was a scruffy, damp council maisonette on a joyless estate in Kent Road, Stirling, five miles away.' Nor had he 'enjoyed the stable, happy childhood apparent in some of the children at Dunblane primary school' (Fergurson et al., 1996).

The 'horror' of the criminal(ised) urban which is said to 'pursue us even here' is symbolised not just by the failure to 'escape' from crime. Within the present reconfiguration of the familial the figure of the single male outsider has increasingly come to appear as the embodiment of social disorder, normlessness and dislocation. However, importantly, it is the very in-adequacy of this iconography of male otherness to *consistently* depict Hamilton as 'outside' the social which becomes glaringly apparent as its very familiarity at times serves to evoke some very different images of the masculine. He is, on one level, immediately recognisable (and is recognised) as a particular type of man. In other contexts, other genres, he would be the 'very stuff' of pulp fiction:

> ... unmarried, 43, a thwarted scoutmaster with an obsessive interest in guns and a habit of photographing very young boys naked from the waist up ... a familiar but dislocated story, the kind usually set in dreary rooming houses across the Atlantic – narratives pieced together after the grisly, ground-breaking crimes that are an American genre. (*The Guardian*, 15 March 1996)

A rich vocabulary exists, known to adults and children alike, through which to depict Hamilton's otherness. Testimonies range from the relatively benign accounts of Hamilton as a 'quiet "anorak" type' (*The Independent*, 18 March 1996), a 'strange moonfaced man' (*Time*, 25 March 1996) who lived in a 'shabby bachelor apartment', to the more overtly dangerous and troubling depictions of a 'vengeful misfit' (*Chicago Tribune*, 20 March 1996) , a ' "Mr. Creepy" or "Weird" man' (*The Guardian*, 14 March 1996) who was driven by 'monsters of the psyche' (*Time*, 25 March 1996). It is the very familiarity of these images which betrays the contingency and fluidity of the over-arching framework of hetero-masculinity which would seek to depict Hamilton as beyond society, outwith the social. Ultimately, as only few accounts noted, Thomas Hamilton 'was not a loner at all. He was the exact opposite. He wanted to run boys clubs. He wanted to run Scout camps. He belonged to a gun club. He wrote peeved letters to everyone. He had his own business. Lots of people knew him. Some loner' (D. Campbell, 1996). Far from having distinguishing marks, the stigmata of his imputed paedophilic intent, Hamilton lived in a community unsuspected. He was *known*.

Reading Hamilton as 'other' is far from straightforward, therefore, when his 'normality' as a man seeps through in representations which themselves reveal much about the dualisms through which ideas of normal masculinity have been constituted. For example, the Cullen Inquiry into the massacre heard frequent reference from a number of witnesses to the 'two sides of child killer Hamilton' (*The Guardian*, 31 May 1996). This notion that a man may have 'two sides' is, of course, a familiar motif within representations of men's criminality. It rests on a dualism between an 'outward face' (the appearance of normality) and a 'dark side' (his 'true' or essential nature). Implicitly, it is asked, 'he seemed to be one thing but he was really another – how could he have acted in such a way?' Hamilton's mother Agnes Watt, aged sixty-five, described him as a 'caring son' who visited her twice a week, telephoned every night and periodically presented her with £50 gifts. Her testimony was, in the light of subsequent knowledge, seen as exemplifying Thomas Hamilton's 'two sides'. However it is also read as emblematic of a darker 'truth' about Hamilton by drawing on a discourse of masculinity in which such 'close' mother–son relationships are seen, simultaneously, as benign (dutiful, caring, appropriate to a middle-aged man) and yet as being potentially problematic (as too close, as the 'mummy's boy', the repressed homosexual). His mother recalled he once had a girl friend 'but she was too serious and he didn't want to know' (*The Guardian*, 31 May 1996; see further the interview with Agnes Watt: 'She Lost a Son at Dunblane, Too', *The Observer*, 1 December 1996).

Just as the mothers of Robert Thompson and Jon Venables had tried, in their accounts to the media and the police, to make their sons 'just like other boys', Agnes Watt sought to establish that Thomas Hamilton was, in many ways, similar to other men. However, were she to succeed in this, the division between the 'monster' (he really was) and the 'normal man' (he at times appeared to be) would itself be revealed as fantasy.[10] The representations of men's otherness constituted through the discourse of hetero-masculinity are multi-layered. Yet, once again, in this process important questions are left begging around why it should be men whose response to the 'bottling up' of emotions should routinely take such violent forms. Violence is banished to a criminal space (the world of the misfit, the *loner*). Such an account is, quite simply, inadequate. In order to develop an analysis of Hamilton's sexed specificity at the level of (social) structure and (individual) psyche it is necessary to explore further how this iconography of otherness played out in terms of notions of the spree killer as a social 'failure' and why men's reaction to that failure should then so frequently be understood to take such violent and destructive forms.

Configuring the 'masculine' subject: Thomas Hamilton as repressed 'failed man'

The classic psychological profile of the spree killer

Though it varies from case to case (Hungerford, Dunblane, Port Arthur) a number of key features recur around the image of the lone gunman as a failed man, 'lonely, angry, resentful and ready to snap':

> The classic profile of the killer as a single, lonely and obsessive man who is unable to articulate his emotions and is desperate for some form of recognition. Very few of these people are psychotic. (*The Guardian*, 29 April 1996)

There is some overlap here with the dominant representation of the serial murderer as a 'resentment killer' out to take revenge on society for some past trauma. Like multiple murderers and serial killers, the spree killer is not generally understood to have been 'ill', at least not in the sense of suffering from schizophrenia, manic depression, and so forth. The following comments are not atypical of those made after Dunblane:

> Where you look in terms of background is at things like isolation, whether he is a loner with a possible desire for revenge, desire for status, a desire to be famous, or infamous, a desire to be a soldier or a commando who idolises guns.[11]

> The man could well be someone who people thought of as odd but not mentally ill who has killed for the sake of it. People who go on spree killings have not entered the mental health community and bottle it up until it all explodes in catastrophe. It could happen to kids who are over protected and not allowed to express themselves. They harbour resentment for a long time while on the face of it they put up with being laughed at.[12]

> They obviously have major problems communicating their feelings and are likely to have all sorts of anger and aggression.[13]

Each of these comments draws on an emotional framework familiar to men and women. After all, it could be argued that we all know fear, uncertainty, desire and envy. In this model rationality and intentionality are imputed to the spree killer. He decides to take 'revenge' on a society which has somehow 'rejected' him.

Such social failures, however, have a distinctly sexed dimension. Within a range of popular cultural texts of the 1980s and 1990s (plays, novels, films[14]) these are emotions associated with a distinctively masculine (and arguably a white, ethnically specific[15]) psychology. It is white men who are, at the present moment, increasingly presumed to be experiencing these kinds of life experiences in a particularly acute form (see Collier, 1996a). The press discourse in the aftermath of the Dunblane massacre shared, and drew on, these more general notions of masculine failure and crisis. Hamilton was an inadequate nobody, a man considered unable to succeed in society – financially, socially, sexually, academically, in sport or in work. Yet within this (gendered) model the sexed specificity of Hamilton continues to be erased, no less powerfully than it had been within the quasi-religious binary of good/evil. The dominant psychological profile model is gendered both in terms of *cause* (what is constructed as the source of rejection and failure in the first place: his sexual, social, work failure) and its *effects* (in his recourse to specifically masculinised forms of violence as response: for example, the use of guns and weapons). There is, moreover, a contradiction emerging here. On the one hand, we have seen, it was said to be 'almost impossible' to pinpoint reasons for the lone gunman's actions. Like the serial murder, the spree killing does not take place in a pre-given rationally ordered society. However, the failed man narrative introduces an emotional framework in which notions of masculine failure are accessible and readily understandable. It imputes an intentionality which is deeply familiar. It can, it would seem, be understood after all.

Ultimately this framework serves to normalise (if not excuse) men's criminality. It does so because it remains within the positivist and modernist crimino-legal frame which does not make the sexed specificity of crime explicit. The dualism of normal/deviant fixes Hamilton as the latter; but there is no engagement with his masculine subjectivity as itself having been in any sense fluid or possibly contradictory (or any sense that men may shift between different subject positions). It negates, crucially, any analysis of what Hamilton may have *shared* with other men at the very moment that it calls upon a normative masculinity by way of explanation for his actions. The failed man model places the spree killer within an understanding of crime as a deviant form of instrumental rationality. The means–ends relation which has typified crime as a modernist discourse thus remains in place. Yet what would happen if we were to re-frame the question asked by the model in such a way as to make sexed specificity problematic? Why, in other words, should it be that *his* social failures take such spectacularly violent and destructive forms? Why is it, in the vast majority of cases, men's anger and despair (and not women's) which manifests itself, with apparently increasing frequency, in the murder of so many 'strangers'?

In the remainder of this chapter I wish to present an alternative reading of the performative strategies in and through which Thomas Hamilton, as a (sexed) subject in a specific (social) location, may have sought to constitute himself as 'a man'. In highlighting the performativity of gender it is possible, I shall argue, to interrogate the interface between the contexts in which Hamilton lived at the level of social structure and the specificities of his own life-history.

The fantasised masculine and the (a)social other: (re)constructing the sexed body of the lone gunman

Thomas Hamilton's life, from what is known, had been dominated by two principal activities: firstly, an involvement in the scouting and the youth club movement, and, secondly, an involvement in gun clubs. In re-reading each of these activities in terms of how gender is performed in specific contexts, both the youth movement and the gun club can each be seen, in different and overlapping ways, as sites for the (hetero)sexing of the male body as 'masculine'.

Thomas Hamilton as surrogate father: childhood, the scouting movement and the youth club

The dominant, indeed exclusive, representation of childhood in the press discourse around the Dunblane massacre is one of 'spotless innocence and hope' (*Time*, 25 March 1996). It is an innocence captured in two images extensively reproduced in television and newspaper accounts. The first is the photograph of Class P 1 of Dunblane Primary School, with their teacher, Gwen Mayor. This was to become a central icon, the reference point for the construction of childhood innocence around which all other images circulated (cf., on the Bulger case, Young, 1996: 116). The second is a freeze-frame taken from a home video recording showing Thomas Hamilton with young boys in a gymnasium assisting them in vaulting over a wooden horse.[16] They are disturbing, haunting and culturally familiar images. It is through our subsequent knowledge, what we now 'know', that they come to tell other, more dangerous stories: of childhood innocence destroyed by a stranger, of evil's destruction of innocence, of a woman who lost her life attempting to protect the children in her class, of a man who sexually desired those in his charge, a man who should not have been allowed to get into such a position of trust, authority and power in the first place.

Such were the dominant interpretations of these images within the press discourse. Yet if each representation is re-framed in a context which renders problematic the sociality of masculinity, what else comes into view? I have argued above that the representation of Hamilton as both (quasi-religious) 'evil' 'grotesque' *and* (secularised) 'social failure' diverts attention from the sexed specificity of the social context in which he lived. With regard to these images, this is a context in which men's presence with children is presently considered problematic in certain scenarios and situations. It is a context in which, moreover, key elements of normative 'idealised' hetero-masculinity are constituted not through contact or association *with* women and children, but via a range of activities primarily located as beyond the 'familial' sphere and which take men *away* from shared physical space with women and children (see further, on criminological theory, Chapter 3, pp. 76–8). The British primary school, in many ways the embodiment of a 'feminised' social space, epitomises this gendering of institution, space and body in terms of the hierarchical structuring of sexual difference. Men remain rare in primary school teaching, except as the head of school. Even before the emergence of high-profile debates around school security in the 1990s, following a number of murders and attacks inside and outside school grounds, the very presence of an unknown man in any school is enough to arouse suspicion. At issue here are more general questions, anxieties and concerns about cultural representations of the paternal relationship which pervade responses to Dunblane. Yet in the case of the press discourse the problematic nature of the relationship between men and children was consistently effaced, notwithstanding the fact that it was central to the social context of Thomas Hamilton's life and actions.

In July 1973 Thomas Hamilton became a leader in the Boy Scouts movement. In 1974, at the age of twenty-one, he was subsequently dismissed as leader of a local scout troop for 'inappropriate behaviour'. In the intervening years he made frequent attempts to be allowed to re-enter the organisation, the last in 1988; he was rebuffed on every occasion. Hamilton was, the psychologist Paul Britton has written, neither 'an altruistic youth leader nor an uncomplicated paedophile' but, rather, 'a person who grew to need to guide direct and control young boys; to influence how their bodies and morals developed'.[17] In so doing, of course, he was not alone. A range of institutions have historically sought to discipline, guide, direct and control the bodies of young boys. Such disciplining has been secured historically by facilitating boys' subjection and bodily proximity to the (suitable) authority of an older man or men. In a more contemporary variant, the search for appropriate male role models for young boys is seen, at a time of widespread 'father-absence', as essential to instilling non-criminal behaviour in male youth. Far from transgressing societal norms, Hamilton's concern with the disciplining and rendering subject to masculine authority potentially 'wayward' male youth can in fact be seen as in keeping with successive British governments' understanding of young men's socialisation 'into crime'.[18]

It is not, in other words, because of any concern to 'discipline' boys *per se* that Hamilton's actions are seen as problematic. The youth clubs he set up exist within a terrain 'outside' the family. They are, however, no less regulated by codes of a familial ideology which ascribes to men particular social roles and functions (as disciplinarian, authority figure, protector and 'friend'). It was by virtue of Thomas Hamilton's imputed sexual transgression that this authority was breached. The symbolic dominance of the father-figure ideal of this authority itself remains in place, however. In the freeze-frame image of a man assisting boys in the gymnasium, Thomas Hamilton encapsulates a paternal presence which is, in other contexts, deemed desirable (as being, for example, a strategy in crime prevention). As both 'surrogate father' in the youth club and 'rogue male' in the primary school, Thomas Hamilton appears the embodiment of, at the same time as he makes visible, the pervasive absence of men from the lives of children, whether in their capacity as (biological or social) fathers or as 'caregivers' to children and welfare workers across a range of institutions and organisations (Pringle, 1995; Skelton, 1994). The 'normality' of men's relationships with young boys is itself deeply contested (to be regulated, policed and rendered subject to surveillance). Indeed, the relationship between men and children constitutes, at present, a problematic (Burgess and Ruxton, 1996) which rests, in part, on a consciousness of men and masculinity as potential threats to the safety, integrity, autonomy and, ultimately, lives of children. These threats cannot be confined to the extra-familial, though it is significant how at present a whole range of stories – hitherto subjugated knowledges – are articulating the point that 'strangers' have been a significant problem in the lives of many young men in terms of sexual abuse in locations such as the youth club, the children's home,[19] the school and the church. It is, nonetheless, from *within* the parameters of the (hetero)sexual family that the rupture between men and children is being most rigorously and pervasively experienced in late modernity/postmodernity. It is the pervasiveness of this threat of the 'dangerous' male which more generally transcends (and in so doing disturbs) the public/private dualism as a meaningful distinction in seeking to locate the crimes of men.

It is in the light of the above that the dominant representation in the press discourse of the community of Dunblane as being somehow beyond, or without, crime assumes a particular significance in terms of its relation to the familial. The dominant image of childhood was, we have seen (and in marked contrast to the Bulger case), one of 'innocence destroyed'. The innocence of childhood secures the body of the child within a particular configuration of the social. Whereas the serial killer, it has been argued, chooses as his victims individuals or groups who can be seen to be somehow 'outside' the social (down-and-outs, hitch-hikers, and so on: Stratton, 1996: 82), Thomas Hamilton chose as his victims the very subjects – children – who constituted the sociality of Dunblane as a phantasmatic community. The representation of Hamilton as a straightforward paedophile appears to restore the order of the (familial) community. It *appears* to efface the rupture caused by a breach of men's (surrogate) paternal trust. Increasingly, however, the family of modernity is itself being displaced as institutional source for the preservation and reproduction of moral (sexual) order. It is in this context that the problematic nature of the relationship between men and children has become something which cannot be sutured by reference to certainties and securities evoked by representations of 'masculinity' constituted through the concepts, categories and binaries which have marked the gender order of modernity. For, increasingly, that which is considered 'dangerous' about men has, it would seem, moved somewhat closer to 'home'.

The cultural framework of idealised masculinity: the 'copycat' spree killer and the gun club

> There are calls for the gun club in a basement under the House of Lords to be scrapped as an example to the nation and turned, of all things, into a crèche.
>
> (*South China Morning Post*, 22 March 1996)

Alongside his involvement in youth clubs Thomas Hamilton had one other abiding interest; a fascination with handguns, many of which he had obtained over a twenty-year period. In the months following the massacre, culminating with the publication of the Cullen Report (1996) in October 1996, an at times intemperate and heated debate over the legal regulation of firearms was rarely out of the news in Britain. It was, and is, a debate in which gender is systematically silenced. Both the 'sporting' and 'lone' gunman appear routinely as de-sexed figures. The debate, it seems, has *nothing* to say of men and masculinity.[20] Certainly, the sport of firearms shooting attracts both women and men among its participants. However, it is an activity framed by a particular gender politics and order.

The above comment in the *South China Morning Post* that 'of all things' there were calls for the gun club in a basement under the House of Lords to be 'turned . . . into a crèche' appears a throwaway comment. It suggests that in Britain the debate over gun control has become far removed from 'reality'. Yet it does, albeit unintentionally, capture an important point. The fact that a decision had been made to install in the basement of Britain's second legislative chamber a gun club, as opposed to any provision for the care of children, is indicative not just of the priorities of those who made that decision. It would be misleading to suggest simply that 'times have changed'. It symbolises the hierarchical structuring of power, resources and access to decision-making positions in terms of sexual difference which cannot be confined to one institution (such as Parliament) or organisation. In the case of the gun club this was, in terms of (empirical) membership/ involvement and prevailing ethos, a pervasively masculinised culture. The Cullen Inquiry noted how the authorities had shown a 'tacit sympathy' towards the prevailing gun culture; the attitudes of the police and gun licensing officers had been 'coloured' by this 'official' (legitimate) gun culture (*The Guardian*, 11 July 1996). Shooting, of course, remains a popular pastime amongst members of the male-dominated judiciary (Labour Research, 1987). Notwithstanding subsequent tightening of the law regulating firearms ownership in the light of Cullen's recommendations, this broader culture highlights a tension between the purported deviance of Thomas Hamilton's involvement with firearms and the 'normality' of other men's actions and attitudes.

This is a tension exemplified by the press discourse as it sought to understand the spree killer in terms of the phenomenon of 'copycat' violence ('Gun Man Obsessed by Hungerford Shot 17 Bystanders', *The Times*, 25 May 1996). Considerable attention was given in the press as to whether

Thomas Hamilton, having witnessed the 'fame' (however fleeting) accorded to other lone gunmen in recent years, had sought to kill in order to achieve his own status, a desire to be famous, or infamous. This model of the copycat killer is, however, like attempts to understand the spree killer in terms of his 'social failure', misleading. It fails to sexualise the social context in which the sexed specificity of men's relationship to violence is established in the first place. As an editorial in *The Independent* newspaper (16 March 1996) noted, 'Hamilton's story, like the story of so much violence in our society, is a tale of men and weapons, sex and repression, power and revenge.' The culture that encircled the school was one of incessant violence in which, it is estimated, 30 per cent of boys between the ages of fourteen and fifteen carry weapons and where a third of teenage boys and two-thirds of girls fear physical attack (Balding, 1996). The broader framework which surrounded Thomas Hamilton and the school is, in short, encoded by representations of potency, privilege and empowerment associated with traditionally public locations for the achievement of an idealised heterosexual masculinity – locations, that is, such as the gun club (or, indeed, the office, the legislature, the sports field or the university).

The 'criminal man' as social (hetero-sexed) subject

The following encapsulates the dominant reading within the press discourse of the events in Thomas Hamilton's life in the weeks prior to the massacre (a reading with which the Cullen Report was subsequently to concur). Hamilton had forcefully resisted the label 'pervert' which, he proclaimed, had been unjustly attached to him. In a sense he 'fought back', protesting his 'normality' to everyone from the Queen to the Ombudsman in a series of 'articulate but increasingly obsessive' letters (*The Times*, 15 March 1996) complaining of his 'damaged reputation'. It was only when this strategy of resistance 'failed' that he finally 'snapped'.

It is possible, I wish to suggest, to read the 'resistance' of Thomas Hamilton in a rather different way. In his account of the murder of James Bulger, *Destroying the Baby in Themselves*, David Jackson has noted how Jon Venables and Robert Thompson, the two ten-year-old boys convicted of the murder, existed 'for much of [the] time within the constraining framework of adult authority, regulation and surveillance' (1995: 9). Thomas Hamilton, in relation to his work, home, family and, it seems, sexuality, may also be seen to have been a dis-empowered subject. However, unlike two ten-year-old children, as an adult male he had access to a range of institutional resources through which he could then seek to establish and exercise power and control over his own (and other) lives. In seeking to carve out an identity for himself 'in a different framework that seemed to offer ... some status and self-respect' (Jackson, 1995: 16), he turned to a range of organisations and behaviour, in and through which he might constitute claims to other sources of power, other subject positions and definitions of masculinity from those through which his 'failure' as a man was otherwise being repeatedly confirmed.[21]

In this active re-negotiation of existing frameworks of masculine identi-fication (in the form, for example, of his participation in youth work and gun clubs), Thomas Hamilton's (sexed, specific) male body is connected with, and ascribed meanings through, notions of sexualised violence and potency. Far from setting him apart, this connected Thomas Hamilton to those other men and boys who on a daily basis, in Jackson's words, long to associate themselves with the power and conventionality of masculine identity 'because of the dominating position that heterosexual masculinity occupies in our Western culture. Practically, this means trying to *heterosexualise* and *masculinise* their . . . bodies' simultaneously (Jackson, 1995: 32). This is a culture pervaded by images of hyper-masculine toughness, which valorises, in multifarious ways, the male body acting on space in conjunction with the skilled use and technical knowledge of weapons, be they guns or knives. Many boys routinely carry weapons. It is not hard to envisage how images of masculine bodies, bulging muscles and empowered actors might be enticing and seductive for men and boys who lack, in so many other respects, any commanding presence and status in the world (see Morrison, 1997). Through the use of weaponry, indeed, the male body is itself transformed. Far from seeing the build-up to the massacre as one of Hamilton *losing* control, therefore, it is to locate the offence as a means of *taking* control (Eastman, 1996). As Cullen himself concluded about Hamilton: '. . . he lacked any real insight into the fact that his (own) conduct had led to the decline in his fortunes . . . he turned his fantasy into reality in order to *achieve control* in one final and terrible manner' (Cullen Report, 1996: para. 5.46, my emphasis).

This was, however, a taking of control which was – most importantly – profoundly masculinised. To adapt and re-write Jackson's argument, this is to see the actions of Thomas Hamilton as closely connected to a 'desperate struggle to become masculine' (Jackson, 1995: 24). Although Thomas Hamilton's killing of sixteen children and their teacher 'was exceptional in degree and intensity', he was not a one-off, devilish, 'freak of nature'. He shared many of the learnt tendencies of aggressive, heterosexual manliness that many insecure young boys and men are desperately striving for today. Although representing a heightened, extremely unusual form of these tendencies, Thomas Hamilton existed firmly within the common continuum of male violence.[22]

To recap the argument at this point: Thomas Hamilton, in trying to masculinise himself within the ideals of traditional heterosexual masculinity, can be read as attempting to forge a more commanding and potent sense of himself as a man (Jackson, 1995: 28). He did this, I have argued, through his involvement in (at least) three major activities: firstly, in his participation in the youth clubs, in which he is constituted as (surrogate) father-figure; secondly, in his involvement with firearms and gun clubs, in which his subjectivity is empowered (however fleetingly) through the constitution of the body as 'masculine'; and, finally, and by way of a combination of each of the above, in his ultimate invasion, re-framing and destruction of the largely feminised space of the primary school at Dunblane which resulted in the death of sixteen children and their teacher.

Concluding remarks: reconstituting the crimes of men *as men*

> What is it about our world that impels men such as Thomas Hamilton to go on random, apparently motiveless killing sprees? This is a new kind of crime, not much more than a decade old, and signs were available long before its emergence.
>
> (Editorial, 'They Deserve Our Answers', *Independent on Sunday*,
> 17 March 1996)

I have argued that a number of oppositions pervade the press discourse in its constructions of Thomas Hamilton. The result is a rich iconography of masculine otherness far more complex than the initial focus on good/evil, normal/deviant binaries would suggest. As a single (unpartnered) man he is not a 'family man' for he is *of* no family. Yet he is understood as Other *through* the family. The crisis of representation of the paternal relation which surrounds the press discourse results from the reconfiguration taking place within postmodernity of the sociality and contingency of those oppositional categories through which hetero-masculinity has hitherto been constituted as a naturalised, essentialist phenomenon. In this process the broader heterosexual matrix which has historically framed understandings of men's crimes and criminality itself appears as, I have suggested, a phantas-matic ideal. The representation of Thomas Hamilton's 'dangerousness' embraces a range of images, behaviours and demeanours which cannot be confined to the 'pervert/paedophile'–'normal' binary. Nor does it fit in with any straightforward representation of Hamilton as a (self-evident) 'psychopath'.

In the suggestion that there is something new and distinct about the spree killing, that it is a 'new kind of crime', it is envisaged that crime has 'transformed itself and mutated'. Crime appears as 'a law unto itself, outside the law, an outlaw' (Young, 1996: 6). Outside the law, beyond reason, a space opens up for speculation about the dark side of 'human nature' which marked so much of the media coverage of Dunblane. Yet what, I have argued, constitutes a more plausible reading of the symbolic power of Dunblane involves locating Thomas Hamilton in relation to a shifting discursive experience of the social: '. . . to the extent that simulation not representation defines the experience of postmodernity, the reified social is the site of the hyperreal' (Stratton, 1996: 79). As the experience of the social is increasingly grounded in the aesthetic, not the moral, the media's shifting and pervasive aesthetization of men's criminality can itself be seen as characteristic, and emblematic, of the end of modernity.

With this in mind it should not surprise that the reconfiguration taking place around representations of men's relationships with children within the postmodern social should involve a re-framing of hitherto self-evident 'dangerous' masculinities. For what is at issue here, I have argued in this and the preceding chapter, is no less than the concept of childhood itself and its relation to the social. From the child's post-Enlightenment positioning as unequivocal source of love, the child of postmodernity has, we have seen, come to signify both 'nostalgia' for an innocence lost (Jenks, 1996) and, notably in the form of the criminality of male youth, social breakdown and moral dislocation (Chapter 3). Each now appears as a symbolic representation for the re-organisation of the patterning of relationships within the social. If the innocence of the child is to be invested with so much, grounding sociality at a time of intolerable and disorientating change, it is no wonder that the deaths of the Dunblane children (and, indeed, James Bulger) should strike at the remaining vestiges of the social bond and surface such an intense, collective pain at the loss of social identity (Jenks, 1996: 21). In contrast to Hamilton's embodiment of evil, the Dunblane children appear as permanent and dependable, the incarnation of a 'nostalgic' vision of the child which has come to jealously preserve no less than the meta-narrative of society itself.

Where does this leave the politics of masculinity, the relationship between masculinity and crime? In this chapter I have presented an interpretative genealogy of how the 'silencing' of masculinity is achieved in one particular context and instance. I have taken the press coverage of Dunblane as illustrative of the broader phenomenon whereby the sociality of men's crimes as the actions of men is routinely effaced. This is a question which traditional political discourse appears to continue to be incapable of addressing, something which itself says much about contemporary understandings of the relation between the crimes of men and the idea of the social. Faced with the events at Dunblane, even the eloquence of politicians seemed to fail: '. . . some public catastrophes', it was stated, 'are out of public reach' (*The Guardian*, 14 March 1996). For others the 'pain for the grieving silenced [traditional] politics' (Editorial, *The Independent*, 15 March 1996).

That which was evacuated, silenced from the very outset was, I have argued, any analysis of Thomas Hamilton not as a 'lone gunman', 'spree killer' or 'monster' but *as a man*. For all the limited engagement it makes with Thomas Hamilton's 'character and attitudes', his 'mood' and 'psychological and psychiatric evidence', there is no trace of such questions in the subsequent Cullen Report into the massacre.[23] 'Traditional' politics seemed to sense, but barely express, the feeling of the betrayal of the vulnerable which runs through the crimino-legal responses to Dunblane and, more generally, to crimes against children. The terms 'no evidence' and 'no action taken' were repeated constantly during the Cullen Inquiry. How is the systematic lack of response to the mothers who made complaints about the actions of Thomas Hamilton to be explained (see Cullen Report, 1996: Ch. 4)? What happened to the knowledge which so clearly existed about his actions and was evident in the accounts of women and children? The dominant representation of the spree killer as (asocial) other fed into a valorising of childhood innocence which, perhaps ironically, itself served to silence the voices of those children who sought to speak of, and be heard in, their testimonies of the crimes of men.

To reconfigure the relationship between men and crime leads, ultimately, to a transformation in how crime is imagined. It leads to a set of different questions and issues which ill fit the traditional formulations of liberal political and crimino-legal thought (in terms, for example, of public/private, mind/body). In one sense Thomas Hamilton is a 'one-off'. Yet from such so called 'aberrant' cases much can be learnt about the crimes of men more generally. Indeed, it is arguably all the more pressing to locate the thread which links such crimes with the fantasies and actions of 'normal' men. We have yet, it appears, to be challenged with what Thomas Hamilton may have shared with other men.[24] What questions might this then raise about the state's responses to knowledge of Thomas Hamilton in terms of competing yet mutually constituted 'masculinities'? To dismiss the lack of response, the failure to 'do something' about Hamilton, as simply a bureaucratic failure or regulatory matter (of firearms, school security)[25] is to misread and to negate analysis of state institutions themselves in terms of sex difference. It is an interesting question as to whether, had the complaints being made about Thomas Hamilton come from women, rather than men, they would have met with similar reception in terms of identification of men's danger-ousness. Far from being a 'one-off', exceptional and not-to-be-repeated event, in (re)locating the 'lone gunman' within a broader framework of sexed subjectivity the recent instances of spree killings can be seen as highlighting not just a failure to protect women and children from the depredations of 'psychopathic' males, but as also raising important, and disturbing, questions about the boundaries of what constitutes 'acceptable' male behaviour in the first place.

Postscript

> Dunblane will happen at any time again, unless decisive action is taken.
>
> (Colin Campbell QC at the Cullen Inquiry, 8 July 1996)

> Teddy Bear Bloodbath . . . Machete Madman hacks picnic kiddies.
>
> (*The Sun*, 9 July 1996)

> Teddy Bears Picnic Terror: Maniac with a machete hacks children in school playground.
>
> (*Daily Mail*, 9 July 1996)

> . . . to hear this thing that has come against him is quite a bit of a shock . . . he seemed like a normal guy.
>
> (School friend of Horrett Campbell, *BBC Television News*, 9 July 1996, 1.00 p.m.)

During the afternoon of 8 July a man scaled a fence and burst into St Luke's Primary School in Blakenhall, Wolverhampton, England, at the end of the school day. He proceeded to attack the class of three- and four-year-olds and their teacher with a machete. Three children and four adults suffered injuries including lacerations and deep hard blows to the head and face. According to one eyewitness, 'he just walked straight towards one of the mothers and slashed at her head . . . he just started hacking at anybody and everybody' (*The Independent*, 9 July 1996). This was the fifth major violent incident in a British school in just over two years. In every case the assailant was a man. The following day a thirty-two-year-old man, Horrett Campbell, was arrested and charged with the attack. By chance, the incident took place within minutes of the judicial inquiry into the Dunblane massacre being told that there existed every expectation that a similar such attack would happen again 'unless decisive action is taken' (*The Independent*, 9 July 1996).

On the same day the British news media reported another story. The body of a nine-year-old schoolgirl, Jade Matthews, had been found dead on a railway siding in the town of Bootle, Liverpool. She had been missing for over eight hours. She had severe head and face injuries and a blood-stained stick was found nearby. Her body was discovered two and a half miles away from the site where the body of James Bulger had been discovered in 1993. As the story broke during the evening of 8 July it became known that the police wished to question three boys, aged between nine and ten, who had been seen in the area. Children, it appeared, might have been involved in the murder of another child: the Bulger murder had 'returned to haunt Merseyside' (*BBC Television News*, 8 July 1996, 6.00 p.m.). By the end of the day it became known that the natural father of Jade Matthews was being held for questioning and the issue was no longer headline news. Later, a thirteen-year-old boy was convicted of the murder of Jade Matthews and was sentenced to be detained indefinitely (*The Guardian*, 8 February 1997).

What was being said about these incidents? What *could* be said? Beyond reason there seemed nothing and yet everything to be said about each event: 'This sick world gets sicker. . . . Today, it seems, you can't let your kids out of your sight' (*The Sun*, 9 July 1996): 'There is no way we can understand these killings' (*Daily Mirror*, 9 July 1996). The echoes with Bulger and Dunblane were deafening. Yet they needed stating and emphasising: 'Not Again . . . After Bulger . . . Cops hunt 3 boys over murder of Jade, 9 . . . After Dunblane . . . machete madman strikes at school' (Headline, *Daily Mirror*, 9 July 1996): 'After Dunblane' came the repeated cry – not again: '. . . Britain, 1996, is a country no longer safe for children. In the streets or at home or at school there is a constant threat. . . . The carefree days of childhood have gone . . . We must turn back from the edge before we plunge into the abyss' (Editorial, 'Innocent Victims of a Sick Society', *Daily Mirror*, 9 July 1996). Parents everywhere would be 'inevitably reminded of the Dunblane shootings' (*BBC Television News*, 8 July 1996, 6.00 p.m.). The attack at St Luke's Primary School was initially depicted as 'an explosion of evil' (*Daily Mail*, 10 July 1996). The innocence of childhood victims, attacked during a 'teddy bears' picnic' in school, placed the attack beyond reason: 'it was here the chuckles and giggles of three and four year olds on a teddy bears' picnic turned to screams and panic as the attacker struck . . . the knifeman could not have struck at a more innocent or defenceless gathering' (*ITN Television News*, 8 July 1996, 10.00 p.m.).

The central issue, to be discussed repeatedly in the television, newspaper and radio accounts in the days following days, was the question of school security ('Attack Confirms the Fears of Teachers', *The Independent*, 9 July 1996). By the evening of 8 July, hours after the attack, the question of why it should have happened surfaced. Attention turned to the attacker himself. Horrett Campbell was an 'eccentric' who 'always remained outside the community, known only as a loner who behaves strangely' (*The Guardian*, 10 July 1996). Testimonies from acquaintances recounted his unusual behaviour: 'He was always so quiet but he wasn't mad. He knew exactly what he was doing.' 'Nobody could remember him having a girlfriend.' He was a 'loner' yet he was known: 'Everyone around here', it was said, 'knew Izzie.' It was, it seemed, a 'copycat' attack. He was a 'Harmless loner' who 'admired mass killers' (*The Guardian*, 10 December 1996). It became known that Horrett Campbell had planned 'a Dunblane style massacre' for weeks. Police who raided his 'seedy flat' found press cuttings of Dunblane ('Machete Madman Obsessed by Dunblane', *Daily Record*, 10 July 1996). Were the media 'giving ideas to people predisposed to violence. . . . What can it be that motivates people to attack children like this?' (*BBC Newsnight*, 8 July 1996, 10.30 p.m.). The 'expert' testimony of the child psychologist Dr Michelle Elliot claimed that such 'people' tend to be

> paranoid individuals who feel they have got some grievance against society. They are certainly inadequate people because they cannot adequately get their griev- ances taken care of in any other way. (*BBC Newsnight*, 8 July 1996, 10.30 p.m.)

A man such as Horrett Campbell, it was stated, notes the publicity given the grievances of 'men like Thomas Hamilton' as empowering – 'If I do that I will be Number One item in the News':

> It may be partly . . . a copycat effect after Dunblane . . . people who have strange . . . aggressive fantasies . . . it suddenly occurs to them that the school setting is an appropriate venue to act out that fantasy . . . we don't know why that is and it is very difficult to predict where the risk will arise. (Michael Levi, *BBC Newsnight*, 8 July 1996, 10.30 p.m.)

Once again the broader frame slides from view. The crime is de-sexed. There is everything, and yet nothing, to be said. Silence falls.

Notes

1. These are distinct from the phenomenon of 'serial killing', on which see further Stratton (1996). On non-politically motivated homicides, including the spree killing, see Gresswell and Hollin (1994).
2. A detailed account of the events can be found in Cullen (1996). Also 'Minutes of Mayhem That Took 17 Lives: Dunblane Inquiry', *The Guardian*, 30 May 1996.
3. See, for example, Young (1996: 111): '... personal reactions to it are as strong as they ever were ... in writing this chapter I have had frequent bad dreams and have felt a deep sense of horror.' Also King (1995: 168).
4. The 'quality' (broadsheet) press tends to seek more liberal, rational explanations in contrast to the more sensationalising tendencies of the tabloids. Given the latter's (considerable) greater circulation, it is open to question what effect this then has on the framing of public opinion. Notwithstanding these differences, each tended to share an initial depiction of Hamilton in terms of 'evil'. On the day Dunblane Primary School re-opened, it was stated that 'the evil has gone' (*The Sun*, 23 March 1996).
5. Mr Justice Moreland, summing up in the James Bulger murder trial (*The Guardian*, 25 November 1993).
6. See, for example, 'Fear Rules in No Go Britain: a report on the parts of the country most people would rather not think about – never mind live', *Independent on Sunday*, 17 April 1994.
7. A number of reports noted how, in a commuter town, the adults who lived in Dunblane tended not to be familiar with each other. The children, in contrast, knew each other and the Primary School had come to be a focus of life in the town. It brought people, who otherwise lived very separate lives, together. As such, the mass murder of the children took on a particular resonance in its symbolic violence against the *idea* of a community which had seemed crime-free.
8. Hamilton had been brought up to believe his natural mother, to whom he was very close, was in fact his sister (see further Cullen Report, 1996: para. 4.2).
9. In October 1996 it was reported that 'being single in Britain in the 1990s means a miserable existence which can lead to heavy drinking, depression and even suicide ...'. 'Singles work harder, are less healthy, through a reliance on convenience foods. Since 1972 the rise in suicide for single males has risen by sixty per cent. Research shows marriage is a preventative measure to suicide. By 2030 one in three men are expected to be single' (*The Independent*, 28 October 1996). See also, reflecting what has become a growing concern about the social problems associated with 'single' men: 'Single Men Responsible for Little But Trouble', *The Independent*, 9 March 1998.
10. A similar argument informs Young's (1996: 125) reading of the mothers of Jon Venables and Robert Thompson, the two boys convicted of the murder of James Bulger.
11. Gerard Bailes, Novik Clinical Forensic Unit, quoted in Younge (1996).
12. Ian Stephen, quoted in Younge (1996).
13. Clive Meux, Senior Lecturer, Institute of Psychiatry, London, and consultant at Broadmoor Top Security Hospital, London, quoted in Younge (1996).
14. See, in particular, on the 1993 film *Falling Down*, Clover (1993: 6–9).
15. According to Clover (1993: 9), the 'Average White Male' 'is the great unmarked or default category of western culture, the one that never needed to define itself, the standard against which other categories have calculated their difference': 'No Travis Bickle this, *Falling Down*'s story is precisely that of *Taxi Driver* ... its whole effect depends on seeing D-Fens [the principal

character in the film, played by Michael Douglas] not as a vet [war veteran] descending into madness, but as a tax-paying citizen whose anger allows him to see, with preternatural clarity, the madness in the society around him' (Clover, 1993: 8).

16. The video from which this image was taken, showing Hamilton involved in a range of activities with young boys in a gymnasium, was later to form the basis of a BBC documentary on Dunblane (*Panorama*, BBC, broadcast 16 September 1996).

17. Notwithstanding that the Cullen Inquiry heard from 171 witnesses unrestrained by libel laws, hard evidence linking Hamilton with sexual abuse of children remained meagre (*The Guardian*, 11 July 1996).

18. See further Chapter 5, pp. 129–31. The stated aims of the 'boot camps' introduced by the British government as a way of instilling military discipline for young offenders, for example, emphasise similar concerns with the disciplining, surveillance and regulation of male bodies.

19. 'Eighty Named as Child Abusers in Clwyd Inquiry', *Independent on Sunday*, 19 January 1997.

20. By way of exception see B. Campbell, 'The Problem with Arms and Men', *The Guardian*, 23 July 1996.

21. In a letter to *The Observer* (24 March 1996) Dr Felicity de Zulueta highlights 'the hidden violence society does its best to ignore. Every week in this country, four children die from parental neglect or abuse. Every week, in my clinic at Charing Cross Hospital, I meet adults whose childhoods read like stories from hell. As small children they were abandoned or beaten, tortured, raped and terrorised by those on whom their lives depended. They come to me overwhelmed by their fears of violence to themselves and others. The violence we see on the streets and in the schools stems from the terror and accompanying rage such children have experienced in their homes.' Individuals like Hamilton, on this reading, seek to 'hang on to a semblance of life by indulging in perverse activities through which they express their childhood rage. By doing horrible things to others, often innocent children', they seek to turn their own 'past terror into power. Take away their access to this last source of human contact and these individuals are thrown back into the states of terrifying helplessness they once knew, and which usually end in madness or suicide. For some, though, final disintegration may be crowned by a final act of revenge – the destruction of others, objects of hatred such as they felt themselves to be.'

22. This section re-writes, in the context of Dunblane, Jackson's (1995) analysis of the Bulger murder.

23. See, for example, paras. 5.2, 5.25–8, 5.37–49. The strategy of the Conservative government had been to regulate the body of the paedophile in some quite specific ways (see the Consultation Paper Sentencing and the Supervision of Sex Offenders, published on 17 June 1996).

24. For a rare exception to this, in another context, see J. O'Sullivan, 'We're Still in the Dark Over West's Madness', *The Independent*, 12 September 1996.

25. Which is, in effect, what the Cullen Report concludes. A senior police officer subsequently resigned in the wake of the comments made on bureaucratic failings in the Report.

5 Absent Fathers, Criminal Sons and Straight Men: The Heterosexual Family and the Family of Crime

It has been a recurring theme in the preceding chapters that the repositioning of the sexed body presently taking place within feminist and queer theoretical scholarship has served to both challenge and disturb dominant ideas of what has been understood to constitute a normative or 'hegemonic' male heterosexuality. This chapter seeks to explore further the nature of that 'normal' male heterosexuality via an investigation of the purportedly fixed, immutable masculinity of 'family' men. In recent years, both across disciplines and from different perspectives, the behaviour of 'straight, white men' has been increasingly problematised. In so doing, I shall suggest, familial politics and the relationship between men, the family and crime have each been opened out to analyses which might transcend those meta-narratives and attempts at grand theorising which have so often sought to understand the crimes of men through reference to a univocal and categorical construct of oppressive masculinity. We have already seen, in relation to the institutional and discursive reproduction of criminology itself (Chapter 2), in debates around youth crime and the 'trouble with boys' (Chapter 3) and in relation to men's violences and notions of the dangerous 'other' (Chapter 4), how a critical refocusing on the 'heterosexuality of masculinity' and 'masculinity of heterosexuality' might shed new light on the framework in which ideas about the relationship between men and crime is conceptualised. This chapter seeks to take forward this analysis of heterosexuality and crime by exploring in more depth the nature of the relationship between the 'politics of the family' and the 'politics of crime'.

The focus of the discussion which follows is an investigation of representation of fathers and fatherhood within a range of discourses presently addressing the crime/family relationship, in particular in the context of the criminality of young men. The schema of the chapter is as follows. In the first section I contextualise the argument to follow by exploring some of the recent associations which have been made between 'absent' fathers, families and crime, by focusing on the ways in which debates have fed into, and articulated, the notion of 'masculine crisis'. The second section examines some of the ways in which the concerns of a range of contemporary fathers' rights organisations, who have been involved in campaigning around men's legal rights, relate to the emergence of a broader 'new men's movement'.[1] This social movement is presently seeking, with I shall argue some success, to influence the wider cultural nexus within which demands for changes in legal, social and criminal justice policies are presently being articulated around a range of issues. Section three seeks to 'unpack' the nature of the representations of male heterosexuality contained in such debates by focusing, in particular, on the nature of the relationship between 'absent' fatherhood, the problem of 'criminal' male youth and a more general negation of the familial. Finally, conclusions will address what I shall suggest are some of the implications of this 'rethinking' of male heterosexuality for developing an understanding of the production of the sexed subject in the context of debates around the family/crime relationship. What concerns me, in short, in this chapter are the ways in which a number of perceived economic, sexual and legal 'threats' to a particular model of paternal masculinity are presently being depicted as developments undermining not just the institution of heterosexuality but ultimately, the social itself, a social in which, importantly, the very *non*-criminality of men has been secured by reference to their positioning within a particular family structure.

Absent fathers and criminal sons

In recent years, both in Britain and elsewhere, there has been an enhanced interest in men's relationship to children. There now exists a considerable body of sociological and historical scholarship, as well as a multitude of popular cultural texts, around the subject of fathers and fatherhood (Burgess, 1997; Burgess and Ruxton, 1996; Lewis, 1986; Lewis and O'Brien, 1987). This work has addressed a broad set of issues: What is 'responsible' fathering? How has the role of fathers in the family changed historically? What is the relationship between families and masculinities (Heward, 1996)? What is the relationship between fathers and divorce (Arendell, 1995; Simpson et al., 1995)? What, ultimately, are fathers 'for'? With specific regard to the relationship between men and *crime*, however, this is a father which has figured above all in relation to one particular question: What is the relationship between 'father absence' (the 'fatherless family') and the subsequent criminality of the – predominantly male – youth of that family? This is an issue which has been raised most prominently in recent debates in Britain within the work of neo-conservative theorists of the 'underclass'. It is, indeed, an association which has become a familiar feature of the British political landscape, a concept used regularly by politicians from diverse political perspectives and by newspaper editorials alike. It is, therefore, revealing at the outset to consider some of the ways in which this explicit linkage of 'families without fatherhood' to the (actual and potential) criminality of urban male youth has been made.

The barbarians at the gate: (or) 'boys will be boys'?

The clearest and most influential statement of the absent father–criminal son correlation has been that made by the North American neo-conservative social commentator Charles Murray (1984, 1990). It has been, largely, from his writings that media accounts, academics and politicians have each based their interpretations of family breakdown, crime and masculine crisis. The general themes of the underclass thesis itself are captured in the following Editorial statement from the British newspaper *The Sunday Times*. It is a passage which is worth quoting at length for the ways in which it encompasses the broad concerns and themes of Murray's argument.

> It is becoming increasingly clear to all but the most blinkered of social scientists that the disintegration of the nuclear family is the principal source of so much social unrest and misery. The creation of an urban underclass, on the margins of society, but doing great damage to itself and the rest of us, is directly linked to the rapid rise in illegitimacy. . . . Of course illegitimacy has increased among all social groups; but the biggest increase has been overwhelmingly among the poorer, the unskilled, the unemployed. As a result they have gone from being merely poor to becoming an underclass. The past two decades have witnessed the growth of whole communities in which the dominant family structure is the single parent mother on welfare, whose male offspring are already immersed in a criminal culture by the time they are teenagers and whose daughters are destined to follow the family tradition of unmarried mothers. It is not just a question of a few families without fathers; it is a matter of whole communities with barely a single worthwhile male role model . . . [F]or communities to function successfully *they need families with fathers*. (Editorial, *The Sunday Times*, 28 February 1993; my emphasis)

Central to this underclass discourse, therefore, is the linking of the criminality of male youth with lone motherhood, 'family breakdown' and the economics of the welfare state. It is Murray's argument that there are three types of behaviour associated with membership of the underclass: illegitimacy, violent crime and a 'dropping out' of the labour force (Bagguley and Mann, 1992). Each, importantly, contains certain assumptions about the relationship between sex, gender and masculinity.

Firstly, young men are, in essence, considered to be 'barbarians'. They are innately brutish, driven by sexual imperatives and, most importantly, civilised by marriage into the social order and 'respectability':

> Supporting a family is a central means for a man to prove himself that he is a 'mensch'. Men who do not support families find other ways to prove that they are men, which tend to take various destructive forms. As many have commentated through the centuries, young males are essentially barbarians for whom marriage – meaning not just the wedding vows but the act of taking responsibility for a wife and children – is an indispensable civilising force. (Murray, 1990: 23)

Secondly, and following on from the above, it is as a result of the widespread (though localised) loss of employment following the shift from manufacturing to service-based economies that these men are said to have lost their 'role'. The 'marriage pool' of young men is thus shrinking because of unemployment. Who would want to marry the man who cannot 'provide' (Phillips, 1995)? These men are, consequently, when robbed of this social role, seen as responding in violent and abusive ways. They are 'good for nothing' except serial impregnation and leaving in their wake a trail of fatherless children who then, it is argued, turn to crime (Dennis and Erdos, 1991). What is bemoaned here is not the loss of employment per se. It is the erosion of a particular (breadwinner) masculine role. Men's contribution to the family destroyed, they turn to the culture of selfishness exemplified by crime and social/sexual irresponsibility. Implicitly, and centrally, it is the family which here functions to make men 'useful' in society. Without work and the taking on of family commitment, all the more so in the context of the prolongation of adolescence resulting from economic restructuring (cf. Hollands, 1990, 1997), the result of the demise of the father is seen to be an increase in the criminality of young men. Work and marriage here combine in providing an appropriate initiation *into* adulthood which militates against the otherwise naturally crimogenic nature of young men. An adult (non-criminal) masculinity is thus bound up within a trinity of work, marriage and social order as the initiation of boys into adulthood is understood in terms of a linear narrative in which a (crimogenic) adolescence gives way to the mature (non-criminal) adult subject.

Thirdly, and as we shall see crucially, it is *father-absence* which denies these essentially 'barbarian' young boys a suitable masculine role model. 'The lack of fathers is associated with a level of physical unruliness that makes life difficult . . . [I]n communities without fathers the kids tend to run wild. The fewer the fathers, the greater the tendency . . .' (Murray, 1990: 12). Young men no longer have a 'respectable' patriarchal father figure (Dennis and Erdos, 1991).

> Little boys don't naturally grow up to be responsible fathers and husbands. They don't naturally grow up knowing how to get up every morning at the same time and go to work. They don't naturally grow up thinking that work is not just a way to make money, but a way to hold one's head high in the world. And most emphatically of all, little boys do not reach adolescence naturally wanting to refrain from sex, just as little girls don't naturally become adolescents naturally wanting to refrain from having babies. (Murray, 1990: 10–11)

This combination of masculine ontology, economic structure and paternal role leads, for Murray, inevitably to certain policy implications. Lone mothers on benefit, he argues, reproduce values of 'welfare dependency' in their children which lead to moral decline and rising welfare costs. Family breakdown is thus, in effect, seen as being *caused* by the welfare state and lone mothers making the 'choice' of dependency (rather than marriage to a man). The solution is clear: firstly, cut welfare payments (a comparison with nineteenth-century constructions of 'odd women' is revealing in this regard: see Showalter, 1992: 19–21; cf. McRobbie, 1994: 138); and, secondly, reinforce or reassert paternal authority – that is, the presence of fathers – in the socialisation of young men. Making the 'father figure' through drawing on his 'natural' disciplinary qualities might then counter the systematic laxness which is seen as prevalent in both 'permissive' school regimes and 'inadequate' parenting practices. The father embodies discipline, control and restraint. His presence is seen as balancing, or diluting, the otherwise essential unruliness of male youth:

> All that we have done is to dismantle the apparatus which was best geared to manage the very difficult task of training young males. We have encouraged the growth of one-parent families by offering almost irresistible incentives to young women to remain single when they become pregnant and to keep their illegitimate babies rather than having them adopted by two-parent families. (*The Times*, 11 August 1994)

What is required is 'constant vigilance and tireless attention' from the father, who is understood to be the 'only really effective restraining presence on young males'. It is, in short, through the disciplining, controlling and rendering subject to appropriate paternal authority of boys that no less than the family itself is to be 'saved'.

The problem of 'father-presence': interrogating the family/crime relation

There is, of course, nothing new to the making of such associations between 'dangerous' male youth, family breakdown and absent fatherhood (Katz, 1993; Macnicol, 1987; Pearson, 1994). However, what is arguably new about the ways in which this underclass thesis has been articulated in Britain, notably during the early to mid-1990s (but also in many respects through to the present day), has not been just the intensity and venom with which never married lone mothers have been scapegoated in a series of demands to restore 'family values' through 'returning' the father to the family. It is, importantly for my present concerns, the increasing prominence of the explicit association which is being made between family breakdown, crime and the more general notion of a crisis of masculinity in which, crucially, the concept of fatherhood has moved centre-stage.

The construction of 'father-absence' as problematic is, in a sense, at the interface of criminology, law and the family. It embraces a nexus of more general concerns around family maintenance, legitimacy, access to children, public spending, delinquency and crime. If the story of criminology has been one of 'dangerous' masculinities (and in particular, as we have seen in Chapter 3, the masculinities of urban male youth), then the representations of masculinity to be found within family law are replete with constructions of 'the good father', that is, of 'masculinities' which have been judicially assigned a positive value usually, though not exclusively, in the context of assessing the desirability of the presence of a certain kind of fatherhood *in* the family (Collier, 1995a). Yet what has remained unspoken in the recent associations which have been made between father-absence and crime has

been any critical analysis of what we actually understand by father-*presence*
– the 'good father' as it were – in the first place. Who is this 'normal father',
this man whose 'love and support'[2] so binds together (his) family? When did
he emerge? Where is he now? The rights and obligations which married men
have historically had over 'their' children must be socially, economically
and politically located in the context of broader changes in family structure.
By the late nineteenth century, for example, the law had already began,
albeit slowly, to move away from the common law 'empire of the father'
position declared by Blackstone (*Commentaries on the Law of England*, Vol.
1: 453, quoted in McKee and O'Brien 1982: 27; see, as the apotheosis of
'absolute father right', *Agar-Ellis* v. *Lascelles* (1883) 24 Ch.D 317). Paternal
authority at this time was naturalised: it needed no explanation, justification
or further deliberation. It was impervious to questioning. The idea of
'modern' fatherhood, in contrast – the father of the egalitarian, 'symmetrical' family, has been constituted through reference to a series of
socially and economically specific ideas of the 'respectable' masculine and
sexual propriety.

I have argued elsewhere (Collier, 1995a) that there have been two
elements to this transformation of fatherhood from the 'pre-modern' pater-
familias to the 'modern' father of the purportedly 'symmetrical' and
egalitarian family. Firstly, it has been necessary to construct father-presence
as desirable and father-absence as problematic. This has been achieved
primarily through reference to fathers' presumed utility as appropriate male
'role models'. Utilising a variant of sex role theory the law has sought to
'attach' fathers to families in a variety of ways. Secondly, it has been
necessary to render fatherhood 'safe' or, more accurately, to make a
distinction between familial paternal masculinities and the other 'dangerous'
masculinities (such as those we have seen in earlier chapters). Through
resorting to the idea of the 'family man', I have argued (Collier, 1995b), it
has been possible to contrast the benign masculinities of matrimonial law
with their antithesis – the 'wild' and 'dangerous' masculinities of criminology. The cost of this bifurcation, however, has been to divert attention from
the problematic nature of what is understood to be normal masculinity and,
in particular, from the socially destructive nature of masculinities *inside* the
family. This has been achieved through assigning to the extra-familial
domain those values which did not accord with this image of the modern and
safe father (Collier, 1995a: 202). It is this bifurcation that the contemporary
'irresponsible' or 'errant father' discourse taps into (Collier, 1994b; Westwood, 1996). 'Masculinities' outside the familial heterosexual matrix are
systematically sexualised; the 'promiscuous' homosexual, the 'irresponsible'
unmarried father who evades his responsibilities, the sexually suspect male
who fails to marry after 'sowing his wild oats' each involve a range of ideas,
notably around questions of bodily hygiene, morality and notions of male
(homo)sexuality as threat to children (Collier, 1995a: 266).

Questions remain, however: Who is this 'good father'? What can be said
of him? What is it about his presence in the family that enables an otherwise

essentially crimogenic male youth to be socialised into respectability? In the following section I shall seek to unpack this masculine subject as he has been propounded by those men who consciously identify *themselves* to be the 'normal' embodiments of just such a 'natural' masculinity. In so doing, I shall seek to explore the nature of (certain) men's responses to the challenges of feminist, gay, lesbian and queer critiques of heterosexuality. Specifically, and by focusing on the ways in which the ideas of masculine 'crisis' and 'renewal' are at present being constructed by proponents of an emerging self-styled 'fathers' rights movement' (Berotia and Drakich, 1993; Foster, 1993), it is my intention in the remainder of this chapter to investigate the masculinities of the (self-identified) 'good fathers' and 'family men' of the domestic sphere and, crucially, how this relates to debates around crime. The subjectivities of those men who feel themselves to be and, importantly, admit to being 'threatened' by the range of social and economic developments reveals much, I shall argue, not just about the nature of men's resistances, it also, I shall suggest, tells us much about the nature of that 'normal' heterosexuality which they seek so vociferously to defend.

Family, law and resistance: the new men's movement

It has been in the arena of family law that a perceived diminution of men's legal rights in relation to women, children and property has been singled out for critique by those who have sought to argue that the law has now swung too far in favour of its hitherto 'spoilt darling'. Given a gloss of legitimacy by the powerful (if empirically questionable) ideology of the 'new fatherhood' (Lewis, 1986; Lewis and O'Brien, 1987) it has been the politics of family law and fatherhood which has, in recent years, become enmeshed within debates around masculinity, crime and ideas of masculine 'crisis'. This crisis of familial masculinity has been presented as, simultaneously, both an explanation of and panacea to a diversity of social ills relating to the growing 'problem of men'. Family breakdown, 'absent fatherhood' and an apparent (though empirically questionable) rising number of 'lawless' urban male youth captured by the evocative 'trouble with boys' thesis have each been depicted as both cause and effect of the contemporary crisis of masculinity. At times, we have seen, both feminist and politically conservative accounts of this crisis have come close, if not merged, in their depiction of a 'new breed' of destructive, anti-social man (Phillips, 1993, 1995) emerging at the intersection of masculine rage, economic disempowerment and the urban underclass. Recent texts from the perspective of 'men's liberation' have simply brought to these debates a particularly bitter and vituperative anti-feminist twist (Farrell, 1993; Lyndon, 1992; Thomas, 1993; see further Faludi, 1992; Roberts, 1992). It is, however, contemporary matrimonial politics which continues to cut to the heart of tensions and contradictions within men's responses to feminism.

The relationship between, on the one hand, the emergence of new social movements based on an explicit concern with men and masculinity (Messner, 1997) and, on the other, a series of political debates around the 'sexual politics' of law reform have, together, taken on a particular significance throughout the 1990s in relation to two (related) questions. Firstly, what is the form and function of the family at the end of the twentieth century? And, secondly, how do changes in this family relate to the crimes of men? In relation to both contemporary father-right (Messner, 1997: 41–9) and mythopoetic practices (Messner, 1997: 17–24), for example, a project of 'masculine renewal' has been seen to entail not a disparagement, but a celebration of traditional forms of masculinity in which it has been a crisis of fatherhood which has become the primary political terrain in which contested meanings of masculinity and heterosexuality are presently being fought. The emergence of both the mythopoetic and fathers' rights strands of the new men's movement thus represents important social phenomena, each deserving of critical analysis in its own right. Nonetheless, what I believe is of particular interest about the fathers' rights movement is the way in which its arguments exemplify the more general trend, identified above, whereby threats to *masculinity* and *heterosexuality* become equated in a way which derives, crucially, from how that which is deemed to constitute 'natural' familial relations has been constituted in the first place. In view of this, the repeated reference to a normative masculine subject position within the father-right discourse presents an ideal opportunity to explore further the nature (and, I shall argue, inherent instabilities) of 'straight' heterosexual masculinity. These are men who seek to affirm a rigid normative sexual position. Yet in so doing they repeatedly make visible the historical contingency, class and racial/ethnic specificity of the form of hetero-masculinity they would maintain is 'normal, 'natural' and 'inevitable'. The notion of 'manhood' the fathers' rights movement seeks to defend is, put simply, confirmed by and inseparable from a model of heterosexual relating predicated on a disavowal, a denial, of the 'other'.

(Re)constructing the 'assertive father': the politics of the family and the defence of 'wholesome' manliness

Within this 'assertive father' discourse (Morgan, 1994) a particular masculine subject is constructed through reference to a number of essentialist presuppositions which presume a fundamental ontological difference between men and women. Specifically, a division is presumed between a normative 'healthy' (natural) masculinity and an impoverished (unnatural) variant, a 'poor relation' somehow 'out of step' with a man's natural, familial state. Implicitly, the idea evoked is of an almost 'feminised man'. This is a man who, in Robert Bly's terms, cannot 'stand up to' the women in his life (Bly, 1990: 63), a 'wimpish' modern male far removed from what was once (and could be again) 'truly' masculine. What is to be celebrated is, in contrast, the 'deep masculine', the culturally universal and transhistorical 'inner essence, a unique combination of temperament, passion and personal experience untouched by society. The idea of a deep, true passionate self [which] has been with us for at least two centuries . . .' (Rotundo, 1993: 285). It is the wholesale neglect of these essential masculine spiritual needs in the organised structures of late twentieth-century societies which is understood as having led to the powerful sense of alienation, loss and disempowerment felt by legions of modern men. In seeking masculine 'renewal', however, the practices of the mythopoetic and fathers' rights movements diverge. Whereas the former involves a journey into the Self, into the 'core' of the masculine (a 'heart of darkness'? – see Showalter, 1992: 83–104) via an embrace of Jungian psychology, the assertive father seeks to heal this 'fracture' or 'rupture' between that which is 'false' and that which is 'truly' masculine through recourse to law and legal reform. In turning *to* law and political activism the assertive father draws on the language of masculine renewal in seeking to challenge what is happening to the 'man's role' in the family.

In their endeavours to 'defend' the patriarchal family and the legal rights of men, contemporary fathers' rights organisations, which exist across western capitalist societies, bemoan above all the undermining of the 'traditional' masculine breadwinner role. The declared intention of one recently formed umbrella organisation in the UK[3] illustrates the movement's wider remit of establishing 'a programme of initiatives to combat . . . policies that are destroying the traditional family through the marginalisation of the male role'. Of particular concern is that which, we have seen above, has been central to the absent father/criminal son association; a perceived erosion of male authority in the family. It is this, it is argued, which has resulted from a number of 'feminist-inspired' assaults on men in the sphere of family law, notably in England and Wales in the years since the 1969 Divorce Reform Act. In the United States, similarly, several groups are at present mounting public-information and political drives to combat what they call 'fatherless America' through a renewed cultural and political focus on fatherhood (*The New York Times*, 19 June 1994). Central to such campaigns is a call for a return to 'the father as provider and disciplinarian'. The central idea of the National Fatherhood Initiative (NFI), for example, is that fathers bring something irreplaceable and 'inherently masculine' to the family. According to the Director of the Campaign, Wade F. Horn, such 'responsible' fatherhood involves the qualities of 'discipline, risk-taking and decisiveness'. 'At times of crisis or stress,' it is declared, 'the traditionally male values – especially the ability to contain emotions and be decisive – are invaluable. . . . Father encourages risk-taking. Mother encourages caution'. Moreover, 'when a child has difficulty at school, a family car is wrecked, or a dispute with a creditor arises, it is often the father who confronts the issue.' The chair of the NFI, David Blankenhorn, continues the theme: '. . . the deep meaning of masculinity for most men is the idea of providing for and teaching children . . . that should be celebrated' (*The New*

York Times, 19 June 1994: cf. Fineman, 1995; see further on the US 'Promise-Keepers', Messner, 1997: 24–36).

Let us be clear about what is being claimed here. The male role is said to have been undermined or marginalised in the very three areas relating to the family in which, we have seen above, masculinity has itself been depicted as now existing in a state of contemporary crisis. That is, in relation to men's *work*, the status of *fatherhood* and with regard to anxieties surrounding male *sexuality*. Each of the three spheres of men's lives singled out for attention in the father-right discourse – work, fatherhood and sexuality – embraces the kinds of notions of men as familial social subjects (as, primarily, economic-ally dominant partner, provider and as heterosexually active) which, we have also seen, have involved historically specific notions of 'manhood'. These are the three areas in relation to which the masculine crisis idea has more generally had the greatest influence in Britain, North America, Australia and elsewhere and is, crucially, that in which the correlation with crime is being constituted. In constructing a crisis in relation to men's work (what jobs are there, in post-industrial societies, for large numbers of young men?), a crisis around fatherhood (do 'families need fathers'?) and a crisis about the 'natural' sexualities of men and women, a resulting familial masculinity is constituted at the intersection of the 'public' and 'private'. Such concerns around men's work, fatherhood and 'natural' (biologically driven) sexuality also, it is important to remember, represent the focal point of a broader neo-conservative 'pro-family' agenda which has, with some success in the 1980s and 1990s, sought to mobilise anti-feminist ideologies through asserting the natural quality of the traditional masculine (breadwinner/provider) role in the family. What we are here dealing with is, in effect, a particular construct of a masculine subject which has been predicated on and defined through a model of hierarchic heterosexuality. In relation to work, fatherhood and sexuality this 'masculinity' has been constituted through a number of (contingent) gendered bi-polarities. However, in relation to each, I wish to now argue, it is possible to see how, at the same times as its 'deviance' is affirmed through legal and/or social censure, that which transgresses this notion of the (hetero-)familial norm can return to haunt the purportedly 'natural' masculinity of the self-confessed 'family man'.

'Economic man': work, authority and the 'good father' ideal

In constructing that which is 'truly' male through reference to a univocal and fixed male subjectivity premised on an essential ontological separation from women and femininity, masculinity is not considered to be a relational concept (defined through its relation to 'femininity,' 'effeminacy', and so forth). The gender polarities of male/female are fixed in such a way that what is masculine is that which is defined apart from (unspoilt through contact with?) the world of women. Within the dominant discourse of the crimino-legal domain, that is, this is a subject divorced from the private sphere of the home and associated with the public world of work. However, such a disavowal of the familial, testified to by the men's movement's repeated negation of 'everyday' heterosexual relations based on reciprocity and co-operation with women, raises some difficult questions about how the heterosexualisation of the familial has itself been achieved through reference to this sexual division of public/private spheres within modernity – at a time when, crucially, the 'good father' is being increasingly called upon to be *both* breadwinner and active participant in child care. It is this negation of men's practical (as opposed to symbolic) involvement in the familial domain which becomes particularly clear when considering how the relationship between men and paid employment is constructed in the father-right discourse.

This point requires clarification, for it relates directly to the argument put forward in the underclass thesis discussed above. Research on the relationship between masculinity and work has recently moved away from the, hitherto dominant, focus on men's manual/physical labour. It has placed, instead, an increasing emphasis on the importance of consumer choice, play and leisured entertainment in the formation of masculine identities in postmodern societies (Ehrenreich, 1983; Rotundo, 1993). It is through shared communities of consumption, for example, that men's experiences of 'masculine community' are now seen to be derived (Mort, 1996; Nixon, 1996). The law, meanwhile, continues in many respects to construct men as primary economic provider and 'breadwinner' (Collier, 1995a; O'Donovan, 1993), notwithstanding the scale and clarity of evidence suggesting that the traditional sexual division of labour (male/breadwinner, female/childrearer) represents nothing like the reality for the vast majority of households in Britain. The legal and cultural dominance of the economic provider discourse in fact entails considerable physical absence from the home for many men. However, by equating men's familial 'presence' with a primary economic nexus, it also renders 'suspect', or signifies as deviant, those households in which the paternal masculine (economic) presence is deemed to be, as it were, 'absent without leave' (absent for reasons other than a man's primary work commitment):

> The construction of father absence as problematic in legal discourse has involved the mobilising of discourses which establish fatherhood as a desirable presence during marriage in the first place. . . . Father absence really signifies something else – the desirability of the presence of masculinity within the family by embodying the three axes of authority, economic responsibility and heterosexuality. It is these which, together, constitute the idea of the 'good father' in law. (Collier, 1995a: 204–5)

In constituting father-absence in such a way, these axes of authority, economic responsibility and heterosexuality become entwined. From the Campaign For Justice On Divorce which took place in Britain during the 1970s and early 1980s (Alcock, 1984), through to the ongoing campaigns of Families Need Fathers and related organisations in the 1990s, lies a concern with men's legal rights in relation to women, children and property.

Underlying such a focus on legal rights and entitlements, however, is a concern with a decline in men's authority in the family. It is this concern with authority which has historically underpinned the father-right discourse. Thus, it is stated in one recent British father-right document, masculine authority in the family has been undermined by the development of an 'intellectually destructive mental attitude that the divorce is not the responsibility of anyone and that it is inevitable' (*RLM*, p. 3).[4] It is as a result of a fashionable 'non-judgmentalism' which has 'developed in the minds of various professional groups and the intellectual culture supporting them' that family law now tends to 'award custody of the children to the mother regardless of her conduct . . . there is no existing psychological theory or legal principle that could remotely justify this cruel and socially damaging policy' (*RLM*, p. 7).

It is, in short, a lamentable decline in men's *control over* familial relations (and in particular women's sexuality) which most disturbs the 'assertive father'. What is sought, however, is greater authority over relationships with women and children, not a qualitative shift in these relationships per se. As Fineman has argued,

> Even the most virulent fathers'-rights discourse does not really seem to be talking much about fathering. What does it mean to be a father from an aspirational perspective, recognizing that access isn't the same as nurturing, and that economic contributions are qualitatively different from sacrificing career and other individual pursuits to care for a child on a day-to-day basis? (1995: 206; see also White, 1994: cf. Fay, 1995)

The 'legitimate status of marital sex' is said to have been destroyed by the husband having no rights over his unborn child conceived during marriage. The 1991 House of Lords ruling making 'marital rape' illegal (*R* v. *R* [1991] 4 All ER 481; [1991] 3 WLR 766) is similarly seen to be 'incompatible with marriage. [It] has placed a legal extortion weapon in the hands of wives' (*RLM*, p. 7).

The male subject who is being evoked here is constituted in terms of his actual or potential control over others. This is, on one level, a familiar model of man as provider and disciplinarian. He embodies a sexual being premised on the ability to define (him)self as self-contained, autonomous and self-assured (a point to which I will return below; see also Collier, 1992; Seidler, 1989, 1995: 170–199). This gendered subject is, of course, very similar to and overlaps with the ideal-typical subjectivity of the 'man of law' (Naffine, 1990: 118). This 'man of law' is premised on the Cartesian model of the rational unitary human subject 'as social and sexual atom, the Kantian man of reason . . . the brain on a stalk, not the soft and vulnerable creature of the flesh' (Naffine, 1994: 16). Given such a construct it is unsurprising that women's social and legal empowerment, resulting in a (however partial) undermining of men's familial authority, should thus be seen as threatening to a gender order in which the male subject has been accorded such a central (and defining) role. This construct of masculine authority is related to the man's assumed position in the public sphere. Yet the idea of economic 'responsibility' central to this notion of the 'traditional role' is, even within its own terms (that this is how men actually behave), increasingly open to question. Considerable evidence testifies, for example, to the widespread failure of significant numbers of men to 'provide' for 'their' families, either during marriage or subsequent to divorce or separation (Simpson et al., 1995). It might be argued that father-absence should be seen as a rule, rather than the exception, when the family 'breaks down'. Men's historical reluctance to 'take on' economic responsibility has itself been viewed as indicative of a 'flight from' commitment[5] (Ehrenreich, 1983) rather than any willing embrace of familial economic responsibility (a reluctance which has been, we must remember, sanctioned to a considerable degree by law: see Smart, 1987b).

I do not at this point wish to argue that present practices which we might deem to be 'masculine' unproblematically assume a symbolic identity of male authority. The ways in which this notion of masculine authority is mobilised within the father-right discourse are quite specific. It is revealing, in particular, how it is the (voluntary) 'taking on' of economic responsibility which has assumed a central significance in the argument that father absence is, per se, problematic. As one British fathers' rights organisation puts it, illustrating this correlation:

> ... it is only through the motivations provided by a stable family that the man can be economically productive for their support ... it is through the father's commitment to this family and the responsibilities he accepts for his children which accrue from that commitment that the children *and the father himself* become socialised. (*RLM*, p. 9; my emphasis)

Men are socialised through taking on economic responsibility which then binds them to the family. Yet, in the present economic climate, this begs an obvious question. It is not simply that the communities of consumption referred to above are mediated by contingencies of class, race and ethnicity. The masculine socialisation process of father-as-provider is *itself* breaking down as a range of cultural and economic developments combine to undermine the traditional masculine 'role' of economic breadwinner. The subject position of the breadwinner is not, importantly, equally available to all men. This is not just a result of the impact of feminism and the increasing proportion of women in the workforce (developments both of which the new men's movement generally deplores). Wider shifts in employment patterns, localised experiences of mass unemployment and the transition from an industrial based to a service economy (as well as the increasing cultural valorisation of leisure time) have all thrown into question traditional ideas of a paternal subjectivity based on the centrality of 'work'. Definitions of work are themselves being transformed as new technologies and economic restructuring shift the boundaries of public and private in relation to paid employment. Not all men can economically 'provide' for their family as they may, or may not, wish (and as increasing numbers of middle-class men in Britain, it would seem, have found during the 1990s: see Hutton, 1995).

Yet it remains the case that the idea of masculine crisis which is evoked by the new men's movement – of crisis as a direct consequence of an undermining of a 'traditional' paternal role – is constructed in quite specific ways depending on just who is, and is not, seen as the object of its discourse. That is, and notwithstanding the considerable homogeneity between communities of consumption shared by men of all sexualities and classes (Campbell, 1993, 1995), the crisis of masculinity thesis appears to be taking different forms contingent on the socio-economic, racial and ethnic positioning of the man who is deemed to be its 'victim'. Nowhere, perhaps, has this been clearer than in relation to the social and economic consequences and the 'problem of crime' which is deemed to follow the problematic of 'father-absence'.

Contemporary literature supportive of the 'pro-family' father-right position, be it of an academic, journalistic or campaigning nature, has consciously evoked what can only be described as the 'contagion by underclass' narrative discussed above (see p. 129). A consequence of the breakdown of the family is thus said to be 'that large numbers of children are being brought up in the absence of their fathers with a consequent lack of parental love, socialisation and proper economic support' (*RLM*, p. 1). A correlation is made between 'father-absence' and 'rising levels' of youth crime, delinquency and general 'yobbish' behaviour (John Major, *The Guardian*, 10 September 1994). It is, of course (and to keep in focus at this point the question of crime), the linking of 'families without fatherhood' to the potential criminality of urban male youth which has now become a, if not the, dominant theme in this literature. Dennis and Erdos (1991) purport to establish a clear link between absent fathers and crime; this, in turn, became a recurring issue in the former British Home Secretary Michael Howard's pronouncements on reform of the criminal justice system. By arguing that it is in communities 'without fathers' that boys tend to be unruly or criminal, the project of 'reclaiming' the place of men in the family itself becomes equated with strategies of crime prevention, social responsibility and the father-right defence of the 'normal' and 'functional' family. Thus, it is argued that professionals, academics and 'the wider society' all now recognise that 'the increasing alienation of youth, with under-achievement, unemployment and delinquency becoming endemic in certain strata of society' (*RLM*, p. 1), occurs *as a direct result of* widespread father-absence.

These associations are, we have seen, familiar. The stigmatising of lone motherhood which has historically accompanied the defence of the 'natural' father's role has a long and well-documented history (Fox Harding, 1993a, 1993b; Phoenix, 1991; Smart, 1987b). Just as the pre-industrial pursuits of an irresponsible and sexually licentious 'dangerous' class had haunted the Victorian imagination (Morris, 1994: Ch. 3), in recent debates around crime in Britain, the 'other' now appears in the form of a contemporary underclass composed of 'errant' or 'wild' masculinities, confined to 'no-go' disintegrating urban areas. In evoking powerful images of transgressive subjects yet to be civilised into the norms of the social order, I have argued in Chapter 3 that some class-based judgements of familial and sexual propriety continue to inform and differentiate between responses to 'masculine crisis'. Indeed, in much the same way as legal discourse has historically sought to valorise a class-specific masculinity (Collier, 1995a; Naffine, 1990), so the fathers' rights movement similarly seeks to characterise men's work through reference to a specific socio-economic construct of male employment. The fact that this familial ideal belongs to a bygone era (presuming it ever existed) seems not to concern those such as the British Cheltenham Group who, in their call to 'Restore Marriage by Recognising Men', seek to maintain that all 'family men' are engaged in 'proper and wholesome employment' (*RLM*, p. 4). Such family men, it is said, have 'proper and wholesome feelings for their children' and a 'wholesome motivation to work and provide for them'. It is legal reforms which have attacked these men's homes built up over many years by their own labours ... [the] rightful ownership over their income'. Without the good example set by (appropriately socialised) fathers, without their 'wholesome motivation to work and provide for' children, without such 'wholesome feeling for children', how could the 'other' men and women of 'a certain strata of society' (those without such feelings? the underclass?) possibly learn respect for marriage and the family?

To recap: the fathers' rights argument shows no awareness of either the historical specificity or cultural contingency of the paternal subjectivity of the 'good father' ideal. Indeed, there is no recognition that the purportedly 'natural' 'proper' model of marriage it seeks to defend has itself been vociferously legitimated and promulgated through familial ideologies which belie any idea (or anthropological evidence to suggest) that it exists as a universal or transhistorical norm. The paternal subject of the 'good father' in law (the father whose absence is here deemed to be undesirable) has historically embodied a 'masculinity' predicated on particular notions of authority and economic responsibility. This is partly why the men and women of the underclass continue to be berated by politicians and social commentators for their 'lifestyle choices' (Davies, 1993), their laziness and 'loose' sexual morality (see Bagguley and Mann, 1992). These are families in which this particular masculine presence is, it is argued, frequently not to be found. It should be no surprise that the new men's movement's most active and vociferous campaigning around law has been in relation to a range of issues which are seen to have 'threatened' or 'undermined' the prerogatives of a primarily middle-class constituency.[6]

In short, the masculine crisis thesis has, in relation to the family, displaced onto a number of familiar folk devils (notably an ill-defined 'feminism', 'political correctness' and a 'fashionable' moral relativism) some deeply felt problems seen to bedevil contemporary 'masculinity'. In so doing an incipient anti-feminism has been aroused by a perceived attack on 'old certainties'. It is these sentiments, a set of (primarily) middle-class grievances, which the new men's movement is largely giving expression to. In shoring up a masculine identity based on the twin pillars of male authority and economic responsibility, however, the men's rights project asserts traditional norms of masculinity, femininity and, I shall argue in the remainder of this chapter, heterosexuality which are becoming increasingly problematic and difficult to sustain. Ultimately they illustrate not the 'natural' quality of this particular familial ideal but, rather, the ways in which men's subjectivities have themselves been historically constituted through a negation of the familial.

'A man's man': (homo)sexuality, motherhood and the negation of the familial

There exists a wealth of evidence within feminist scholarship and the sociology of masculinity which has suggested that 'men's sexual engagement with women is coded first and foremost as an affirmation of healthy "manhood", making heterosexual practice, so often, so little to do with men pleasing women' (Segal, 1994: 239–40). Within feminist, sexological and sociological texts, sexuality has long been located as a central facet of male gender identity, and a diverse range of cultural discourses continue to position certain heterosexual practices (notably genital intercourse) as signifiers of 'manhood', as ways of 'proving' or 'accomplishing' a (normative) masculine subject position of being 'straight' (see Collier, 1992; Person, 1980).

Within the discipline of criminology any critical engagement with heterosexuality has remained curiously absent. As in the social sciences generally, the area of 'crime and sexuality' or 'law and sexuality' has usually been taken to be a 'handy euphemism' for discussion of the relationship between lesbian, gay and bisexual studies and the subject matter in question (Stychin, 1996). In recent years, however, the study of heterosexuality in its own right has emerged as, in the words of one recent text, 'a new research agenda' (Richardson, 1996; cf. Maynard and Purvis, 1995; Wilkinson and Kitzinger, 1993). Within one strand of this work (specifically, that informed by developments in queer theory) a particular (hetero-)sexed subjectivity and the process of being 'sexed' – as having, or, rather, obtaining/taking up a heterosexual sensibility – has been seen as 'not merely defined by private sexual acts . . . [it] is a public process of power relations in which everyday interactions take place between actors with sexual identities in sexualized locations' (Bell and Valentine, 1995: 146; Smart, 1996a, 1996b). Within this work, it is no longer simply counter-hegemonic or subordinate sexualities which are thought of as 'marking' their bearers in some way. The 'straight sensibility' of masculinity has itself become a meaningful object of concern in analysis of how sexual borders are patrolled and constructed, sexual identities assigned and sexual politics formulated (Robinson, 1996; Waldby, 1995).

At this stage, and in the light of this literature, it is possible to consider further some of the aspects of the relationship between 'heterosexuality' and 'masculinity' discussed above. The crimino-legal arena, we have seen, is a site of confrontation on a number of different issues around heterosexuality. Just as 'law desires' 'the production through discourse of the figure of the homosexual – sadomasochistic, polluted, addicted to his desires, self-destructive, and yet terrifyingly seductive' (Stychin, 1996: 139), so too does the discursive constitution of the 'heterosexual' norm (as 'not' other) reveal the contingency of heterosexual identity and the sociality of the hetero/homosexual sexual binary itself. What we have seen above, in the arguments of both the fathers' rights movement and the (overlapping) concerns of the neo-conservative underclass theorists, are some of the ways in which the heterosexual centre 'has a particular intransigence with respect to giving up its privileges' (Stychin, 1996: 2). Yet at issue, I have argued, has been the privilege of a heterosexual imperative inscribed within the naturalised binary divisions of modernity. The crimino-legal has 'desired' the 'good father' as an embodiment of the heterosexual norm. The new men's movement's search to recover an 'essence' to this manliness rests, I have argued, on an idea that there *is* something to be reclaimed; something, that is, which could be said to be 'truly' masculine. It is to be found, depending on what aspect of the mythopoetic or father-right strands of the movement one subscribes to, in another 'uncorrupted' time or place.[7] It is a search which has historically assumed both temporal and geographic dimensions. It is in the past (a different era) or in a different place (such as the hills and woods) where one will find that which is truly male: it is unlikely to be 'at home'. Yet, in seeking the 'truly' masculine from within communities of men, this quest is itself fraught with dangers. Not the least of these is in relation to the (ever present) other of homosexual desire.

To clarify: I have argued thus far in this book that discourses of (hetero)sexuality have been established via oppositional and hierarchically defined categories of gender. As a consequence, aberrations, or deviations, from the heterosexual norm have been met with efforts to silence or negate difference (in the form, for example, of legal censure). Such a heterosexual 'world-mapping' envisages that

> every given person, just as he or she was necessarily assignable to a male or female gender, [is] considered necessarily assignable as well to a homo- or hetero-sexuality, a binarized identity that was full of implications, however confusing . . . [and] that left no space in the culture exempt from the potent incoherences of homo/heterosexual definition. (Sedgwick, 1994: 2)

Between the (normative) heterosexual male body of law and its (censured) other – the 'homosexual' – thus lies a (heavily policed) line, a dangerous terrain dividing the 'legitimate' solidarities of homosocial bonding and the 'perversions' of homosexuality. It is in this domain that the 'potent incoherences of homo/heterosexual definition' are to be found.

In such a context the intense homosociality of an avowedly, and almost exclusively, heterosexual new men's movement or, indeed, of crimino-legal

cultures more generally (be it of government, the prison or the criminological academy: see Chapter 2) takes on a particular significance when seen
in relation to homosocial heterosexual culture more generally. Indeed, as
Sedgwick (1985) notes, the negation of homosexuality has historically
existed in direct proportion to its centrality to those heterosexual cultures
which seek to denounce it. The relentless repudiation of the feminine which
marks so many crimino-legal institutions could thus, like the mythopoetic
and father-right strands of the new men's movement, be interpreted as
illustrating a rather wider ambiguity about men's commitment to heterosexual relating. With this in mind, and to locate this issue in the context of
the widespread father-absence discussed above, the ambivalence on the part
of the men's movement to relationships with women and children raises
some interesting questions about the ostensibly 'natural' quality of the
(hetero-)masculine subject in the first place.

By 'ambivalence' to women and children I am not simply referring to the
general depiction within much of the father-right literature of 'mendacious
mothers' or 'alimony drones', women prepared to resort to 'legal extortion'
(*RLM*, p. 7) of their husbands in order to achieve their own ends. Recurring
images in new men's movement rhetoric and texts are of, on the one hand,
the beleaguered, helpless and 'misunderstood' father, full of only 'wholesome feelings for his children' (*RLM*, p. 5); and, on the other, the self-
interested, vengeful and frequently deceitful mother who, whatever her
conduct, nonetheless gains custody of 'his' children, sometimes notwithstanding 'physical assault of the children, adultery and lesbianism . . . [each]
deemed to be no bar to her fitness' (*RLM*, p. 2). The attitudes expressed by
some fathers' rights organisations certainly sit most uneasily with the
'wholesome feelings for . . . children' (*RLM*, p. 5) presented elsewhere in the
literature. The Cheltenham Group, campaigning on behalf of British fathers,
declare that an otherwise paramount 'welfare of the children' principle can
be downgraded in importance whenever it is in 'conflict with the rights of
the husband and the father' (*RLM*, p. 5).[8] Children come first, it would seem,
apart from when their interests conflict with those of men. This argument
might, at the present moment, be illustrated by the ways in which the
economic interests of men and the state have historically tended to override
the welfare of children in ongoing debates around the provision of child
support in Britain (Collier, 1994b; Westwood, 1996).

It is also however possible to locate men's 'ambivalence' to the familial in
the context of a wider, and pervasive, cultural and legal disparagement of the
feminine, the familial and the domestic sphere. Indeed, it is just such a
negation of the familial and of relations of *inevitable dependency* (see
Fineman, 1995) which marks the gender regime of public institutions. This,
in turn, has a number of implications for understanding how the good father/
unruly mother binary is constituted in particular instances. For example, and
as we have seen above with regard to the socio-economic contingency of
this masculine subject, heterosexual identification, per se, is not in itself a
sufficient guarantor of securing familial status. In constituting the familial

through reference to the twin signifiers of social/economic propriety and father-presence, a particularly venomous vilification has been reserved for working-class lone mothers. These are, it has been declared, 'related to every known social pathology in children' (*RLM*, p. 6). There is no recognition that the present proliferation of non-normative heterosexual parental and familial structures might equally be cast as a sign of the 'expanded possibilities of being female, a category which marks a changed society and a changed mode of familial organisation' (McRobbie, 1993: 138). They are, rather, casually dismissed: 'there is nothing good one can say about these states' (*RLM*, p. 6).

In seeking to valorise an essential and fixed masculine subjectivity, that which constitutes the 'other' to the familial ideal is systematically purged. This is not simply a matter of rendering homosexuality, and other masculinities marked down as 'unmanly' diversions, as 'outwith' the law. Because of the way in which the idea of the 'family' has been heterosexualised in the first place, following this argument, all 'families without fathers' are ultimately deemed to be outside the bounds of what is said to be 'proper and legitimate modes of behaviour' (*RLM*, p. 7). This, crucially, has a number of implications for understanding how this male subject has been constructed in relation to women and, in particular, to the idea of Woman as *Mother*. The construction of Woman as other to a (normative) male subject cannot be confined to father-right discourse. Far from being 'out of step' with this father-right position legal discourse, for example, shares such attitudes in many respects. Law has also sexualised the female body by, for example, defining the purpose and function of female sexuality in terms of reproductive biology (Smart, 1987b; Stanworth, 1987). Indeed, it has been in seeking to expose and challenge the social values and norms to which the female body is used as a point of entry in law that feminist scholars have sought to challenge the phallocentric and heterosexual nature of both legal and criminological discourse. The father-right discourse, like law and recent political debates about family, welfare and public spending, has reserved especial contempt for the apotheosis of the 'good father' – the 'unruly mother' (Smart, 1995: 221). Yet the new men's movement is, in this regard, perhaps not so new for history reveals a predictable familiarity to men's resistances. From the very beginnings of the family law reforms in England and Wales which sought to (formally) equalise the positions of men and women in the late nineteenth century, through to present-day campaigns around maintenance and care and control of children, a notion of masculine crisis, and the men's liberationist thesis on which it draws, has been constituted around the 'good father/bad mother' binary. Notwithstanding the complex amalgam of pleasures, fears and anxieties heterosexual relations hold for men and women, within this rhetoric of men's 'loss' and women's (unjust) 'gain', and through the language of righteous anger, the blame and responsibility for disturbing the 'natural' state of patriarchal marriage and the family continues to be projected onto a representation of a legally (and unjustly) empowered 'new woman' or 'phallic female'.

It is at this point that an important, and difficult, question arises. The very real anger of the men committed to the fathers' rights agenda is beyond doubt. The question remains to be asked, however: why should it be that significant numbers of men feel so threatened by this 'phallic female', a 'growing feminist tidal wave . . . a sustained and remorseless attack against the institution of marriage and the patriarchal family based on it'?[9] Why should the 'unruly mother', 'mendacious wife' or 'alimony drone' attract such condemnation in this way? It is insufficient to explain the depth of feeling simply by reference to a (misleading) perception of men's economic disadvantage seen to have resulted from women's increased participation in the workforce; nor simply to relate it to a consequence of changes in entitlements on divorce. In seeking to understand men's responses in this area, that is, it is insufficient to limit explanation to a rational calculation of men's economic self-interest (however significant this might be in particular instances). In order to begin to answer such questions it is revealing to bring into the analysis that which has hitherto been absent – the social and contingent nature of the masculinity/heterosexuality relation discussed above. Accordingly I wish, in this next section, to draw together the points raised thus far in this chapter in an endeavour to seek to go 'beyond' the dualisms of the heterosexual imperative and develop a more complex understanding of the construction of the male heterosexual subject.

Post-heterosexuality? (Re)constructing men's resistance

To recap the argument thus far: I have argued that a form of male hetero-sexuality has come to serve both as a confirmation of ideas of 'manhood' and, importantly, as a signifier of normative heterosexuality. The arguments of the new men's movement, and in particular the strand of it concerned with the assertion of fathers' rights, illustrate in a particularly clear way the nature of this ideal-typical male subject. In recent years, a perceived increase in women's control and authority in familial relations, notably with regard to children, property and calls upon men's 'hard-earned' finances, has been seen as bringing with it a loss of control in men's relationships with women. It is, in particular, around the changing status of fatherhood that the battle-ground has been formed for those engaged in 'struggling with the demands of . . . masculinities on their developing identities in the difficult and danger-ous terrain of heterosexual relating' (Hollway and Jefferson, 1994: 1).

Why should it be that, at present, apparently increasing numbers of men are being attracted to men's rights organisations? It is not possible to begin to answer such questions without recognising the broader changes which are redrawing the terms through which the politics of heterosexuality are expressed. Some, for example, have argued that the new men's movement is symptomatic of a wider anti-feminist 'backlash' (Faludi, 1992). This 'backlash thesis' has been influential. It is certainly initially appealing, having an explanatory power in seeking to explain a range of cultural phenomena of the 1980s and 1990s. Yet it is of limited use in seeking to engage with the question of *why* the father-right agenda should have 'struck a chord' with so many men. In order to address this issue, and in seeking to understand why subjective commitments may be formed in relation to particular social identities, critical tools are required which might manage to bring together individual agency with a recognition that 'experience' is itself mediated through discourses of power which are (re)produced structurally; that subjectivity, as the lived experience of a psychical and libidinally mapped body which gives meaning to subjects, is itself socially and culturally inscribed (see further the approach detailed in Chapter 1).

To begin to analyse the formation of individual commitments to new men's movement politics it is necessary to accommodate an understanding of both individual life-history and social structure (Connell, 1995). In seeking to address the construction of the male subject within 'pro-family' father-right discourse I have argued in this chapter that it is possible to see individuals as being located within a variety of discursive relations; that the heterosexual male social subject is, as it were, composed of multiple and contradictory positionings or subjectivities. The 'good father' can, for example, co-exist with representations of other 'dangerous' masculinities, just as today's 'family man' can so very easily, if he misses a few mainten-ance payments, be tomorrow's 'deadbeat dad'. Identities are precariously achieved and never fixed (Chapter 1, pp. 29–30).[10] Analysis of the ways in which the father-right discourse has mobilised this subject thus renders political and accountable the very categories with which we are operating in these debates: for example, the 'family man', 'absent father', the 'lone mother' or, indeed, 'men's rights activist'. Let us be clear: in Britain in the 1990s fathers' rights groups such as the Cheltenham Group, Families Need Fathers and others are engaged in a political struggle. There is no ambiguity about the kind of social changes which they seek. They are engaged in a project of mobilising collective identities, manipulating fears and anxieties around men's disempowerment, appealing to men through the representation of *all* men as actual or potential victims of social change and 'feminist-inspired' legal reforms. It would, on one level, be mistaken to overestimate their political influence. However, it is also important not to underestimate just how the rhetorical power of men's liberation and masculine crisis is, at the present moment, preceding political change in both the United States, Europe and Australia. When allied to a 'pro-family' political agenda, abortion, homosexuality, divorce, legislation seeking to protect cohabitees from violence, sex education and 'pornography' are all swept up (and to be swept away) in a defence of the patriarchal family and marriage.

Does this mean, however, that these men are, to adopt the seem-ing prevalent language of the 'war between the sexes', the 'enemy' of feminism? To dismiss those involved in advocating the father-right dis-course as being, at best, peripheral but harmless extremists or, at worst, anti-feminist misogynists is to misread the pervasive nature of the broader cultural nexus in which the idea of masculine crisis, on which their liberationist rhetoric draws, is presently being legitimated. It is also, most importantly, miscalculated in that it fails to address and connect with the level of many men's experiences of 'family life', work and sexuality – with what is actually 'going on' in many men's lives in the 1990s. The emergence of the new men's movement, and the considerable media attention it has received, is testimony to what appears to be a very real disjuncture between the facts of power and the very real experience of personal disempowerment which appears to exist on the part of many men. In terms of theorising the sexed subject it is unhelpful to deny these men's experiences simply by, for example, dismissing them as products of masculine 'false consciousness' or straightforward misogynistic intent. Certainly, for a politics of heterosexuality to fail to address what is happening at the level of the experiential here is to 'give up' this terrain to the arguments of those who, like the new men's movement, would seek to construct a masculine subject through reference to old certainties and securities (something which is part of the undoubted appeal of the neo-conservative 'pro-family' agenda). It is also to lose as potential allies to feminist projects considerable numbers of men who do not recognise anything of themselves in the various accounts of masculinity which both feminist and self-consciously 'anti-sexist' literature written by men has at times produced.

It would, in other words, be most unfortunate if, because of an unwillingness to recognise the complexity of subjectivity, 'critiques of masculinity, however well-intended, [were to] fall on deaf ears' (Jefferson, 1994a: 11). What is possible, and I would argue desirable, is to utilise theories of subjectivity, identity and agency in order to rethink the ways in which cultural values are ascribed to particular gendered identities. This enterprise does, crucially, address issues of social and legal policy. In focusing on the instability and multiplicity of social identities, the ways in which social practices constitute bodies as masculine/male are themselves rendered contingent and socially accountable. With this in mind it is possible, I have suggested, to re-read these debates from a position which does not reject out of hand (as 'false consciousness') the grievances of considerable numbers of men (through, for example, depicting them as the 'bad', as opposed to the 'good', pro-feminist, anti-sexist men). Nor, crucially, does this approach entail any acceptance or further legitimation of a political agenda which is, in so many respects, oppressive, anti-feminist and frequently misogynistic and which seeks to maintain and reinforce the power and privileges of an already dominant social group. It is, however, neither politically useful nor accurate to construct a monolithic 'heterosexuality' as being inherently and essentially oppressive. Depicting heterosexuality, in the words of a recent British feminist text, for example, as 'not a happy place to be', declaring that 'a happy heterosexual is hard to find', or maintaining that a 'stream of heterosexual misery' (Wilkinson and Kitzinger, 1993) is incompatible with feminist and progressive struggles, does not open up the (much needed) space in which the sociality of heterosexuality may be discussed. Rather, it closes it down through failing to engage with the complex and diverse experiences of and multifarious dimensions to women's and men's (hetero)-sexual desires at the level of practice and fantasy.[11]

The politics of heterosexuality/ies

I have argued that, far from seeing heterosexual relations culturally desig-nated as 'familial' as being, in each and every case, a site of (male) power and (female) submission, it is also possible to recognise (and in so doing empower) the multifarious resistances of both women and men to existing configurations of gender. To recognise, that is, that what may be empower-ing in one context may be disempowering in another, and that 'within broad cultural paradigms there are often localised situations where gendered attributes can be reversed' (Gutterman, 1994: 221). Such an approach is not to reify or celebrate a heterosexual matrix which is, for so many gays and lesbians (and, arguably, heterosexuals), oppressive and destructive. Just as 'straight' identities are never fixed, certain or free of the 'other's 'perverse dynamics', so that which is formed in resistance inscribes, at the moment of its articulation, the body of the heterosexual. As Young (1993: 37–9) has noted, for example, questioning the dominant binary of hetero/homosexual in such a way is not to deny the powerful experiences of a fixed sexual identity. It is, rather, to remember that heterosexuality is itself relational, 'constituted in a matrix formed by the intersection of negotiated situations, desires, fears and attitudes'. If social 'identities', far from being 'natural', are grounded instead by this series of discursively produced oppositional binarisms (such as man/woman, hetero/homo[sexual]), then what is rendered social and political is the question I have asked above in relation to the new men's movement and neo-conservative thought: How do individual men come to take up particular discursive positions? How does the formation of subjective commitments to particular social identities relate to historical shifts in sexual practices and familial roles which have been sexually scripted (such as the family 'breadwinner')? What does it mean for these men to maintain that certain family forms are, or are not, 'natural'? Or that the crimes of men, in certain social situations, may be 'normal' and inevitable consequences of family 'breakdown'?

This approach, I have suggested, 'writes in' to the analysis of men and crime the agency of the social subject. It presumes an identity which is always partial, uncertain and fragmented, constituted through reference to its dependency on that which is defined as 'other' (Gutterman, 1994: 221). This is not to argue that the opportunities to 'transcend', disrupt or disturb dominant sexual hierarchies are available equally to hetero- and homosexual identified individuals. Any heterosexual 'performative practice' mirroring developments in queer theory would, it seems to me, be more likely to reinforce rather than 'parody' or 'subvert' the heterosexual matrix. However, and notwithstanding the limits to such deconstructive inversions in a society marked by rigid structural inequalities, it is nonetheless in the performative nature of heterosexuality itself, its comedic and potentially subversive manifestations, that a progressive politics of heterosexuality, rather than resigned submission to its present contours, lies:

> Straight sex, with its tactile, olfactory, oral and visual bodily connections, can be no less 'perverse' than its 'queer' alternatives. Ridiculing hierarchies of sexuality and gender, it too can serve as a body-blow to the old male order of things (Segal, 1994: 318).

Such a politics does not reduce debates around sexuality to battles over meaning and representation. It is to see the body 'as the *interface* between internal forces (whether conceived as psychic, libidinal or whatever) and [the] external social forces which mould and give meaning to them' (Segal, 1994: 184; original emphasis). Recognising the contingent nature of existing social arrangements, and the complex contours of social, cultural and libidinal mappings of the male body, involves embracing a politics which is aimed at transforming and reconfiguring social power at every level. The creation and sustaining of non-patriarchal cultures, for example, does not simply take place at the level of individual performance/practice but also occurs in social, collective ways. Such an approach does not lead to a turning away from the politics of heterosexuality but, rather, to a recognition that there are alliances between heterosexuals, gays, lesbians and bisexuals 'that can and must be made, as we seek to confound the expectations of straight sex, and slip through the binaries linking sexuality and gender' (Segal, 1994: 260–1). Such a

> dialogically-oriented ontology recognises that the possibility of finding or nego-tiating common ground inheres not in the firming up of a prescriptive commonalty but in the dialogical exchange . . . the recognition that there is enough common ground between individuals and groups, at specific times and places, to authorise political demands *without* falling into the essentialist trap. (Sandland, 1995: 25–6; original emphasis)

To think beyond the conceptual limits of the present and to embrace new possibilities, new ways of being 'straight', entails recognising how hetero-sexual men and women can move *between* different subjectivities, all of which might involve making claims to being 'straight' (whatever that might involve) in different contexts and in differing ways. This is not to deny the powerful experience of identity but, rather, to recognise that ' "post-structuralist feminism" contemplates a dialogue between the "post" dis-courses and modernism, or, if you prefer, between the absence of self (or Other) and a situated, value-laden, interest driven self' (Sandland, 1995: 15). Rather than see heterosexuality and homosexual identities as fixed and immutable categories of gender, an 'appropriation and redeployment of the categories of identity themselves' (Butler, 1990: 128), a simultaneous recognition of the significance of both social structural response (embracing law) and the experiential domain (at the level of psyche, subjective commit-ment) might together facilitate a 'going beyond' of heterosexuality in the sense that the idea of a singular, knowable 'straight' self is itself revealed as a convergence of multiple sexual discourses.

Concluding remarks

Where does this leave the relationship between men, masculinity and crime? It is possible to make a number of (tentative) conclusions about the relationship between heterosexuality, the family and crime. Ideas of what constitutes a 'family', I have argued, are dependent upon and interwoven with a complex network of other structured heterosexual social practices which derive legitimation from existing social arrangements. I have argued elsewhere (Collier, 1995a) that the heterosexualities of men have been constituted through inscribing meaning on the body in ways far more complex than simply through reference to the signifying of sexual status in terms of either/or hetero/homosexual. On closer analysis, a diversity of heterosexualities/masculinities have themselves been encoded, accorded value or denigrated through reference to this normative, familial and hierarchic order. The 'family man' ideal, we have seen, embodies a subject position which is, at present, conferred considerable social power (hence the willingness of so many men to take up such a position). Being a 'family man' is to be shielded (albeit with considerable contingency) from accusations of association with other 'lesser' masculinities (from being, notably, homosexual). There is, ultimately, no one 'fatherhood' within recent representations of the masculine crisis. Indeed, we have seen, diverse ideas of fatherhood co-exist in present debates around crime and the issue of whether 'families need fathers'. Frequent reference continues to be made to ideas of 'absent fathers', 'new fathers', the 'assertive father' and, somewhat less visible, the 'abusing father' (Morgan, 1994). Yet it remains this lack of any fixed meaning which has rendered the concept of fatherhood itself, ultimately, something of a cipher in debates about masculinity. As Fineman has noted, '. . . even in a climate of reconsideration generated by social changes and the women's movement . . . there has been no corollary reconstruction or reconsideration of the institution of fatherhood' (1995: 202).

In this chapter I have sought to explore how the social construction of paternal masculinity in western culture provides a fascinating (and disturbing) example of how a 'drive to convert difference to otherness' has functioned (Gutterman, 1994: 229). The 'heterosexuality' of 'fatherhood' epitomises many aspects of this drive. A familial masculine subject has been produced and sustained by interwoven discourses of sexuality and gender which are rooted in dualistic configurations which pervade liberal legal thought and which, we have seen, are central to the father-right discourse. The father-right argument reproduces, in a startlingly rigid way, a gendered assignation of male/female attributes in a hierarchical manner. The concept of the 'family man' the new men's movement seeks to defend, the example taken in this chapter, has been constituted through a range of discourses which position heterosexual men, however fleetingly, as 'masculine' by tying up male gender identities with certain historically specific ideas of heterosexuality. Yet it is important to remember that this familial masculinity is itself, as the grievances of the fathers' rights movement illustrate only too clearly, surrounded by painful contradictions and ambivalences. It is these tensions which become particularly evident at the point of relationship breakdown, not the least of which relate to the separation of men from children/child care within the economic provider discourse, a separation which in turn informs the gendered strategies of men and women in negotiating divorce and separation and, for many divorced fathers, what appears to be their sense of a need to 'be a man' in coping with separation. Arendell (1995), in her study of divorced fathers in the United States, notes the significance for the vast majority of men of preserving a sense of 'masculine' identity in their adoption of a gendered strategy, the discursive themes and actions of which constitute no less than what she terms a distinct *masculinist discourse* in the negotiation of divorce and the end of heterosexual relationships:

> Related to both their victimization and belief in differences between men and women, divorce was understood as a battle – a 'war between the sexes,' in general, and with the former wife, in particular ... despite the situational ambiguity and stressful circumstances related to divorce, the men adhered to a definition of self that required a persistent demonstration, in action and comportment, of authority, confidence, and competency. They were not just being men, but were 'doing gender' ... and because these identities had been brought into question by divorce in dramatic and far-reaching ways, they expended major efforts to re-establish and reassert their identities as men. (Arendell, 1995: 14)

Some of the destructive effects of such a 're-establishing' or 'reassertion' of 'their identities as men' are, it seems, all too clear.[12] The concern of those who advocate the masculine crisis thesis is not to challenge existing social structures which continue to sustain and promote such separations. It is to reproduce quite 'traditional norms of masculinity and femininity, of heterosexuality, and, in Western culture, monogamous marriage' (Kimmell and Kaufman, 1994: 269). The focus of the father-right discourse is thus not the assumption of responsibility, including the responsibility for self-definition, but of *control*, both in and of men's relationships with women and children. Moving 'beyond these traditional hierarchical meanings of fatherhood', in contrast, may be to

> forge social and political meanings that are corollaries to the challenges presented by single mothers ... to raise questions about, perhaps challenge the whole conceptual basis of the 'private' family and to recognize the need for systemic societal reform to address inevitable dependencies. To be a nurturing father is to concede the importance of mothering. (Fineman, 1995: 205)

The repeated references to individual choice, free will and 'normality' within the men's movement rhetoric should not surprise: those to whom power is bequeathed have historically tended to ascribe merit and social status to individualistic accounts of de-gendered human agency by way of justification of existing social structures (and, of course, judicial espousal of these values is not hard to find). What the implicit construct of 'threatened normality' within the new men's movement testifies to is not the 'natural' quality of any 'traditional man's role' in the family but, once again, its fragility and historical specificity. Any crisis of the masculinity which exists, be it on inner-city council estates or in the leafy suburbs of the middle classes, is not 'because' of feminism. It cannot be confined to a particular socio-economic group. It has more to do with the ways in which men have not learnt new roles, new ways of 'being' men in families, in the light of the social and economic changes discussed in this chapter.

In her book *Straight Sex: The Politics of Pleasure*, Lynne Segal (1994) asks of those who would seek to maintain that there is just one 'heterosexuality', 'How Dare You Assume What It Means To Be Straight'. The question, she asks,

> is whether heterosexuals can recognise themselves as part of both a compulsory system and an intrinsic comedy. For until they can, the comedy hides only tragedy – for everyone – with the most difficult and painful roles reserved, still, for women and gay men. (Segal, 1994: 212; see also Soper, 1995)

I do not interpret this accusation as being directed at lesbian and gay critiques of heterosexuality so much as the endeavours of those who, like the new men's movement, seek to promote one 'wholesome' paternal masculinity and one place for women in their relations with men and children. I have argued in this chapter that at the present moment in Britain the rendering otherwise of 'dangerous' male youth within underclass theory, the vilification of 'unruly' lone mothers and single sexual females, and the continued negation of homosexuality have become important elements in the 'patriarchal reconstruction' advocated by the dominant political grouping. It is this which has been an unspoken, hidden dimension to the debates presently taking place around masculinity and crime. It is in such a context that the deconstruction of gendered bi-polarities and the rethinking of heterosexuality I have attempted in this chapter must take place. It is no wonder that, for those who have most to lose from such challenges to existing social arrangements, the return of that which has been repressed in the constitution of male heterosexual 'normality' should prove so disturbing and threatening; nor that, when pushed far enough, such anger and hatred should be unleashed towards those whose (inescapable) presence serves continually as a reminder of the fragility, contingency and uncertainty of the very 'normality' of 'straight' male heterosexuality.

Notes

1. The burgeoning literature on masculinity which has emerged during the 1980s and 1990s has no one politics or method (see Chapter 1, pp. 6–7) and it would

be erroneous to group together a disparate collection of texts and practices under the umbrella 'men's movement'. The idea of a 'new men's movement' has, nonetheless, assumed a common currency in recent accounts of both mythopoetic practice and, in particular, in relation to a range of internationally based fathers' rights organisations. It is with reference to these developments that I am using the term here. On the particularly virulent anti-feminism of the UK men's movement in the 1990s, see 'Militant Men Declare War on the "Social Evil" of Feminism', *The Independent*, 4 February 1997; ' "Much of Feminism is Hitlerism and Nazi": Here Comes Trouble', *The Guardian*, 13 February 1997.

2. In July 1993 the then Cabinet Minister John Redwood prompted a high-profile and apparently orchestrated political row when he suggested that some single women were deliberately becoming pregnant, with no intention of marrying, in the knowledge that they would then be supported by the state. Moreover, he declared, lone mothers should not receive state benefit until the 'errant father' had been found and forced to return to the family. Fathers, Redwood proposed, should be required to return to the household so that they might offer what he called 'the normal love and support that fathers have offered down the ages' (*The Guardian*, 3 July 1993; see further Collier, 1995b).

3. In November 1994 a conference took place in London, England, entitled 'Restoring Marriage by Recognising Men'. The conference was organised around a central claim; that the legal 'reassertion' of fatherhood must be central to 'defending' the family from the threat it is now under from 'powerful lobbies drawn from the social science and legal professions whose value systems are either non-supportive of the values underpinning marriage or are actively hostile to them'. The conference was organised by the Cheltenham Group, an organisation made up of representatives of a number of self-styled 'pro-family Men's Organisations' including Families Need Fathers, Dads After Divorce, the Family Law Action Group, Parents Forever (UK) and the United Kingdom Men's Movement. The group itself had been formed after a meeting on 30 April 1994 in Cheltenham, initially as a response to the Child Support Act 1991 and the proposals for divorce contained in the discussion papers *Facing the Future* (1988, no. 170) and *The Ground For Divorce* (1990, no. 192). As a result of the perceived success of the conference a discussion paper, *Restoring Legal Marriage* (*RLM*), was produced in which the Cheltenham Group set out their arguments in favour of a reintroduction of what they call 'a moral base to marriage and divorce involving the incorporation of conduct into both the grounds for divorce and its consequences'. The arguments put forward in *RLM* are discussed here as being generally illustrative of the father-right engagement with law reform in Britain.

4. *Restoring Legal Marriage.* See note 3.

5. The underclass theorists' moral panic about this father has been ignited, Campbell has suggested, not by their flight and failure – that after all was nothing new – 'but by their redundancy. . . . To reveal the redundancy of the fathers is the crime of the mothers' (Campbell, 1993: 313–14).

6. The mythopoetic movement, for example, has been described as 'nothing more than a bunch of white, upper middle class professionals chanting and dancing around bonfires' (Kimmell and Kaufman, 1994: 260).

7. Within the mythopoetic celebration of male creativity there is, in the end, and most significantly, no need for women at all. In going 'back to the woods', these 'spiritual warriors' enter a world devoid of women and the regulations of heterosexual familialism. The circulation of mythopoetic texts between male writers and audiences is inscribed with female exclusion. Women have no place in the reconstitution of the father/son bond central to mythopoetic practice. The narrative closure is here one of masculine 'self-mothering',

(re)birth through the symbolic male body and the community of men. Within a world in which fathers and sons are reunited, mothers are literally and allegorically banished. As Kimmell and Kaufman note (1994: 276), mytho-poetic initiation rites are decontextualised, removed from the cultural context in which they existed. The practices relies on racial, and racist, stereotypes (see further Bonnett, 1996; Collier, 1994c).

8. The idea that the welfare of the child should be paramount, enshrined in legislation from the 1925 Guardianship of Infants Act through to the 1989 Children Act, is considered in *RLM* to be 'superficially attractive ... [but] dangerously destructive'. Children's rights, it is argued, only accrue from the child being a member of the family.

9. R. Whitcombe, *The Guardian*, 24 January 1994. Whitcombe has also expressed similar sentiments during a BBC Television debate on 'The Redundant Man' (13 February 1994). The three objects of his contempt are what he terms 'lone mother pseudo-families', the House of Lords ruling against marital rape, and, of course, the Child Support Agency, set up in 1991.

10. The section borrows from the argument of Jefferson (1994a).

11. Contemporary culture, and perhaps in particular popular music, is of course redolent with paeans to the vulnerability and confusion of the modern, white western male: 'Should a love be tender and bleed out loud?/Or be tougher and tough and prouder than proud?/If I'm troubled by every folding of your skirt/ Am I guilty of every male inflicted hurt?/But I don't know how to describe the modern rose/When I can't refer to her shape against her clothes/With the fever of purple prose' (Prefab Sprout, Cruel, 1984). Amongst the multitude of similar expressions of the confusions of heterosexual men in popular music see also, for example, Aztec Camera, How Men Are (1987), Bruce Springsteen, 'Walk Like a Man' (1987). According to Robinson (1994), Springsteen can in fact be seen as a central figure in an emerging form of popular art which explores what it means to be a man 'in a feminist age'. On the relation between law and popular culture generally, see Redhead (1995).

12. There is some evidence that men involved in bitter family recriminations appear increasingly likely to seize their children and former partners as hostages, thus provoking what have become known as 'domestic' sieges ('Angry Fathers Blamed for Domestic Sieges', *The Guardian*, 16 June 1997). In the Netherlands concern has grown over the number of men who have killed their children 'as the ultimate act of revenge against their wives' ('Dutch Fathers Kill Children for Revenge', *The Sunday Times*, 16 February 1997).

6 Concluding Remarks: 'Taking Masculinity Seriously'? Theory, Practice and the (Hetero)Sexing of Criminology

> Can you imagine a world without men? . . . No crime, just lots of jubilant sisters!
>
> (Postcard, on sale in the Tyneside Cinema, Newcastle upon Tyne, July 1997)

In June 1995 a one-day conference took place in Newcastle upon Tyne, the British city in which I have lived for the past seven years and in which much of this book has been written. Entitled 'Deprived or Depraved?', it was an attempt to explore a range of issues around crime and criminal justice with a particular focus on the phenomenon of youth crime in the north-east of England.[1] The event brought together individuals working in a range of criminal justice agencies with academics, journalists and other interested parties each concerned to address and, through discussion and the sharing of experience, hopefully begin to understand more about crime in Britain. As the day progressed one issue emerged within the discussion, repeatedly, as being central to this project: the question of 'masculinity' or, more specifically, the inseparability of the relationship between men, their 'maleness' and crime. Within the presentations of the speakers, in the performance of a play and in the questions from the floor, this masculinity/crime relation emerged as *the* issue which would have to be addressed if, in the words of Lea and Young (1984), something was at last going to be 'done about law and order'.

During the evening after the event and throughout the following day extensive local (and some national) media coverage of the conference chose to highlight other topics which the day was considered to have been 'about'. Each was, certainly, an important and familiar feature of the criminological and criminal justice landscape. The sentencing of young offenders, 'family breakdown', social disorganisation and urban disorder, prisons policy, the treatment of victims in the criminal justice system, the fear of crime and issues around working with offenders – the 'usual suspects' of criminological thought, the traditional subject matter of criminology conferences. And yet, in so representing the discussion about crime which had taken place, issues raised about the 'sex' of crime by the 'masculinity question' were themselves somehow rendered invisible, unspoken. That which had been so central to the impassioned, powerful testimonies of those who had sought to speak of the overwhelming 'maleness' of crime became that which could not (or would not) be spoken of. The sex of crime appeared again as the problem with no name.

In this book I have sought to address this silence: to surface the ways in which such knowledges have historically been, and continue to be, systematically effaced from conversations about crime. In Chapters 1 and 2 I have attempted to bring to bear to an account of the institutional and conceptual development of the discipline of criminology an analysis of the underlying configurations in and through which the men/crime relation has (and has not) been constructed as an object of concern. The argument has not been that the discipline of criminology has simply *failed* to address the relationship between men and crime. Far from it: men have long constituted, we have seen, the primary subjects of criminological knowledge. Within much of sociogenic criminology, moreover, this is a relationship which has indeed been explored through reference to the concept of masculinity. Issues which are presently being associated with the emerging topic of 'masculinity and crime' – learning to 'be a man', the 'unruliness' of male youth, links between the 'gender' of men and their aggression, questions of competitiveness, violence and the importance of 'masculine' honour – each can be seen as having long been the 'very stuff' of sociogenic criminology. What criminology has tended *not* to do, I have argued – at least until recently (Daly, 1997) –, is to frame its engagement with the crimes of men via any explicit recognition that this has been a discussion premised all along by the making of a particular distinction between 'sex' and 'gender'. Criminology is replete with texts which are rich in representations of the gender of men, whether it is couched in terms of their 'social roles' or 'scripts', their 'masculinity' or their 'machismo'. The problem facing criminology's present (if nascent) pro-feminist 'men and crime' debate, I have suggested, stems not so much from a hitherto *absence* of gender but, rather, from the *ways in which* this relationship between men and crime – criminology's 'sex question' itself – has been and is now being conceptualised.

What I have termed the 'pre-history' of criminological research on crime and masculinity had tended to reflect the positivist and frequently functionalist frame of the moment. This was a position in which a normative heterosexual masculinity was presumed. The construction of men and their masculinity as a problem per se – the politic*ising* of masculinity, as it were, of holding men to account for their actions – was an issue later put on the criminological agenda by feminism. In revealing hitherto hidden pains and suffering, and in highlighting the manifest and manifold harms caused by the behaviour of men – its consequences for women, children and, indeed, other men –, feminist scholarship gave voice to a range of previously subjugated knowledges. In so doing, understandings of 'crime' and 'criminal justice', questions of criminological practice/method and theory/concepts, were each subjected to a powerful critique. Within this feminist project, I have argued, the concept of masculinity was itself to assume a central, iconic and emblematic status. Certainly, the conceptualisation of masculinity has differed between the various strands of feminist thought. However, in 'naming' the problem of men in this way, masculinity has become a powerful tool within feminist critique. Law, crime and the state each appear at various moments in feminist scholarship as 'masculine', 'masculinist', as being suffused with an ideology of 'masculinism', and so forth.

It is this feminist conceptualisation of the 'masculinity' of crime which is, I have argued, itself presently being undermined by the challenges of postmodernism, not just to the 'Woman' of feminist discourse but also to feminism's *'Man'*. Attendant to this has been, I have suggested, the project attempted in this book: a reappraisal of the analytic utility of the concept of 'masculinity/ies' per se premised on an emerging critique of the sex/gender distinction and the growing influence of what has been termed the 'sexed bodies' or 'corporeal feminist' approach (Daly, 1997). Feminism's 'whopping political headache' resulting from the postmodern critique of a collective 'gendered' project (Murphy, 1996: 58) cannot, in short, be confined to questions of the well-documented (in)authenticity of 'Woman'. It also, I have argued in this book, raises some revealing and disturbing questions about the (in)authenticity of both feminism's *and* criminology's 'Man'. What kind of investments have been made in this 'masculinity', by both women and men? Of what desires, fears and fantasies has a politics of masculinity come to speak? And what is the discipline of criminology really seeking to achieve in its attempts to 'take seriously' the 'masculinity of crime'?

By way of concluding remarks, and in the light of the above brief overview of some of the central themes of this book, I would like to explore further what I believe to be a number of the implications of this engagement with masculinity. I wish to do so in the context of what might be termed aspects of 'everyday' practice and policy within the field of criminal justice. In this final chapter I shall, by way of bringing together the primarily theoretical themes and arguments of the preceding readings, seek to address what this surfacing of criminology's 'sex question' might mean in terms of developing an understanding of the relationship between men, crime and the state. The chapter is in three sections. The first will summarise the principal arguments of the book by way of rethinking the 'epistemological crisis' presently facing criminology in the light of the above questioning of sex-specific corporeality and, importantly, what I have suggested throughout has been the mutual discursive construction of heterosexuality, the family and masculinity. The second section seeks to relate this 'theory' to the question of 'practice' in the context of exploring what it means to change or to work with men *in terms of their gender* in the specific context of the sphere of criminal justice. Via an engagement with the 'sexing' of criminal justice discourse, this section seeks to further question the ambiguities and conceptual limitations of masculinity in the light of rethinking the relationship between the body, subjectivity and power. Finally, and by way of conclusion to the book as a whole, I wish to address the limits of the 'crisis of masculinity' thesis itself and critically assess just where, I will suggest, the present 'masculinity turn' taking place within criminology may in fact be leading.

Paradigms lost?:[2] beyond heterosexuality, gender and the 'problem of criminology'

I have argued in this book that it is in the context of the epistemological crisis presently facing both feminism and aetiological criminology that recent attempts to 'take masculinity seriously' must ultimately be assessed. The appeal of 'masculinity' for criminology is certainly understandable at the present moment. Notwithstanding the well-documented troubled relationship between men and feminism more generally, an explicitly 'pro-feminist' engagement with the concept of masculinity appears to offer some comfort, with the context of a bureaucratised (post-marxist?) critical academy, to those for whom 'the experience of being left out, on the sidelines, was the new and threatening reality for many a young male radical, no longer feeling as certain as he had in the 1960s of his own participation in the making of history' (Segal, 1990: 280). The question remains, however, as to precisely what is at issue within criminology's present recourse to the concept of masculinity. The answer to this question is dependent, I have suggested in Chapters 1 and 2, on how the discipline of criminology is conceptualised in the first place.

It is, of course, commonplace for criminological texts to embrace a recognition of the partial and limited nature of the discipline's past engagements with the phenomenon of crime. Introductory student texts routinely refer to such issues as the epistemological crisis, the 'fragmentation', 'failures' and troubled 'futures' of criminology (see, for example, Muncie et al., 1996). The very parameters and, indeed, *possibility* of criminology has been subjected to intensive scrutiny. It could itself be considered a 'main-stream' issue. Criminology now frequently appears with caveats; what is presented is not, and could not, be the 'whole story'.[3] The rationalism of the modernist narrative, aspiring to progress, peace and prosperity – a society without crime –, has long been recognised as an unattainable fantasy, an ideological construct.

Yet, and notwithstanding such debates, Anglo-American criminology as depicted in those 'reflections' of the discipline discussed in Chapter 2 broadly remains within a post-Enlightenment, modernist frame (cf. Henry and Milovanovic, 1996; Naffine, 1997: 75). It is this 'scientific' criminology which, we have seen, remains the dominant form of investigation. It is the concepts and categories of modernity which continue to structure criminological thought. The 'whole *raison d'être* of criminology', Smart has argued, is that it:

addresses crime. It categorizes a vast range of activities and treats them as if they were all subject to the same laws – whether laws of human behaviour, genetic inheritance, economic rationality, development or the like. The argument within criminology has always been between those who give primacy to one form of explanation rather than another. *The thing that criminology cannot do is deconstruct crime.* (1990: 77; my emphasis)

'Explaining' crime remains at the core of criminology's Lombrosian tradition (Garland, 1994). Criminological positivism in the twentieth century may not have sought 'deep laws'. It may have turned instead to 'immediate indications' and 'factors' deemed to be associated with, or disposing an individual to, criminality. It has remained, however, no less positivist in its belief that the search for the truth about crime has been, and remains, a viable project. It may be recognised that criminology might not be able to produce one truth about crime; it can, however, produce truth. The problem for such a criminology at the present moment, Smart (1990) has suggested, relates to the ways in which postmodernism has not just challenged the foundationalist understandings of previous criminological theories but has done so in such a way as to question what it means to make such claims to knowledge about 'crime' in 'society' in the first place. In the context of the concerns of this book, far from seeking to 'explain' men's actions by providing an ultimate 'truth' – be it about 'crime' or 'masculinity' – encounters with postmodernism have redrawn debates about how 'crime' is imagined by reconfiguring conceptualisations of ideas of criminology, masculinity, subjectivity, community and power, and so forth, in the first place (see, for example, the approach of Young, 1996). Crucially, in so doing, the kinds of claims towards the establishing of truth about crime which criminology has attempted have themselves been rejected as incapable of 'dealing with difference in a sufficiently subtle way. They are wedded to giving priority to one form of oppression over others in the last instance' (Smart, 1989: 190). Or, as Leng puts it:

The point is *not* to replace one truth with another, a strategy that would merely reproduce the phallic economy whereby one authority speaks for all other epistemological and subjective positions. In disrupting phallocentric beliefs, the goal is to offer *the possibility of sexual difference.* (1995: 56; original emphasis)

Integrating such a 'possibility of sexual difference', I have argued in this book, must be central to any project which would seek to develop an understanding of the sexed specificity of crime. It is this question of sex difference which, in turn, leads us to the limitations of criminology's recent 'masculinity turn' itself.

It is Smart's (1990) contention that, although criminology might accord priority to forms of explanation (its 'answers') at particular historical moments, it is 'of the essence' of the discipline that it cannot *deconstruct* crime. What criminology cannot do, that is, is locate specific crimes with particular domains. Thus, criminology is unable to locate crimes such as rape or child sexual abuse in the domain of sexuality, or a crime such as theft in the domain of economic activity, and so forth. In order to address crime within such specific contexts what becomes necessary is to reject the unified problem of 'crime' and, along with it, the possibility of there being any unified response or intervention. In so doing, however, that which gives the discipline of criminology its own epistemological or foundational unity – 'crime' – fades away (Smart, 1990: 77; see also, generally, Naffine, 1997). The focus shifts instead to the construction of 'Woman', 'Man', femininity, masculinity, corporeality, sexuality, and so on. In seeking to surface the sexed specificity of crime, such a deconstructive project, it is clear, cannot be confined to understandings of Woman. It involves a reassessment, I have argued, of the ways in which the subjects 'Man' and 'men' have themselves been constituted and made to signify within particular discourses as, I have suggested, inherently crimogenic concepts. In the preceding chapters we have seen no one reading of men and crime, just as there is, I have argued, no 'one' masculinity. This book has sought to address, in contrast, some subjugated knowledges, some different stories, by way of looking to different positions from which it might be possible to speak of that which has been unsaid in accounts of the 'masculinity of crime'. My aim has thus been to deconstruct criminology's truth claims about men in this area and, my concern later in this chapter, to assess the effects of these claims on the materiality of social practice.

Ultimately, criminology's engagement with the concept of masculinity has been premised around some of the familiar dualisms which have structured western philosophical thought in general. Amongst the recurring binaries in this field, we have seen, have been those of sex/gender, nature/nurture, mind/body, public/private, work/home, rationality/irrationality, hetero/homosexuality, autonomy/dependence and, of course, man/woman. The recognition of and engagement with questions of sexual difference and corporeality which has been advocated in this book begins, in a sense, from the disturbing of these binaries. It is through these (hierarchical) divisions that understandings of 'masculine' identities have been constructed (as *not* feminine, *not* homosexual). Yet (re)conceptualising men's specifically *heterosexual* subjectivities within both feminist and mainstream criminology raises, I have suggested, some very different questions about men and crime from those which have previously framed criminology's engagements with masculinity. It is these questions – about corporeality, sexual difference and the nature of the (hetero-)sexed subject – which have constituted the principal themes of this book.

To review the general argument: rejection of the sex/gender, mind/body distinction has entailed a reconfiguring of the idea of the sexed male body, understood here not as a pre-discursive, pre-theoretical corporeal artefact (the position in mainstream criminology),[4] but as, rather, a body which is constituted in *discourse* and *made to signify* in particular ways and at specific moments. Sex and biology, I have argued, are not 'outside' the social, somehow beyond power relations. They are themselves constituted discursively, in and through relations of power (Smart, 1990; Woodhull, 1988). To argue as much is not to suggest that the body is a *tabula rasa* on which discourses can be simply written or inscribed. Nor is it to give free rein to voluntarism or performativity at the expense of any analysis of social structure. It is to recognise that the materiality of the body and the lived experience of (sexed) subjectivity, the 'lived-in'-ness of a psychical and libidinally mapped body, must itself be central to addressing the sexed specificity of crime (or, indeed, to understanding experiences of 'family', 'work', and so on). In the integration of a recognition of sexual difference, such a focus on corporeality leads to a questioning of the fluidity of, and interaction between, a range of (supposedly) fixed categories which make up the above hierarchic binaries of modernity. The readings of men's subjectivities which have been presented in this book have sought to valorise a 'lived' body which is sexed as 'male', as 'inscribed by culture *and* determined by nature' (Murphy, 1996: 61). Crucially, I have argued, in so doing, a potentially different male body comes into view from that which has previously dominated criminological and much of feminist thought (the body as constituted through the binarisms of modernity).[5] This is not a body which is, as in some 'radical' feminist accounts, invariably empowered and oppressive, a body positioned as the repository of men's patriarchal power. Nor is it the body of men's liberationist and neo-conservative thought (Chapter 5), the body-as-victim, the *dis*empowered male. Nor, importantly, is this the 'de-sexed' 'ungendered' body of social constructionism, whether seen from the perspectives of feminist or men's anti-sexist politics (see below). It is, rather, a body which embraces a recognition of the complexity and contradictory nature of subjectivity and lived experience itself, the ways in which subjects presently constituted as 'male' may be simultaneously 'oppressive' and 'caring' (see the readings of fatherhood in Chapter 5), transgressive and conformist (the heterosexual[ised] violent body in Chapter 4), capable of resistance to the social order *at the very moment* that they reproduce dominant and oppressive sexual cultures (the 'lads' and their 'wild' masculinities discussed in Chapter 3). These are bodies which have an active part in accruing subjectivity rather than being replaced or inscribed by it. They do not exist pre-discursively to be 'explained' by the criminologist or social commentator.

Such a rethinking of corporeality leads, I have suggested, to some further explorations of the ways in which the actions of men are (or are not) deemed to be constituted as criminal at particular moments and locations; that is, are themselves criminal*ised*. In following feminism's important questioning of the fixity of the distinction between criminal and non-criminal men, I have sought to challenge the processes whereby certain male bodies are, and others are not, encoded and experienced in ways associated with the range of qualities which the masculine has been variously made to signify at particular moments. In so doing, this project has involved repositioning and reconfiguring the meanings of 'masculinity' itself. The refusal or transgression of the pre-ordained binary pairings which have hitherto informed understandings of the masculine has, I have argued, major implications which cannot be confined to the field of criminology and/or feminism. To surface the discursive constitution of sexual difference in this way is to look towards a future in which theory is itself *always already* a sexual, textual, political and historical production, to look to a recognition of the 'sexuatedness' (Leng, 1995: 56) of discourse, to the recognition that the relation we have to our bodies organises both our subjectivity and our systems of knowledge and representations – knowledge and representations such as those which, we have seen, have been produced by male criminologists who have sought to understand the inside/outside of their (male-dominated) discipline (Chapter 2).

Although this is a project which may certainly threaten those who adhere to the values of phallocentrism, it is also clear that it is an approach which may open up hitherto unimagined sites, sources and tools for theoretical exploration. In this book, and in a study of the relationship between men, masculinity and crime, I have argued that two (interrelated) such tools or sources have been the *heterosexualisation* of 'masculine' subjectivity and the refiguring of the boundaries of *the family* which is taking place within the conditions of postmodernity. In relation to each, I have argued, understandings of the 'social' – the 'context', that is, of crime and law – are themselves being transformed as a shift takes place in representations of what are taken to constitute both 'safe' and 'dangerous' men and their masculinities. Throughout modernity, Jenks has argued (following Virilio, 1986),

> time was measured and contained, it came to be expressed in minutes, days, weeks, years and in categories such as generations. We marked out our personal ability, responsibility, functionality, mortality and general expectations of self, and others, through such divisions. (Jenks, 1996: 18; see further Frosh, 1995; Osborne, 1995)

Within the conditions of postmodernity, in contrast, the pull of nostalgia has served to reconfigure some familiar imaginings of the past: the past of the (nuclear and extended) family, the past of consensus and social order, the past of a (relatively) 'crime-free' world it is presumed we have 'lost', a past of unquestioned and unchallenged (hetero)sexuality, a past in which gender 'roles' were understood as a function of ontology.

In this book I have sought to explore aspects of the reconfiguration presently taking place around the 'past' of masculinity in terms of a transformation around the interrelations of the 'familial' and 'childhood', of marriage and the family, of divorce and disorder (Chapters 3–5). What we have seen within this reading of the transformation of heterosexual social relations has been the changing significance accorded to, alongside the increasingly problematic nature of, the relationship between *men and children*. It is this relationship which, I have suggested, has come to constitute one of the major political conversations of the day. And as this conversation has itself been played out in debates around men, male youth and crime, the idea of a crisis of 'the family' (seen as being engendered by feminism) has itself been politically counterposed with a celebration and cultivation of a social experience of heterosexuality, fatherhood and child-hood as nostalgia. Media responses to the deaths of children, we have seen in Chapters 3 and 4, embody just some of the ways in which in this process the child, as Beck has suggested, has become the source of the

> last remaining, irrevocable, unexchangeable primary relationship. Partners come and go. The child stays. Everything that is desired, but is not realisable in the relationship, is directed to the child. . . . The child has become the final alternative to loneliness that can be built up against the vanishing possibilities of love. It is a private type of re-enchantment, which arises with, and derives its meaning from, disenchantment. (Beck, 1992: 118)

In relation to responses to both men's apparently random violence (Chapter 4) and debates around youth crime (Chapter 3), we have seen some of the contours of this 'disenchantment' (notably, a shifting and sexed good/evil binarism, a division of boy-children into 'rat boys' or 'little angels'). It is this reconfiguration of the child which has been, I have argued, central to the construction of the contemporary masculinity problematic. Men are, on the one hand, increasingly perceived as being no longer 'safe' – *because they are men* – in relation to children. At the same time, however, other discourses are seeking to *resecure* men's 'natural', ontological status both within and beyond the family. In so doing, the ghosts of modernity are, I have suggested, all too clear in the resulting shifting and contested repre-sentations of the 'otherness' of men not just inside/outside the familial but, increasingly, in relation to ideas of the 'community' itself. For, let us be clear, the battleground for the reconfigurations which have taken place in the 1980s and 1990s around criminal justice, social exclusion, family/child, fatherhood and crime has been not that of 'the state' but, increasingly, that of the terrain of 'community' (see, generally, Benhabib, 1992; Cornell, 1991; Frazer and Lacey, 1993).

The discipline of criminology has, of course, long engaged with the idea of there being distinctive 'communities' of crime (traditionally associated with the homogenised values and working-class households of earlier periods). Yet as the idea of community is now being reformed, Young (1996) has suggested, one consequence has been a growing belief that urban society has precipitated physical degeneracy, producing a corporealised 'community body' powerless in the face of the 'Daily Diet of Crime' which it is now said to face. This community body is the context for the 'contagion' of the new underclass (along, of course, with their 'maverick' masculinities) discussed in Chapters 4 and 5. Such a community body pervades the range of discourses presently visible within the crimino-legal sphere (evident, for example, in debates around community policing, neigh-bourhood watch, community crime prevention, community sentences, and so forth). It is doing so, however, at the very moment that the concept of 'community' is itself being put into question in some specifically sexed ways because of the growing recognition of the 'maleness' of crime. In making this connection it is becoming easier to see, perhaps, just why the question of the gender of men's crime should have assumed an iconic significance in broader debates around social (dis)order. The existence of the (male) offender turns *everyone* into victims: '... the lines are rigidly drawn between those who belong to the law (and the community) and those who do not: the outlaws' (Young, 1996: 9). The trouble is, I have argued, that this boundary between safe/dangerous, criminal/non-criminal masculinities is itself always and inevitably blurred and shifting. What we have seen in the reading of Thomas Hamilton in Chapter 4 is an 'outsider' who wanted 'in', but who remained beyond, outwith the community; in Chapter 3 we have seen how constituting the 'urban wastelands' of contemporary Britain as sexed (or different) communities surfaces some class-based fantasies of corporeality, order and belonging. The dangerous/criminal masculine calls into being its antithesis, 'a simulacrum of a community; a phantasm that speaks of a nostalgic desire for oneness and unity, while at the same time structuring itself around its dependence upon fear, alienation and separateness' (Young, 1996: 10). Crimino-legal conceptualisations of masculinity, I have argued in this book, have perpetuated 'the stranglehold grip of Cartesian-style dualisms by trading in uneven oppositions around the mind and the body, the real and the romantic, the scientific and the fantastic' (Murphy, 1996: 57). This in/outside of gendered community is just one of a range of binaries which have structured criminological understandings of the men/crime relation more generally.

Criminological engagements with masculinity have, in short, been pervaded by a series of distortions and closures. To disturb such boundaries does not simply entail a re-reading of criminology's past. It is not *simply* that generations of 'expert' professional (usually male) criminologists have been constructing complex taxonomies of 'the masculine'. It involves a more disruptive, dangerous and perhaps threatening project, one which ultimately refigures understandings of criminal justice practice and intervention itself. Theory and practice cannot be separated: '... ideas about crime ... are a product of society that develop in a particular context and then have their consequences for social policy' (Lilly et al., 1995: 225). Thus far this chapter has sought to provide an overview of and expand on what has been a largely theoretical engagement with the relationship between men, masculinities and crime. It is now necessary, by way of conclusion, to make explicit questions of social policy in addressing some of the implications of this theoretical frame.

Rethinking the relationship between men, the state and criminal justice

Analysis of the relationship between masculinities, crime and the state is an area in which, Walklate has suggested, 'much more ... work needs to be done' (1995: 181; cf. Liddle, 1996; Messerschmidt, 1993). The following comments by Sumner capture well some of the dominant themes of the conceptualisation of the state as they have occurred within both the sociology of masculinity and 'masculinity and crime' literature. The state, Sumner argues, is

> profoundly masculine in that its fundamental organizing concepts, institutions, procedures and strategies are historically imbued with, and are themselves descriptive of, an ideological notion of masculinity that is hegemonic (over other ideas of masculinity and all femininity); and that this hegemonic masculinity which contributes to the very form of state power is not so much an effect of men's economic power as an overdetermined historical condensation of the economic, political and ideological power of ruling-class men. . . . (1990: 35)

A broadly similar conceptualisation of the 'state as masculine' has informed the influential work of Connell, who pertinently asks:

> How can we expect democratic reform of gender relations from an institution that is dominated by those who benefit from the present gender order? What kind of reform process could possibly transform the gendered character of the state, without being trapped by the politics of social control in which the state is enmeshed? (What politician would survive, with a policy of taking the police *off* the streets?) (1993: xvi; original emphasis)

In each case the concept of masculinity is evoked, in what has become a now familiar move within the masculinity turn, in such a way that a range of concepts and practices are unified through making a division between what Sumner terms 'hegemonic' and 'other ideas' of masculinity. The problem with such an analysis, I have suggested in Chapter 1, relates to the ways in which the complexities and multi-layered nature of men's subjectivities are themselves here side-stepped. Within such a characterisation of the relationship between men and the state, power tends to be understood as a material possession (as something which, in effect, men – or at least 'ruling-class men' – have 'more of' than women). Men's subjectivities are, within Sumner's account, graded hierarchically as being (relatively) powerful or powerless (as, following Connell, 'hegemonic' or 'subordinated' masculinities, for example). The state itself, however, continues to be conceptualised as somehow expressing men's interests, albeit that these are interests mediated by class, sexuality and/or 'race', ethnicity. It is the state which simultaneously embodies and reproduces a particular form of (hegemonic) masculinity. What tends not to be evident in such accounts, however, is an engagement with the possibility that, within the conditions of postmodernity, 'the shaping of wills, desires, aspirations and interests, *the formation of subjectivities and collectivities* [may be] more typical than the brute domination of one will by another' (Rose, 1987: 69; my emphasis). What would it mean to carry over to an analysis of the state 'as male' a recognition that men may be simultaneously powerful *and* weak/vulnerable? What would this mean for the 'sexing' of criminal justice discourse? How have discourses of masculinity framed the ways in which economic policy agendas have been expressed? And how does this, in turn, impact on what it means to 'work with' men in terms of their gender in this particular field?

The example of 'being tough' on crime

In the analysis of the masculinity of criminology discussed in this book we have seen some of the ways in which a range of behaviour relating to men 'being hard' has historically been associated with the qualities deemed 'masculine' at particular moments. Indeed, this iconography of the 'tough', the study of the 'hard man', can itself be seen as the dominant motif of criminological work on masculinity and crime. For men, in short, it is being 'tough' which is (at the very least) associated, if not equated, with both criminality and being 'masculine' (Ryder, 1991). Yet what does 'being hard' actually mean? What does it signify in different contexts? Within some recent pro-feminist accounts a notion of 'toughness' has been seen as uniting *all* men (whether inside/outside state institutions such as the police, prisons) with both the organising principles and form of state power (for example, Sim, 1994: 116–17). For the politician, meanwhile, and in terms of public rhetoric around crime and penality, some value-laden notions of 'being tough' on crime have become the dominant language through which debates around criminal justice are now being conducted. It is through the avoidance of the (feminised) other – the charge of being 'soft' on crime – that politicians of all quarters in Britain are presently articulating policies in the sphere of criminal justice.[6]

There are, clearly, different discourses at work here. Being 'hard' or 'tough' does not *necessarily* mean, as a host of studies have made clear, actually engaging in physical conflict. It might relate, rather, to questions of mental 'control', to an attitude underlying which is a potential threat of violence/ridicule which will then make others submit. The values of the 'tough' cannot be confined to one socio-economic group (for example, young, urban, working-class men). The phenomenon of men 'being hard' cuts across society, traversing the corporate boardroom, the street 'gang' and the courtroom (Thornton, 1996), the university seminar and academic conference (Collier, 1991, 1998). At times, we have seen, it is this quality of 'toughness' which has been taken to denote the masculine/male over and above other gendered attributes; as 'being tough' becomes emblematic of what men (and boys) do, albeit that they might do so 'differently' depending on class or race positioning (Messerschmidt, 1993, 1994).

To suggest there is a problem with this construction of 'being tough' is not to argue that men do not routinely dominate, terrorise, threaten and enact violence. It is, however, to question the ways in which a certain unity is here being accorded to a masculine subject by the attribution of these qualities of over-arching toughness, bravura, and so forth; the qualities which are, we must remember, then deemed to associate the masculine with the criminal in specific contexts. What much of criminological scholarship has made clear, albeit at times implicitly rather than explicitly, is the contradictory nature of the power presently accorded men in society. In the accounts of young offenders 'in their own words' (Graef, 1992), in accounts of damaged boys (and even more damaged men), what appears alongside the testimonies of undoubted empowerment and privilege is also rich and disturbing evidence of some of the psychic subjective costs of 'being a man' in contemporary society (on the complexities of the idea of the 'hard man' in prison, for example, see Sim, 1994). Implicit here is a notion of psychological and frequently physical pain. Such 'pain', Walkerdine (1995) has suggested, can be usefully conceptualised not so much as an individual *pathology* that needs to be corrected, but as part of 'everyday' experience. It is, of course, precisely such/a politics of the 'everyday' which has surfaced in feminist accounts of interpersonal violence by men (Stanko, 1985, 1990). Yet this idea of the 'everyday' can also, I wish to suggest, be of use in seeking to understand something of the diversity of the experiences of the male sexed self within contemporary society; and in so doing, the focus shifts away from a unified (constituted as 'tough') masculine subject to a growing awareness of the lasting psychic effects of the routine, actual and threatened violence which surrounds (but is so often unspoken of in) the 'everyday' experiences of men.

This is not, to repeat, to efface the significance of the existence of continuous systematic and organised assaults by men on peoples singled out as 'less than' fully male/masculine. Nor is it, in any way, to seek to excuse men's violence. It is, however, and bearing in mind the socio-economic specificity of the criminal masculine subject of criminology to date as it (he) has played out in terms of implications for criminal justice policy, to ask some questions of

> the consequences of living that daily humiliation and for children to grow up watching their parents face it. . . . How do they live watching parents do without, face hardship, be hurt or killed at work, never stop working, become drudges, old before their time and so forth? *Why are not these the questions that are being asked?* (Walkerdine, 1995: 326–7; my emphasis)

Masculine 'toughness', it is to be remembered, has been historically associated in criminology with lower/working-class masculinities. It has been seen as a key factor in 'their' gendered disposition to crime, to 'their' fighting, bravado, the importance of 'honour' in 'their' cultures, and so forth. Only more recently has the criminological gaze turned, drawing notably on feminist perspectives, towards some cross-class engagements with gender, where these masculine qualities have instead been seen to traverse socio-economic groups (Campbell, 1993; see further Chapter 3). Yet reconceptualising such a gendered attribute as 'toughness' in the way Walkerdine (1995) suggests in some important respects undermines this notion of the 'strong' masculine subject in the first place. It is clear that women and men, girls and boys experience violence and humiliation in ways which are mediated by sexual difference. However, in recognising the possibilities of the mutual constitution of vulnerability and empowerment, the co-existence of pain and joy, a rather insidious form of self-regulation is here being established at the very moment that particular socio-economic groups of men are being subjected to the gaze of the state in the field of criminal justice. In seeking to 'make public the psychic effects of living in and under oppression', groups such as the working class, Walkerdine has argued, survive in a way which means that they come to recognise themselves as lacking, deficient and deviant, as being *where* they are in society because that is *who* they are: '. . . genocidal persecution is not required to elicit psychic defence', she suggests, 'daily mundane humiliation will do' (Walkerdine, 1995: 326). To relate this point to the discursive construction of masculinities within criminology and the crimino-legal domain more generally, such an analysis does not simply shed new light on the 'daily mundane humiliation' which was experienced by boys such as Robert Thompson and Jon Venables, the murderers of James Bulger, during their lives (see Morrison, 1997; or, indeed, on the humiliations experienced by Thomas Hamilton discussed in Chapter 4). It surfaces, importantly, a sexed dimension to the 'everyday' criminality of those (largely) working-class men who *continue* to constitute the primary object of criminal justice and criminological knowledge; that is, the men who make up the bulk of prison statistics and the men whose (largely property-related) crimes constitute the majority of known offenders generally.

To recognise this complexity is not to accord either to men who commit crime or to men in general any victim status (a status which has itself been culturally encoded as female). Far from *ignoring* the all too real costs of men's actions, be it for women, children and other men, it is to seek to try to understand men as subjects in ways which may be far more complex than the qualities of a unifying gendered 'toughness' which has been so central to the idea of hegemonic masculinity as it is presently being used. In terms of seeking justification for the violence of law itself, the state's call for retribution in criminal justice policy, it is to collapse these binaries of guilt and innocence which have facilitated the construction of young men as deserving of punishment, as 'vermin, scum, nasty' individuals, as venal 'rat boys', as 'barbarians' (that is, the very 'tough' young men, it is to be remembered, a significant number of whom then go on to take their own lives rather than live this violence of the state).[7] These are men and boys whose lives have *already* in many ways been dominated by violence and amongst whom, as mounting evidence is revealing, many will have experienced abuse by those who have been in positions of care and trust whether in their capacity as parents or other care-givers. In Britain, where surveys of the prison population suggest as many as one in four prisoners have been in local authority care, it has become increasingly apparent that such state 'care' has itself frequently been the location for widespread and systematic physical and sexual abuse.[8] Amongst the male population generally what is unquestionably clear is that, while many boys are hit, yelled at, teased and goaded into fighting, the very experience of *being* a boy is frequently one in which, as countless adult and childhood testimonies now reveal, a conviction is established that the boy child *will* be violated until he learns to 'protect' himself. And it is in the very nature of this self 'protection' that sexed specific processes of 'routine humiliation' and violence can be seen to reproduce themselves. They do so, importantly, in ways which *draw on* the broader discursive constitution of the 'masculine' as an priori, inherently crimogenic gender attribute. Those who fail to walk this thin line between danger and conformity, who fail to act, that is, 'like a man', appear invariably to meet the derogations of hetero-masculine culture – of 'fag', 'queer', 'mam's boy', 'girl', 'puff', and so forth. This is, I have argued, a *heterosexualisation* of the process of 'becoming' a (straight) man. Criminology, education research and sociology generally are replete with texts in which boys of *all* classes depict it as being a challenge, an expectation that, in this process of 'becoming', they fight or use other resources (such as intelligence and/or educational credentials) to 'prove themselves' as 'manly'. These are not the voices of unproblematically 'powerful' subjects, the embodiment of a 'tough' hegemonic masculinity. They are masculine subjects pervaded by, indeed *constituted through*, a fear of identification with that which is other, that which is not (which is less than) the culturally masculine.

In seeking to surface such voices it is necessary to recognise that 'defences are not only produced but are necessary. Necessary, but not without contradictions' (Walkerdine, 1995: 327). The transition from boyhood to heterosexual manhood, I have suggested, is not seamless or unproblematic. It is fraught with dangers. Difference and dominance are fused in the ways in which the hierarchical binaries which construct the masculine are played out in terms of psychic defences, contradictions and projections. Criminology, however, has tended to miss the ways in which

> routine humiliation . . . constitute[s] the subjectivity, defences and coping practices of most of the population. So busy looking at a progressive/reactionary dichotomy and working with, not taking apart, this fiction which functions in truth [it seems] . . . not to see the ways in which subjects cope, produce defences against extreme conditions . . . . (Walkerdine, 1995: 329)

Criminology has historically understood such 'defences', we have seen in Chapters 2 and 3, in terms of class relations. It has been as a result of feminism that gender has entered the (critical) criminological frame. Yet the crimes of men continue to be conceptualised by the discipline, as we have seen in this book, in terms of a division between 'hegemonic' masculine and 'other' masculinities in ways which, in so many respects, continue to talk about 'working-class' fantasies without ever analysing criminology's own.

*Changing men as changing masculinities? Crime prevention and the
'de-gendering' of men*

This making of a systematic association between men and 'toughness' has
had a number of consequences in constructing understandings of specific
criminal populations at particular moments. In reconceptualising change in
gender relations in the light of such an understanding of a simultaneously
heterosexual(ised) and *criminal(ised)* subject, I wish to return at this point to
some of the problems of the dominant sex/gender frame of analysis outlined
in Chapter 1. I wish to return, in particular, to what I have suggested has
been criminology's underlying – and problematic – conceptualisation of
sexual difference as pre-discursive.

Both the state and a range of voluntary bodies at present work with male
offenders in a number of diverse ways. One increasingly prominent strategy
of intervention in Britain has taken the form of what might loosely be
termed 'gender awareness' programmes (Murphy and Joels, 1993; Pearce,
1993).[9] Engaging with questions of masculinity can be seen in this context in
relation to men who are in very different positions within the criminal justice
system. In relation to *male offenders*, for example, programmes designed
to rehabilitate men have drawn on a range of different theories and
methods. Those based on cognitive-behavioural approaches, that is, tackling
deficiencies in offenders' 'ways of thinking', reasoning and associated
behaviour, are now being increasingly favoured in the criminal justice
system. Such cognitive-behavioural methods, it has been suggested, are
generally more successful in modifying patterns of thinking and behaviour
than more traditional counselling and therapy (Vennard et al., 1997).
Although it may not always be explicitly addressed as an engagement with
masculinity per se, by 'gender awareness' in this context I am referring to
those interventions with offending in which the key idea underlying practice
in changing 'ways of thinking' has been a foregrounding of the issue of
'changing' masculinity (Wolf-Light, 1996). This gender frame has been
particularly prominent in relation to conceptualisations of intervention in the
context of men's violences (Dobash et al., 1996), though gender questions
have also been increasingly significant in relation to working with male
youth (notably with regard to 'joyriding' and related car crimes: Chapman,
1993). Yet such attempts to *challenge* men's gender (their masculinity)
cannot be confined to *offenders* in the criminal justice system. Considerable
efforts are also presently being put into challenging practices and cultures of
those men who are *working* within the criminal justice system whose
behaviour is seen to exclude or otherwise discriminate against women. Here
questions of sexism, harassment and discrimination have been particularly
evident in relation to the police (facing the well-documented problems of
'cop culture': Fielding, 1994; Ryder, 1991; Westmarland, 1997), the armed
forces, the legal profession, the judiciary and, indeed, parliament itself.
There now exists a rich literature on sex difference within the criminal
justice system (Cavanagh and Cree, 1988; Knight, 1997; Martin and Jurik,

1996) in which issues of equality and the development of policies and strategies to address widespread and pervasive discrimination have been conceptualised, first and foremost, as questions of challenging a dominant form of 'masculinity'. In short, and at the risk of over-simplifying what are complex and diverse programmes, working *with* men is here seen to involve changing the kinds *of* men these are. Implicitly, it is men's 'gender' which is, at the very least, a if not *the* most significant part of the problem to be tackled.

Without in any way underestimating either the scale of the problem or the value of the various interventions which have been and continue to be made around these issues, what interests me here are the possibilities, and limits, of such de- or re-gendering strategies *when seen in the light of* the above critique of the sex/gender distinction. Part of the appeal of the sex/gender distinction for feminism has been, we have seen, the way in which it configures or imagines social change. In contrast to 'sex', seen as a biological category denoting essentialism and a pre-given, ordained (patriarchal) social structure, 'gender' has appeared to be a social category which is open to contestation, challenge and resistance. Challenging gender – in this case masculinity – is thus seen as opening out society to a range of 'progressive' political interventions aimed at questioning, and transforming, the ways in which 'gender roles' are presently constituted. The task within gender feminism, whether in relation to criminology, law or other disciplines, has been one of challenging the 'naturalness', the 'inevitability' of the characteristics of gender (masculinity, femininity) at any particular moment. The fact that there has been a certain historical constancy or continuity to the 'masculine' values associated with men does not, in theory, negate the viability of de-gendering and gender neutrality per se. Such a social constructionist approach to gender envisages *precisely* the kinds of strategies of re-education of men discussed above as part of a programme for viable social change.

Yet such a de-gendering project is, Gatens (1996) has argued, itself profoundly problematic as soon as the underlying sex/gender distinction is disturbed. For de-gendering to be successful (or theoretically tenable), Gatens suggests, one would have to allow the validity of two unargued assumptions assumed by 'degendering feminists' (Gatens, 1996: 7). Firstly, that the body is neutral and passive with regard to the formation of consciousness. This is, implicitly, a rationalist view of the subject which, I have argued in Chapter 1, conceives of the body in a particular (and ultimately problematic) way (see pp. 24–30). Secondly, this approach assumes that one can definitively alter the effects of the historical and cultural specificity of 'lived experience' 'by consciously changing the material practices of the culture in question' (Gatens, 1996: 7). Were each of these assumptions to be correct, then, Gatens accepts, it may indeed be possible to claim that the cultural and historical significances or meanings attached to masculinity receive their expression in, or are made manifest by, an essential neutral (ungendered or 'before' gender) consciousness which, in turn, acts upon an (initially) 'ungendered', neutral body.

There are, however, several problems with each of these propositions. Such a 'de-gendering' strategy is premised on a 'top down' rationality which rests on the assumption that it is possible to alter the effects of the historical and cultural specificity of an individual's lived experience. Such an effectively behavioural conception of subjectivity itself presumes a causal relationship between the body and mind which rests upon the given of an a priori, neutral and passive subject – in this case a (male) subject conceived of as being a passive recipient of (masculine) gender roles or scripts (which are themselves seen as products of, variously, the media, peer group pressure, a 'respectable' paternal presence, and so forth).[10] Such a tactic presumes that consciousness is primary and that, within the context of these re-education strategies, not only that men might *want* to change but also that what is at issue here in effecting change is the question of men's 'gender' (Brooker, 1995). Individual 'will', as it were, might, given certain societal encouragement, eradicate the effects of patriarchal socialisation. Yet underlying such a position, Gatens (1996) argues, is a dubious voluntarism which underestimates the *unconscious* embedding of these 'patriarchal' imperatives.[11] To state as much is *not*, importantly, to suggest that 'men cannot be changed'. It is, however, to highlight the ways in which a behaviourist conception of 'gendered' conditioning presumes the existence of a passive (non-signifying subject), a subject which might then be trained to respond 'appropriately' (in a non-sexist, non-criminal way for example) and be relied on, crucially, to *consistently* respond in such a manner. The gender concept 'masculinity' is here conceptualised as operating somehow at the level of ideas, premised on a distinction between 'mind/consciousness' and 'the body'. However, as some accounts have recognised (Sim, 1994), as soon as the relationship between the 're-educa*tor*' and the 're-educa*ted*' is questioned, this renders problematic the nature of the relationship between what is taken to be the 'pathological' masculine and the 'normal' culture which surrounds it (the hegemonic and 'other' masculinities discussed above for example: see further, in relation to the criminological academy, Chapter 2).

To relate this to the field of criminal justice, at the present moment re-gendering *as* rehabilitation is being equated in many ways with a process of feminisation; in effect, making men less 'like men' and more 'like women' (that is, it is presumed, non-criminal).[12] Yet given the disparagement of the feminine within the broader culture, it is at the very least open to question to what extent individual men may seek to take up a subject position which has been, in so many ways, already constituted as less than masculine, as less than male, as less than the 'normal' masculine to which so many had already been presuming that they were *adhering* in their criminal behaviour all along. As Sim notes (1994: 109), if an aim of the criminal justice system is to rehabilitate male offenders, then the question must be 'rehabilitate to what'? Is it to reproduce 'normal' men, 'normal' masculinities? If so, then this means engaging with what must be considered normal about a culture in which, according to one recent survey, thirty-two out of 142 convicted rapists believed that the raped woman had been harmed and in which less than half reported displaying any compassion for their victims (Sim, 1994: 116).

It is at this point that the crimogenic dimensions to what is taken to be the 'normal' masculine become clearly significant. It is not just criminology but society itself which is, in many ways, deeply ambivalent about male offending. To state as much is not to argue that any simple or straight-forward correlation exists between 'masculinity' and 'criminality' (cf. Oakley, 1972, quoted in Box, 1983: 175 and Messerschmidt, 1993: 27). Nor is it to efface what are the very real links between the culturally masculine and many – but by no means all – aspects of men's offending. It is, rather, to look beyond the assumptions underlying particular constructions of the masculine to the ways in which, I have suggested, both masculinity and crime have been made to signify at particular moments. Crime does not *necessarily* require 'strength', 'toughness' 'aggression' 'violence', and so forth. Indeed, other values may, in certain instances, be encoded as mascu-line within the context of crime (qualities such as cunning, patience, deceit, an ability to empathise). At other moments, other times, these may be seen as feminine qualities. Whilst, however, what might be termed the 'stereo-typically' masculine can be seen as having been overplayed in relation to crime, what we have also seen in this book has been something of the pervasive, systematic violence which nonetheless surrounds, and which is part of the lives of so many (if not, arguably, all) men and boys: something of the way in which, time and again, men and boys say that they are supposed to be tough, aggressive, in control, that they are not to express any feelings except anger, not to cry, and never to ask for help.[13] If part of 'being a man' is, in a sense, to walk that thin line between danger/deviance and 'respectable' conformity (Sim, 1994; Stanko, 1994), it is nonetheless a line which is always shifting, dependent on other contingencies and maintained at considerable cost. Ultimately, I have argued, it is a line which is policed in very different ways depending on the class, 'race' and ethnic positioning of the particular, always contingent, masculine subject.

Concluding remarks

Through engaging in a deconstructive reading of the masculinity/crime relationship, a reading which has focused in particular on the mutual discursive constitution of the categories of both 'men' and 'crime', this book has not sought to efface the significance of other issues and concepts which continue to be important in how identities are constructed. Questions of sex/gender may not *necessarily* be the most significant in seeking to understand crime in any specific context. A recurring concern in this book has been to question the ways in which processes of criminalisation taking place at the present moment have themselves been premised on the identification of politically and economically marginalised groups within advanced capitalism. It has been, in particular, groups of 'underclass' or lower-class men whose masculinities are seen as having been 'sharpened' or 'heightened' by the social/economic and cultural changes of the past decades. It is these men who are seen as reaffirming collective male violence, misogyny and homophobia. They are, in a sense, familiar folk devils. Yet the current association of the crisis of *masculinity* with, primarily, these groups is itself profoundly misleading. As Walklate has argued:

> ... the following question should be asked: what makes the often rude and belligerent *behaviour* of the old boys network in the House of Commons any different from the lads who shout, whistle and jostle hanging about on the street corner? The reply has to be that in behavioural terms, very little. As expressions of masculine behaviour, the reply also has to be very little. What differs, of course, is their public and political *acceptability*. (Walklate, 1995: 178; original emphasis)

At the present moment, I have argued, the 'dangerous' masculinities of working-class and underclass youth are in fact mediating complex concerns around the economy, the family, the idea of the social and this seemingly ubiquitous concept of the 'crisis of masculinity'.

Beyond the 'crisis of masculinity'

> Britain is increasingly witnessing the consequences of the current crisis for men. Growing male unemployment has brought an end to the traditional 'breadwinner' role, leaving more men on the margins of society. Crime is predominantly a male activity. At schools, girls now generally outperform boys. At home, the numbers of families without fathers are rising. Mental health problems and suicide are increasingly common amongst young men, whilst men generally neglect their health and lead shorter lives as a consequence.
>
> (Publicity material for the Working With Men conference 'What Next for Men?', 25 October 1996)

The much-heralded 'crisis of masculinity', so central to recent debates around men and crime, has been a cipher for some wider anxieties. The terrain of masculine crisis encompasses a broad range of concerns and issues relating to a perceived diminution of points of attachment to collective life or, at the very least, the transitory nature of such points of attachment. As it is presently being articulated in relation to the crimes of men, this masculine crisis discourse evokes some powerful images; of anti-social unpartnered men living alone (outwith the family), of 'unmarriageable' underclass males (rejecting the family), of 'wild' youth and 'dangerous' masculinities, of men who are increasingly unable to cope, whether after marriage breakdown or on the loss of employment, of other men who are seeking to assert their 'true' masculinities, be it as assertive and controlling fathers, through involvement in crime or, for some, in the mythopoetic self-actualisation of those who seek to celebrate the 'deep masculine' as a source of ontological security in an increasingly uncertain world. Culturally, during the 1990s, the 'new barbarianism' of the underclass has come to co-exist with the 'new laddishness' of the affluent male consumer: the latter denotes the playfulness of a (heterosexual) irony and distanced performativity, of 'men behaving badly'; the former a more insidious, dangerous masculinity. Yet each speaks of a profound tension around just what it means for men to behave 'badly' in the first place.

Across socio-economic groups the judgement of 'manliness' has become dispersed, fragmented and de-traditionalised. Its meaning has come to float free from what were once (or at least appeared to be) established sources of masculine identity (the 'good father', the breadwinner, the sexually potent man, and so forth). In this process the cognitive, ethical and aesthetic reconfiguration of the men/gender relation, and of the individual and collective experience of 'being' a man in western society, has itself come to take on the language of crisis, contestation and resistance. Ideas about men's achievements and social status – previously indelible markers of masculine social experience – have been relativised through the pressures of economic and cultural shifts which have resulted in a profound re-evaluation of what 'being a man' is about (Hearn, 1996). Within this process, I have argued, crime has had a powerful, symbolic significance at the very moment – indeed, it has been enmeshed with – the ways in which the crisis of masculinity discourse has become a cipher, a catch-all term bound up with the transitions and tensions which have marked postmodernity. The idea of the 'crisis of masculinity', I have argued, is an essentially contested notion which has facilitated and been mobilised within some politically diverse interpretations of the men/crime relation. Whatever it may mean for criminology at the turn of the century to seek to 'take masculinity seriously', it is essential that it address the double-edged and potentially reactionary nature of the ways in which these ideas of masculine 'crisis' and 'renewal' are presently being articulated in debates around men's crimes and criminality.

Whither criminology?

Where does all this leave criminology? We have seen above (p. 18) how R.W. Connell, writing the foreword to James Messerschmidt's *Masculinities and Crime*, had sought to praise Messerschmidt's text as 'part of a conceptual revolution in the social sciences, reflecting profound changes in our understanding of everyday life . . . a time when questions of gender and sexual politics, femininity and masculinity, have been brought out of obscurity and seen as key issues in our society' (Connell, 1993: vii). The publication a year apart of Newburn and Stanko's edited collection *Just Boys Doing Business?* (1994a) and Messerschmidt's *Masculinities and Crime* (1993) can certainly be seen as a sign that the 'conceptual revolution' within the social sciences to which Connell refers – the study of men *as men* prompted (in large part) by the second wave of feminism – has at long last (and rather belatedly) reached the shores of criminology (see also Messerschmidt, 1997). Judging from the frequency with which this masculinity/crime relation is presently being referred to, I have suggested in Chapter 1, it might appear to the casual observer that a veil of ignorance has been (or is about to be) lifted as, thanks largely to feminism, a 're-vitalised' criminology can now begin to critically engage with that which had been before it all along – the maleness of crime. Criminology is at long last, it would seem, seeking to 'take masculinity seriously' by addressing the pervasive, overwhelming, apparently obvious, and yet seemingly so difficult to explain, 'maleness' of crime and the institutions of criminal justice (the pervasive masculinism, for example, of the police, courts and the prison system). It has become almost a truism, the mantra of (critical, post-feminist?) criminological enlightenment, to declare an awareness of that which had been before us all along – the fact that the vast majority of crimes are committed by men and that crime is, in so many ways, a matter of 'just boys doing business' (Newburn and Stanko, 1994a). Increasingly, it would seem, even the most 'mainstream' and traditional texts of the criminological establishment can no longer ignore the 'masculinity question' (see, for example, Carlen and Jefferson, 1996; Goodey, 1997; Maguire et al., 1997).

Such a 'masculinity turn' in criminology, an overtly pro-feminist *critical* study of men and the social construction of masculinity/ies, I have argued in this book, is problematic in a number of respects. The note of caution I have sought to sound arises, firstly, from a concern with the problematic way in which 'masculinity' is presently being theorised within this work (broadly, through reference to the sex/gender binary); and, secondly, to the ways in which this 'masculinity turn' within criminology is, more generally, itself conceptualising existing feminist critiques of masculinity and criminal justice. The issues raised by this engagement with masculinity are fundamental. They pertain not just to debates about the 'maleness of crime' but also to questions about the viability and future of the discipline of criminology per se as well as those present 'public' and high-profile political debates which are taking place around crime, social in/exclusion and the social bond.

This book has sought to do something different. I have argued that it is misleading to construct men as 'criminal' or, indeed, as 'non-criminal' social subjects in such way as to presume a simple association between biological men and an authoritative or oppressive identity (or, indeed, a 'hegemonic' masculinity). Nor can it be presumed that this identity relates unproblematically to a range of activities which may be deemed 'masculine' in any particular context. What is necessary, I have suggested, is to address the ways *in which*, and the kinds of bodies *on which*, specific subjectivities are constituted at particular historical moments. In so doing, I have argued, social constructionist arguments of sexual identity, in which the notion of gender is privileged over sex, can themselves be seen as being implicitly phallocentric (Gatens, 1996; Grosz, 1994). In such accounts, we have seen, femininity appears as a learning of certain kinds of 'feminine' behaviour, masculinity as a learning or 'accomplishing' of certain kinds of 'masculine' behaviour. In terms of the resulting politics, we have seen in this chapter, such an approach has tended to replicate the feminist tactic of 're-socialisation'; that is, one of re-socialising or re-gendering men away from their 'oppressive' masculinity, making men 'more like' women. Much of the emerging work on masculinities and crime carries on in the long line of 'gender feminists' in this regard, using 'masculinity' for various descriptive and analytic purposes but seldom engaging with what I have suggested is the problematic concept of masculinity itself in terms of its implicit *hetero*sexual normativity. Such accounts assume that consciousness is primary and, importantly, that the historical and cultural specificity of a sexed (as different) experience can itself be transformed through a conscious change in behavioural practices. De-gendering as a programme, it has been suggested, presumes that the sexed body – in this case, the sexed (as) male body – is passive and completely irrelevant in determining consciousness. In this concluding chapter I have sought to explore what some of the implications of this approach may be for seeking to understand 'gendered' intervention in the field of criminal justice and, in particular, to how this relates to what I have suggested has been this neglected question of the (hetero)sexuality of both 'masculinity' and, indeed, 'crime' (cf., in sociology, Stein and Plummer, 1996).

There is, of course, a history to all this and to begin to make sense of the present masculinity and crime debate it is instructive to look to the past. This book, therefore, has sought to engage with criminology's conceptual and institutional development. I have suggested that the undoubted insights and many valuable contributions towards understanding the men/crime relation which have emerged from the present 'masculinity turn' may themselves, ultimately, be limited by a conceptual grounding in, and continued faith in the viability of, a modernist and positivist criminological project. In their endeavours to reconceptualise masculinity what has emerged is a perspective which continues to be based on a sex/gender dualism. It is this dualism which (amongst others) has become increasingly problematic within recent postmodern feminist and queer theoretical scholarship. It has been a central argument of this book that it must be open to question whether, bearing in mind the institutional nature of the discipline (Chapter 2), criminology will ever be able to 'take masculinity seriously' whilst keeping in place the assumptions, methodologies, concepts and categories of those very systems of thought which have, thus far, proved to be so inadequate in seeking to account for the 'sex question'. It is, I have argued, the inherent vagueness and instability of the concept of 'maleness/masculinity' *itself* which is at the heart of these tensions which pervade the engagement with masculinity. Repeatedly citing 'hegemonic masculinity' as an indicator of theoretical *nous* cannot, importantly, wish away these tensions and contradictions. Although both criminology and criminal justice practice may tentatively be addressing 'masculinities and crime', this engagement is taking place in such a way that questions of sex, difference and power continue to remain marginal and peripheral. Ultimately, I have suggested, it is likely that any calling of *men* to account for their crimes will itself continue to be systematically negated as long as the focus of analysis is the concept of masculinity.

The question remains therefore: where does this leave criminology? The masculinity and crime agenda may, I have suggested, ultimately obfuscate as much as it reveals about the relationship between men and crime. The 'politics of masculinity' are at present so vague and uncertain that, whether it be in conversations or in academic conferences and seminars (in criminology or otherwise), people often appear to be talking about different things; what masculinity is, or rather what it signifies, is deeply contested and uncertain. Ideas of masculinity – even purportedly progressive, liberationist and pro-feminist ones – are themselves embedded within modernist and policing discourses concerned with constructing 'appropriate' or 'inappropriate' (be it feminist, patriarchal or 'anti-sexist') models of a 'gendered' practice – of what men can/should do. In each case this question of the 'appropriateness' of an individual man's gender identity is brought into issue in particular ways (Hearn, 1996: 207). Can men be pro-feminist? Are men 'sexist'? What do men want? Why is he writing about 'masculinity'? Are men the 'new victims' of complex social change? Has feminism itself gone 'too far' in its critique of men? Such questions *abound* in this work and in these debates. Yet ultimately the search to unpack or understand the 'masculinity of crime' continues to remain a bit like trying to square the circle.

This is not to end on a note of pessimism. It is, in part, to recognise that men 'turning to' feminism in search of a conceptual grounding for an engagement with masculinity and crime is itself fraught with difficulties. At present, it is clear, feminism faces some difficult questions. In contrast to reproducing social constructionist feminist accounts based on sex/gender, it is a focus on sexual difference and sex-specific corporeality which, I have argued, can provide some powerful conceptual tools which might facilitate an engagement with the crimes of men. Such an analysis is not removed from questions of policy and practice; it is not a matter of a deconstructive parlour game, divorced from questions of the materiality of discursive practices. Although the critical projects of Anglo-American feminism have for some time been trying to cope with the displacement of Woman (Murphy, 1996: 59), this project has also entailed, I have suggested, reconfiguring the position of 'Man' within feminism. Such a questioning has been long overdue in both law and criminology. The male subject represented both in criminology and within much of feminism remains within a grip of identity binarisms. This, in turn, has important implications for the ways in which feminism's political subject 'Woman' and feminist criminology's subject 'Man' have been constructed. Just as feminism's 'Woman' has purported to represent the experiences of 'real' women, so feminism's 'Man' has been seen as representing the experiences of 'real' men. However, I have argued, this Man – and the (hegemonic) masculinity with which he has been associated – is a self which remains a phantasm, based on a distortion of the relationship between sex and gender. As Murphy writes, '... we have reached a time where identity can no longer be forged from the violent imbalance of the sex/gender binary pair, or from its reduction, or from the illusion of harmonious fusion' (1996: 63).

To conclude: it has not been my intention in this book to underestimate the importance and strengths of much of the recent work which has sought to tackle the issue of masculinity and crime. The questions this work has raised – about men, women, power and crime – are crucial. It is ultimately important to keep in mind, however, where this 'masculinity turn' in criminology may be leading. Is it to be the 'saving grace' of a humanist criminology, a criminology which remains wedded to positivist (and, for some, masculinist) assumptions? To merely replace one 'truth' about 'men and crime' with another would be to reproduce the dominant political economy in which one authority has *already* come to speak for all other epistemological and subjective positions. As it stands, feminism has challenged the very idea of 'criminology' by exposing the epistemological failings of a discipline whose hitherto sociological engagement with 'masculinity' had, in any case, taken place through reference to a range of concepts and categories which were inextricably linked with, and bound up in, dominant knowledge formations. Sex/gender are just two of the binaries which have structured this discourse. Perhaps, in the end, what we face here is something of a paradox. The 'masculinity turn' in criminology would appear to be undermining, at the same time as it is held out as potentially 'saving', a discipline which has been and remains wracked with doubt about the ways in which its masculinist 'explanations' of crime have historically been constituted; explanations which have so obviously failed to account for the crimes of men as men as well as, quite spectacularly, the crimes of women. It is, alternatively, possible to seek to reposition the sexed body and the status of sex within discourses around crime, offer the possibility of sexual difference and, in so doing, seek to understand the criminal(ised) bodies of men *and* women in cultural and psychical terms. Such an approach might highlight 'the manner in which sexual difference becomes socially, politically and ethically significant ... [an approach] ... capable of opening the present to different ways of being a woman or a man, along with different ways of negotiating that difference' (Gatens, 1996: 148). Without an adequate conceptual framework it is likely that any attempt to 'take masculinity seriously' will collapse before it begins.

Notes

1. The city of Newcastle upon Tyne, christened the 'birthplace of ram-raiding' (*The Independent*, 17 May 1995), has for a long time been frequently associated with crime and criminality within a range of representations of

youth crime and disorder in the British media: see, for example, Kershaw and Macbeth (1993); 'Brave New World on the Tyne', *The Independent on Sunday*, 4 December 1994. For an alternative, and critical, view of such associations between Newcastle and 'otherness', see Campbell (1992).

2. This phrase is borrowed from the title of a conference stream at the Law and Society Association Annual Conference, St Louis, 1997. On the idea of 'post'-heterosexuality see Collier (1996a); Smart (1996a, 1996b).

3. Walklate (1995: 182), for example, concludes her discussion of gender and crime with the recognition that, one hundred years on, there are many questions which still 'remain to be answered' by the discipline. The search for a general theory of crime is explicitly rejected; far from engaging in a search for 'broad (and brave) assertions', what is advocated is a 'focused specificity of the relationship between particular crimes and particular context(s)' (Walklate, 1995: 183).

4. As, indeed, it is within a range of public debates around the meaning of sex difference: for example, 'Genes Say Boys Will Be Boys and Girls Will Be Sensitive', *The Guardian*, 12 June 1997; see Orbach and Schwartz (1997).

5. Note the seeming inability of the criminal justice system to deal with the case of the transsexual prisoner ('Jail Nightmare for Prisoners of Gender', *The Independent*, 8 May 1995). The fixity of the man/woman, straight/gay dualism more generally was particularly evident in the controversy surrounding the Bishop of London's pronouncement in 1995 that his sexuality was 'ambiguous' (*The Guardian*, 4 March 1995).

6. In Britain, as elsewhere, it has led to an apparently insurmountable rise in prison numbers and fashion for US-style 'boot camps' and electronic tagging. It can also be seen in the context of the emergence of a transnational 'corrections-commercial complex' (Lilly et al., 1995: 221) in which lucrative private corporations, by increasingly providing goods and services to corrections institutions, themselves profit economically and can thus be seen as having a vested interest in the perpetuation of criminal justice 'tough-speak'. Within the terms of the dominant dualism, the alternative – being 'soft' on crime – appears an increasingly unattractive and politically unacceptable option.

7. See, for example, *The Independent*, Editorial 30 August 1994; 1 September 1994, letter from Vivien Stern.

8. In Britain growing evidence of abuse in state-run children's homes, going back at least twenty years, prompted the inquiry by Sir William Utting. The subsequent report, published in 1997, chronicles accounts of widespread poor education and health, high rates of mental illness, bullying and intimidation, and the threat of 'sexual terrorists', men who it argues still work in the care system preying on young, vulnerable victims. It is estimated that nearly five thousand care workers and former care workers are now on a government 'black-list', all having received convictions or police cautions (*The Independent*, 20 November 1997; 'Care System Fails Children', *The Guardian*, 20 November 1997; also Snow (1996)).

9. Generally, on therapeutic regimes in criminal justice, see, for example, *HMP Grendon Therapeutic Community: A Reconviction Study*, Home Office Research and Statistics No 53, 1997. Also Vennard et al. (1997). As examples of the 'gender awareness' strategy in practice, note the various 'Education for Parenting' classes held at youth prisons and aimed at 'education for fatherhood'. Also a range of Detached Youth Work projects: see Longbenton Youth Project (1994). Of all the areas in which working with men has been addressed in relation to crime, the most discussed and contentious area perhaps remains that of responses to men's violence against women and children (see Braithwaite and Daly, 1994; on programmes specifically designed to work with

violent men aimed at changing their abusive behaviour, see Dobash et al., 1996).

10. 'If we conceive the body to be neutral and passive and consciousness to be socially determined, then we are at least halfway to a behavioural conception of subjectivity' (Gatens, 1996: 8).

11. This issue has been central to debates around the treatment of sex offenders (see, for example, 'Penis Test for Deviancy Keeps Lifers Behind Bars', *The Observer*, 28 May 1995; 'Castration by Knife May Be the Kindest Cut After All', *Independent on Sunday*, 20 July 1997; 'Child Sex Attackers Face Castration', *The Guardian*, 10 October 1997; see further Hedderman and Sugg, 1996).

12. Asking 'how to make men socially acceptable?', *The Independent* newspaper suggested capturing the underlying assumption of this approach, that the answer may simply be to 'teach them some manners and get them to hang out with the girls – but keep their genes out of it' (*The Independent*, 13 June 1997).

13. It has been estimated that most school pupils in Britain have been bullied by the age of 12 and that school bullying can start from the age of three (*The Guardian*, 27 October 1995; *The Independent*, 27 October 1995). This problem is particularly acute in relation to the bullying of pupils who are gay or believed to be gay. More than 80 per cent of schools taking part in a study of homophobia in schools reported verbal bullying to be common: *The Guardian*, 13 March 1998. It has also been estimated that weapons are now carried in one in ten British schools (*Violence in Schools*, Department of Education, London; Suzy Lamplugh Trust as reported in *The Guardian*, 7 October 1997). One third of adult prisoners and one half of young offenders report being beaten or threatened ('Culture of Bullying Endemic in Prison', *The Guardian*, 3 October 1996). In 1996 Vijay Singh, a thirteen-year-old schoolboy, hanged himself from a banister in his home in Manchester, England. In the days before his death he had written this poem about his suffering at the hands of bullies:

> I'm frightened and scared
> my body has been shaking
> my mouth open wide and
> frozen, the tears drop as
> they destroy my face
> take my money and flee
> to ware they can go. Bullies
> I call out they have no feelings at all
> (Poem about Bullies by Vijay Singh, reproduced in *The Daily Telegraph*, 17 October 1996)

Bibliography

Acker, J. (1990) 'Hierarchies, Jobs, Bodies: A Theory of Gendered Organization', *Gender and Society*, 4 (2): 139–58.

Adkins, L. (1995) *Gendered Work*, Milton Keynes: Open University Press.

Alcock, P. (1984) 'Renumeration or Remarriage? The Matrimonial and Family Proceedings Act 1984', *Journal of Law and Society*, 11 (3): 357–68.

Alder, C. and Polk, K. (1996) 'Masculinity and Child Homicide', *British Journal of Criminology*, 36 (3): 396–411.

Allen, H. (1987) *Justice Unbalanced*, Milton Keynes: Open University Press.

Allen, J. (1987) ' "Mundane" Men: Historians, Masculinity and Masculinism', *Historical Studies*, 22: 617–28.

Allen, J. (1989) 'Men, Crime and Criminology: Recasting the Questions', *International Journal of the Sociology of Law*, 17 (1): 19–39.

Arendell, T. (1995) *Fathers and Divorce*, London: Sage.

Ashton, D., and Lowe, G. (eds) (1991) *Making Their Way: Education, Training and the Labour Market in Canada and Britain*, Milton Keynes: Open University Press.

Askew, S. and Ross, C. (1988) *Boys Don't Cry: Boys and Sexism in Education*, Milton Keynes: Open University Press.

Atkins, S. and Hoggett, B. (1984) *Women in Law*, Oxford: Blackwell.

Audit Commission (1996) *Audit Commission Executive Briefing: Preventing Crime Among Young People*, London: HMSO.

Bagguley, P. and Mann, K. (1992) ' "Idle Thieving Bastards": Scholarly Representations of the Underclass', *Work, Employment and Society*, 6 (1): 113–26.

Balding, J. (1996) *Young People: 10th Report*, Exeter University, Schools Education Unit.

Barker, P. (1996) 'Loner in Our Midst', *The Guardian*, 15 March.

Bauman, Z. (1992) *Intimations of Postmodernity*, London: Routledge.

Beck, U. (1992) *Risk Society: Towards a New Modernity*, London: Sage.

Becker, H. (1973) *Outsiders: Studies in the Sociology of Deviance*, New York: Free Press.

Beirne, P. and Messerschmidt, J.W. (1991) *Criminology*, San Diego: CA: Harcourt, Brace Jovanovich.

Beirne, P. and Sumner, C. (1997) 'Editorial Statement', *Theoretical Criminology*, 1 (1): 5–13.

Bell, C.M. (1995) ' "All I Really Need to Know I Learned in Kindergarten (Playing Soccer)": A Feminist Parable of Legal Academia', *Yale Journal of Law and Feminism*, 7: 133–6.

Bell, D. and Valentine, G. (1995) 'The Sexed Self: Strategies of Performance, Sites of Resistance', in S. Pile and N. Thrift (eds) *Mapping the Subject: Geographies of Cultural Transformation*, Routledge, London.

Bell, V. (1991) 'Beyond the "Thorny Question": Feminisms, Foucault and the Desexualisation of Rape', *International Journal of the Sociology of Law*, 19: 83–100.

Bem, S. (1974) 'The Measurement of Psychological Androgyny', *Journal of Clinical Psychology*, 42 (2): 155–62.

Benhabib, S. (1992) *Situating the Self: Gender, Community and Postmodernism in Contemporary Ethics*, London: Routledge.

Benhabib, S., Butler, J., Cornell, D. and Fraser, N. (1995) *Feminist Contentions: A Philosophical Exchange*, New York: Routledge.

Benoit-Scott, D. (1996) 'Shattering the Instrumental-Expressive Myth: The Power of Women's Networks in Corporate Government Affairs', *Gender and Society*, 10 (3): 232–47.

Berotia, C. and Drakich, J. (1993) 'The Fathers' Rights Movement: Contradictions in Rhetoric and Practice', *Journal of Family Issues*, 14 (4): 592–615.

Bird, S. (1996) 'Welcome to the Men's Club: Homosociality and the Maintenance of Hegemonic Masculinity', *Gender and Society*, 10 (2): 120–32.

Bly, R. (1990) *Iron John*, Shaftesbury, Dorset: Element Books.

Blyth, S. (1996) 'The Law of Feminist Theory: Men, Masculinities and Feminist Theory (or) "Speaking Softly and Carrying a Big Stick" ', paper presented to 'Women and the Law' conference, University of Durham, August.

Bonnett, A. (1996) 'The New Primitives: Identity, Landscape and Cultural Appropriation in the Mythopoetic Men's Movement', *Antipode* 28 (3): 273–91.

Boone, J. (1992) 'On Me(n) and Feminism: Who(se) is the Sex that Writes?', in D. Porter (ed.) *Between Men and Feminism*, London: Routledge.

Booth, W. (1976) 'In Darkest England', in P. Keating (ed.) *Into Unknown England 1866–1913*, London: Fontana.

Bourdieu, P. (1977) *Outline of a Theory of Practice*, Cambridge: Cambridge University Press.

Bourdieu, P. (1984) *Distinction: A Social Critique of the Judgement of Taste*, Cambridge, MA: Harvard University Press.

Bourgeois, P. (1996) 'In Search of Masculinity: Violence, Respect and Sexuality Amongst Puerto Rican Crack Dealers in East Harlem', *British Journal of Criminology*, 36 (3): 412–27.

Bower, L. (1994) 'Queer Acts and the Politics of "Direct Address": Rethinking Law, Culture and Community', *Law and Society Review*, 28: 1009.

Box, S. (1983) *Power, Crime and Mystification*, London: Tavistock.

Braidotti, R. (1989) 'The Politics of Ontological Difference', in T. Brennan (ed.) *Between Feminism and Psychoanalysis*, London: Routledge.

Braithwaite, J. and Daly, K. (1994) 'Masculinities, Violence and Communitarian Control', in T. Newburn and E.A. Stanko (eds) *Just Boys Doing Business? Men, Masculinities and Crime*, London: Routledge.

Brake, M. (1984) *Comparative Youth Cultures: The Sociology of Youth Culture and Youth Subcultures in America, Britain and Canada*, London: Routledge and Kegan Paul.

Bristow, J. (1992) 'Men After Feminism: Sexual Politics Twenty Years On', in D. Porter (ed.) *Between Men and Feminism*, London: Routledge.

Brittan, A. (1989) *Masculinity and Power*, Oxford: Basil Blackwell.

Brod, H. (ed.) (1987) *The Making of Masculinities: The New Men's Studies*, Boston: Allen and Unwin.

Brooker, E. (1995) 'Mindful of Violence: Can Violent Men Be "Cured" Through Therapy?', *The Guardian*, 3 April.

Brown, B. (1986) 'Women and Crime: The Dark Figures of Criminology', *Economy and Society*, 15: 355–402.

Brown, B. (1990) 'Reassessing the Critique of Biologism', in L. Gelsthorpe and A. Morris (eds) *Feminist Perspectives in Criminology*, Buckingham: Open University Press.

Browne, R. (1995) 'Schools and the Construction of Masculinity', in R. Browne and

R. Fletcher (eds) *Boys in Schools: Addressing the Real Issues, Behaviour, Values and Relationships*, Sydney: Finch Publishing.

Burgess, A. (1997) *Fatherhood Reclaimed*, London: Vermilion.

Burgess, A. and Ruxton, S. (1996) *Men and Their Children: Proposals for Public Policy*, London: Institute for Public Policy Research.

Burgess, E.W. (1928) 'The Growth of the City', in R. Park, E.W. Burgess and R. MacKenzie (eds) *The City*, Chicago: University of Chicago Press.

Busch, K. and Cavanaugh, J. (1986) 'The Story of Multiple Murder: Preliminary Examination of the Interface Between Epistemology and Methodology', *Journal of Interpersonal Violence*, 1: 5–23.

Butler, J. (1990) *Gender Trouble: Feminism and the Subversion of Identity*, London: Routledge.

Butler, J. (1992) 'Contingent Foundations: Feminism and the Question of "Postmodernism" ', in J. Butler and J.W. Scott (eds) *Feminists Theorize the Political*, New York: Routledge.

Butler, J. (1993) *Bodies That Matter: On the Discursive Limits of Sex*, London: Routledge.

Butler, J. and Scott, J.W. (eds) (1992) *Feminists Theorise the Political*, New York: Routledge.

Cain, M. (1990a) 'Realist Philosophy and the Standpoint Epistemologies or Feminist Criminology as Successor Science', in L. Gelsthorpe and A. Morris (eds) *Feminist Perspectives in Criminology*, Milton Keynes: Open University Press.

Cain, M. (1990b) 'Towards Transgression: New Directions in Feminist Criminology', *International Journal of the Sociology of Law*, 1: 1–18.

Cain, M. (1994) 'The Symbol Traders', in M. Cain and C. Harrington (eds) *Lawyers in a Postmodern World*, Milton Keynes: Open University Press.

Campbell, A. (1984) *The Girls in the Gang*, Cambridge, MA: Basil Blackwell.

Campbell, B. (1992) 'Lost in Translation', *The Guardian*, 8 December.

Campbell, B. (1993) *Goliath: Britain's Dangerous Places*, London: Virago.

Campbell, B. (1995) 'Boys Learning to be Boys', *New Times*, 8 July: 2–3.

Campbell, B. (1996) 'The Problem with Arms and Men', *The Guardian*, 23 July.

Campbell, D. (1996) 'He Was a Loner: He Kept His Clichés to Himself', *The Guardian*, 13 July.

Canaan, J.E. (1991) 'Is "Doing Nothing" Just Boys' Play? Integrating Feminist and Cultural Studies Perspectives on Working-Class Young Men's Masculinity', in S. Franklin, C. Lury and J. Stacey (eds) *Off-Centre: Feminism and Cultural Studies*, London: HarperCollins.

Canaan, J.E. (1996) ' "One Thing Leads to Another": Drinking, Fighting and Working Class Masculinities, in M. Mac an Ghaill (ed.) *Understanding Masculinities*, Buckingham: Open University Press.

Canaan, J.E. and Griffin, C. (1990) 'The New Men's Studies: Part of the Problem or Part of the Solution?', in J. Hearn and D. Morgan (eds) *Men, Masculinities and Social Theory*, London: Unwin Hyman.

Carlen, P. (1983) *Women's Imprisonment*, London: Routledge and Kegan Paul.

Carlen, P. (1988) *Women, Crime and Poverty*, Milton Keynes: Open University Press.

Carlen, P. and Jefferson, J. (eds) (1996) *British Journal of Criminology: Special Issue – Masculinities and Crime*, 33 (6).

Carlen, P. and Worrall, A. (1987) *Gender, Crime and Justice*, Milton Keynes: Open University Press.

Carrigan, T., Connell, R. and Lee, J. (1985) 'Towards a New Sociology of Masculinity', *Theory and Society*, 14: 551–604.

Carrington, K. (1993) *Offending Girls: Sex, Youth and Justice*, St Leonards, NSW: Allen and Unwin.

Cavadino, M. and Dignan, J. (1997) *The Penal System: An Introduction*, London: Sage.

Cavanagh, K. and Cree, V. (eds) (1988) *Working with Men: Feminism and Social Work*, London: Routledge.

Chambliss, W.J. (1973) 'The Saints and the Roughnecks', *Society*, 11 (1): 24–31.

Chambliss, W.J. (1975) 'Toward a Political Economy of Crime', *Theory and Society*, 2: 152.

Chapman, T. (1993) 'Toys for the Boys: Gender and Car Crime', in *Masculinity and Crime: Issues of Theory and Practice*, Conference Report, Brunel University, Centre for Criminal Justice Research: 143–50.

Chodorow, N. (1978) *The Reproduction of Mothering: Psychoanalysis and the Sociology of Gender*, Berkeley: University of California Press.

Clover, C. (1993) 'White Noise', *Sight and Sound*, May: 6–9.

Cloward, R. and Ohlin, L. (1961) *Delinquency and Opportunity: A Theory of Delinquent Gangs*, London: Routledge and Kegan Paul.

Cohen, A. (1955) *Delinquent Boys: The Culture of the Gang*, New York: Free Press.

Cohen, E.G. and Farrington, D.P. (1994) 'Who are the Most Influential Criminologists in the English-Speaking World?', *British Journal of Criminology*, 34 (2): 204–25.

Cohen, P. (1972) 'Subcultural Conflict and Working-Class Community', *Working Papers in Cultural Studies*, 2: 5–52. Centre for Cultural Studies, University of Birmingham.

Cohen, P. (1981) 'Policing the Working-Class City', in M. Fitzgerald, G. McLennan and J. Pawson (eds) *Crime and Society: Readings in History and Theory*, London: Routledge and Kegan Paul.

Collier, R (1991) 'Masculinism, Law and Law Teaching', *International Journal of the Sociology of Law*, 19: 427–51.

Collier, R (1992) ' "The Art of Living the Married Life": Representations of Male Heterosexuality in Law', *Social and Legal Studies*, 1 (4): 543–63.

Collier, R (1994a) 'Ten Years On: What Is To Be Done About Law and Order?', *Northern Ireland Law Quarterly*, 45 (3): 308–16.

Collier, R. (1994b) 'The Campaign Against the Child Support Act 1991: "Errant Fathers" and "Family Men" ', *Family Law*, July: 384–7.

Collier, R. (1994c) 'Back to the Woods and on to the Streets: Change and Continuity in Ideas of "Crisis" and Renewal', paper presented to the Legal Identities/Global Cultures conference, University of Warwick, September.

Collier, R. (1995a) *Masculinity, Law and the Family*, London: Routledge.

Collier, R (1995b) 'A Father's "Normal Love"? Masculinities, Criminology and the Family', in R. Dobash, R. Dobash and L. Noakes (eds) *Gender and Crime*, Cardiff: University of Wales Press.

Collier, R. (1996a) ' "Coming Together?": Post-Heterosexuality, Masculine Crisis and the New Men's Movement', *Feminist Legal Studies*, 4 (1): 3–48.

Collier, R. (1996b) 'Just (More) Boys Doing Business? Gender, Sex and the "Masculinity Turn" in Criminology: Review Article', *Social and Legal Studies* 5 (2): 271–8.

Collier, R. (1997a) 'After Dunblane: Crime, Corporeality and the (Hetero)Sexing of the Bodies of Men', *Journal of Law and Society*, 24 (2): 177–99.

Collier, R. (1997b) '(Un)Sexy Bodies: The Making of Professional Legal Masculinities', in C. McGlynn (ed.) *Legal Feminisms: Theory and Practice*, Aldershot: Dartmouth.

Collier, R. (1998) ' "Nutty Professors", "Men in Suits" and "New Entrepreneurs": Corporeality, Subjectivity and Change in the Law School and Legal Practice', *Social and Legal Studies*, 7 (1): 27–53.

Collinson, D. and Hearn, J. (1994) 'Naming Men as Men: Implications for Work, Organisation and Management', *Gender, Work and Organisation*, 1 (1): 2–32.

Collinson, D. and Hearn, J. (eds) (1996) *Men As Managers, Managers As Men: Critical Perspectives on Men, Masculinities and Managements*, London: Sage.

Collinson, M. (1996) 'In Search of the High Life: Drugs, Crime, Masculinities and Consumption', *British Journal of Criminology*, 36 (3): 428–43.

Connell, R.W. (1987) *Gender and Power*, Cambridge: Polity Press.

Connell, R.W. (1989) 'Cool Guys, Swots and Wimps: The Inter-play of Masculinity and Education', *Oxford Review of Education*, 15 (3): 291–303.

Connell, R.W. (1993) 'Foreword', to J.W. Messerschmidt, *Masculinities and Crime: Critique, and Reconceptualization of Theory*, Lanham, MD: Rowman and Littlefield.

Connell, R.W. (1995) *Masculinities*, Cambridge: Polity Press.

Coote, A. (1994) *Families, Children and Crime*, London: IPPR Publishers.

Cornell, D. (1991) *Beyond Accommodation: Ethical Feminism, Deconstruction and the Law*, London: Routledge.

Corrigan, P. (1979) *Schooling with the Smash Street Kids*, London, Macmillan.

Cousins, M. (1980) '*Mens Rea*: A Note on Sexual Difference, Criminology and the Law', in P. Carlen and M. Collinson (eds) *Radical Issues in Criminology*, Oxford: Martin Robertson.

Coward, R. (1994) 'Whipping Boys', *The Guardian*, 3 September.

Cullen Report (1996) *Report of the Public Inquiry into the Shootings at Dunblane Primary School on 13 March 1996*, Cmnd 3386; Chair: The Hon Lord Cullen.

Daly, K. (1993) *Gender, Crime and Punishment*, New Haven: Yale University Press.

Daly, K. (1997) 'Different Ways of Conceptualising Sex/Gender in Feminist Theory and Their Implications for Criminology', *Theoretical Criminology* 1 (1): 25–53.

Daly, K. and Chesney Lind, M. (1988) 'Feminism and Criminology', *Justice Quarterly*, 5 (4): 498–538.

Davies, C. (1996) 'The Sociology of the Professions and the Profession of Gender', *Sociology*, 30 (4): 661–78.

Davies, J. (ed.) (1993) *The Family: Is It Just Another Lifestyle Choice?* London: IEA Health and Welfare Unit.

Dennis, N. and Erdos, G. (1991) *Families Without Fatherhood*, London: Institute of Economic Affairs.

Dingwall, R., Eekalaar, J. and Murray, T. (1986) *The Protection of Children: State Intervention and Family Life*, Oxford: Basil Blackwell.

Dinnerstein, D. (1978) *The Rocking of the Cradle and the Ruling of the World*, London: Souvenir Press.

Diprose, R. (1994) *The Bodies of Women: Ethics, Embodiment and Sexual Difference*, London, Routledge.

Dobash, R.P., Dobash, R.E., Cavanagh, K. and Lewis, R. (1996) *Research Evaluation of Programmes for Violent Men*, The Scottish Office Central Research Unit, Edinburgh: The Scottish Office.

Dollimore, J. (1986) 'Homophobia and Sexual Difference', *Oxford Literary Review*, 8: 5–22.

Donzelot, J. (1980) *The Policing of Families*, London: Hutchinson.

Douglas, T. (1994) ' "New Men" and the Tensions of Pro-Feminism', *Social Alternatives*, 12 (4): 32–5.

Downs, D. (1966) *The Delinquent Solution*, London: Routledge and Kegan Paul.

Downes, D. and Rock, P. (1988) *Understanding Deviance*, Oxford: Clarendon Press.

Dowsett, G.W. (1993) ' "I'll Show You Mine if You Show Me Yours": Gay Men, Masculinity Research, Men's Studies and Sex', *Theory and Society*, 22: 697–709.

Duncan, N. (ed.) (1996) *Body Space: Destabilising Geographies of Gender and Sexuality*, London: Routledge.

Eastman, N. (1996) 'Madness or Badness?', *The Guardian* 22 October.

Eaton, M. (1986) *Justice for Women? Family, Court and Social Control*, Milton Keynes: Open University Press.

Eaton, M. (1993) *Women After Prison*, Milton Keynes: Open University Press.

Edley, N. and Wetherell, M. (1996) 'Masculinity, Power and Identity', in M. Mac an Ghaill (ed.) *Understanding Masculinities*, Buckingham: Open University Press.

Edwards, A. (1989) 'Sex/Gender, Sexism and Criminal Justice: Some Theoretical Considerations', *International Journal of the Sociology of Law*, 17: 165–84.

Edwards, T. (1990) 'Beyond Sex and Gender: Masculinity, Homosexuality and Social Theory', in J. Hearn and D. Morgan (eds) *Men, Masculinities and Social Theory*, London: Unwin Hyman.

Edwards, T. (1994) *Erotics and Politics*, London: Routledge.

Ehrenreich, B. (1983) *The Hearts of Men*, London: Pluto.

Faludi, S. (1992) *Backlash: The Undeclared War Against Women*, London: Chatto and Windus.

Farrell, W. (1993) *The Myth of Male Power: Why Men are the Disposable Sex*, New York: Simon and Schuster.

Farrington, D.P. (1972) 'Delinquency Begins at Home', *New Society*, 21: 495–7.

Farrington, D.P. (1994) 'Human Developments and Criminal Careers', in M. Maguire, R. Morgan, and R. Reiner (eds) *The Oxford Handbook of Criminology*, Oxford: Clarendon Press.

Fay, R. (1995) 'The Disenfranchised Father', *American Journal of Family Law*, 9 (1): 7–33.

Fergurson, E., Harrison, D. and McKay, R. (1996) 'Dunblane: the Story That Need Never Have Been Told', *The Observer*, 17 March.

Field, S. and Southgate, T. (1982) *Public Disorder*, London: Home Office, HMSO.

Fielding, N. (1994) 'Cop Canteen Culture', in T. Newburn and E.A. Stanko (eds) *Just Boys Doing Business? Men, Masculinities and Crime*, London: Routledge.

Fineman, M. (1994) 'Feminist Legal Scholarship and Women's Gendered Lives', in M. Cain and C. Harrington (eds) *Lawyers in a Postmodern World*, Buckingham: Open University Press.

Fineman, M. (1995) *The Neutered Mother, The Sexual Family and Other Twentieth Century Tragedies*, New York: Routledge.

Flax, J. (1990) 'Post-Modernism and Gender Relations in Feminist Theory', in L. Nicholson (ed.) *Feminism/Post-Modernism*, London: Routledge.

Foster, P. (1993) 'Are Men Now Suffering from Gender Injustice?', in A. Sinfield (ed.) *Poverty, Inequality and Justice: New Waverley Papers*, Social Policy Series No. 6, Edinburgh: University of Edinburgh Press.

Fox Harding, L. (1993a) ' "Alarm" versus "Liberation"? Responses to the Increase in Lone Parents – Part 1', *Journal of Social Welfare and Family Law*, 2: 101–12.

Fox Harding, L. (1993b) ' "Alarm" versus "Liberation"? Responses to the Increase in Lone Parents – Part 2', *Journal of Social Welfare and Family Law*, 3: 174–84.

Fraser, N. and Nicholson, L. (1990) 'Social Criticism Without Philosophy: An Encounter Between Feminism and Post-Modernism', in L Nicholson (ed.) *Feminism/Post-Modernism*, London: Routledge.

Frazer, E. and Lacey, N. (1993) *The Politics of Community*, Hemel Hempstead: Harvester Wheatsheaf.

Frosh, S. (1995) 'Time, Space and Otherness', in S. Pile and N. Thrift (eds) *Mapping the Subject: Geographies of Cultural Transformation*, London: Routledge.

Frye, M. (1983) *The Politics of Reality: Essays in Feminist Theory*, Trumansburg, NY: The Crossing Press.

Fuss, D. (1989) *Essentially Speaking: Feminism, Nature and Difference*, New York: Routledge.

Game, A. (1991) *Undoing the Social*, Milton Keynes: Open University Press.

Galanter, M. (1983) 'Mega-Law and Mega-Lawyering in the Contemporary United States', in R. Dingwall and P. Lewis (eds) *The Sociology of the Professions*, London: Macmillan.

Garland, D. (1985) *Punishment and Welfare*, Aldershot: Gower.

Garland, D. (1994) 'Of Crimes and Criminals: The Development of Criminology in Britain', in M. Maguire, R. Morgan, and R. Reiner (eds) *The Oxford Handbook of Criminology*, Oxford: Clarendon Press.

Gatens, M. (1983) 'A Critique of the Sex/Gender Distinction', in J. Allen and P. Patton (eds) *Beyond Marxism? Interventions After Marx*, Sydney: Intervention Publications.

Gatens, M. (1996) *Imaginary Bodies: Ethics, Power and Corporeality*, London: Routledge.

Gelsthorpe, L. (1986) 'Towards a Sceptical Look at Sexism', *International Journal of the Sociology of Law*, 14 (2): 125–52.

Gelsthorpe, L. (1989) *Sexism and the Female Offender*, Aldershot: Gower.

Gelsthorpe, L. and Morris, A. (1988) 'Feminism and Criminology in Britain', *British Journal of Criminology*, 28 (2): 93–110.

Gelsthorpe, L. and Morris, A. (eds) (1990a) *Feminist Perspectives in Criminology*, Milton Keynes: Open University Press.

Gelsthorpe, L. and Morris, A. (1990b) 'Introduction: Transforming and Trangressing Criminology', in L. Gelsthorpe and A. Morris (eds) *Feminist Perspectives in Criminology*, Milton Keynes: Open University Press.

Gibbs, J.T. and Merighi, J.R. (1994) 'Young Black Males: Marginality, Masculinity and Criminality', in T. Newburn and E.A. Stanko (eds) *Just Boys Doing Business? Men, Masculinities and Crime*, London: Routledge.

Giddens, A. (1991) *Modernity and Self-Identity*, Cambridge: Polity Press.

Gilmore, D. (1993) *Manhood in the Making: Cultural Concepts of Masculinity*, New Haven, CT: Yale University Press.

Goodey, J. (1997) 'Boys Don't Cry: Masculinities, Fear of Crime and Fearlessness', *British Journal of Criminology*, 37 (3): 401–18.

Graef, R. (1992) *Living Dangerously: Young Offenders in Their Own Words*, London: HarperCollins.

Graham, J. and Bowling, D. (1996) *Young People and Crime, Home Office Research Study 145*, London: HMSO.

Gramsci, A. (1971) *Selection From the Prison Notebooks*, London: Lawrence and Wishart.

Greenwood, V. (1981) 'The Myth of Female Crime', in A. Morris and L. Gelsthorpe (eds) *Women and Crime*, Cambridge: Cambridge University Institute of Criminology.

Gregory, J. and Lees, S. (1994) 'In Search of Gender Justice: Sexual Assault and the Criminal Justice System', *Feminist Review*, 48: 80–93.

Gresswell, D. and Hollin, C. (1994) 'Multiple Murder: A Review', *British Journal of Criminology*, 34 (1): 1–14.

Griffin, C. (1993) *Representations of Youth: The Study of Youth Culture in Britain and America*, Cambridge: Polity Press.

Groombridge, N. (1993) 'Car Crime: Is Joyriding a Male Driving Disorder?', in *Masculinity and Crime: Issues of Theory and Practice*, Conference Report, Brunel University, Centre for Criminal Justice Research, September: 25–35.

Groombridge, N. (1997) '(Br)others in Crime: Masculinities, Crime and Criminology', paper presented to the British Criminology Conference, Queen's University Belfast, July.

Grosz, E. (1987) 'Feminist Theory and the Challenge to Knowledge', *Women's Studies International Forum*, 10 (5): 208–17.

Grosz, E. (1990) 'A Note on Essentialism and Difference', in S. Unew (ed.) *Feminist Knowledge, Critique and Construct*, London: Routledge.

Grosz, E. (1994) *Volatile Bodies: Towards a Corporeal Feminism*, St Leonards, NSW: Allen and Unwin.

Grosz, E. and Probyn, E. (eds) (1995) *Sexy Bodies: Strange Carnalities of Feminism*, London: Routledge.

Gutterman, S. (1994) 'Postmodernism and the Interrogation of Masculinity', in M. Kimmell and M. Kaufman (eds) *Theorizing Masculinities*, London: Sage.

Gwynn, C. (1993) 'Women and Crime: The Failure of Traditional Theories and the Rise of Feminist Criminology', *Monash University Law Review*, 19 (1): 92–103.

Hagan, J. and Kay, F. (1995) *Gender in Practice: A Study of Lawyers' Lives*, New York: Oxford University Press.

Hahn Rafter, N. and Heidensohn, F. (eds) (1995) *International Feminist Perspectives in Criminology: Engendering a Discipline*, Buckingham: Open University Press.

Hall, S. and Jefferson, T. (1976) *Resistance Through Rituals: Youth Subcultures in Postwar Britain*, London: Hutchinson.

Hanke, R. (1992) 'Redesigning Men: Hegemonic Masculinity in Transition', in S. Craig (ed.) *Men, Masculinity and the Media*, London: Sage.

Harding, C. (1992) *Wingspan: Inside the Men's Movement*, New York: St Martins Press.

Harding, C. and Koffman, L. (1995) *Sentencing: Texts and Materials* (2nd edition), London: Sweet and Maxwell.

Harding, S. (1986) *The Science Question in Feminism*, Milton Keynes: Open University Press.

Harding, S. (ed.) (1987) *Feminism and Methodology*, Milton Keynes: Open University Press.

Hartley, R. (1959) 'Sex Role Pressures and the Socialisation of the Male Child', *Psychological Reports*, 5: 457–68.

Harvey, D. and Haraway, D. (1995) 'Nature, Politics and Possibilities: A Debate and Discussion with David Harvey and Donna Haraway', *Environment and Planning D: Society and Space*, 13: 507–27.

Haywood, C. and Mac an Ghaill, M. (1996) 'Schooling Masculinities', in M. Mac an Ghaill (ed.) *Understanding Masculinities*, Buckingham: Open University Press.

Hearn, J. (1987) *The Gender of Oppression: Men, Masculinity and the Critique of Marxism*, Brighton: Harvester Wheatsheaf.

Hearn, J. (1992) *Men in the Public Eye*, London: Routledge.

Hearn, J. (1993) 'The Politics of Essentialism and the Analysis of the "Men's Movement(s)" ', *Feminism and Psychology*, 3 (3): 405–9.

Hearn, J. (1994) 'Research on Men and Masculinities: Some Sociological Issues and Possibilities', *Australia and New Zealand Journal of Sociology*, 30 (1): 47–70.

Hearn, J. (1995) 'Imaging the Ageing of Men', in M. Featherstone and A. Wernick (eds) *Born Dying: Images of Ageing*, London: Routledge.

Hearn, J. (1996) 'Is Masculinity Dead? A Critique of the Concept of Masculinity', in M. Mac an Ghaill (ed.) *Understanding Masculinities*, Buckingham: Open University Press.

Hearn, J. and Melechi, A. (1992) 'The Trans-Atlantic Gaze: Masculinities, Youth and "the American Imaginary" ', in S. Craig (ed.) *Men, Masculinity and the Media*, London: Sage.

Hearn, J. and Morgan, D. (eds) (1990) *Men, Masculinities and Social Theory*, London: Unwin Hyman.

Hebdige, D. (1979) *Subculture: The Meaning of Style*, London: Methuen.

Hedderman, C. and Sugg, D. (1996) *Does Treating Sex Offenders Reduce Offending?*, Home Office Research and Statistics Directorate, No 45: London, HMSO.

Heidensohn, F. (1985) *Women and Crime*, London: Macmillan.

Heidensohn, F. (1987) 'Women and Crime: Questions for Criminology', in P. Carlen and A. Worrall (eds) *Gender, Crime and Justice*, Milton Keynes: Open University Press.

Heidensohn, F. (1989) *Crime and Society*, London: Macmillan.

Heidensohn, F. (1994) 'Gender and Crime', in M. Maguire, R. Morgan and R. Reiner (eds) *The Oxford Handbook of Criminology*, Oxford: Clarendon Press.

Heidensohn, F. (1995) 'Feminist Perspectives and Their Impact on Criminology and Criminal Justice in Britain', in N. Hahn Rafter and F. Heidensohn (eds), *International Feminist Perspectives in Criminology: Engendering a Discipline*, Buckingham: Open University Press.

Henriques, J., Hollway, W., Urwin, C., Venn, C. and Walkerdine, V. (1984) *Changing the Subject: Psychology, Social Regulation and Subjectivity*, London: Methuen.

Henry, S. and Milovanovic, D. (1996) *Constitutive Criminology: Beyond Postmodernism*, London: Sage.

Heward, C. (1996) 'Masculinities and Families', in M. Mac an Ghaill (ed.) *Understanding Masculinities*, Buckinghamshire: Open University Press.

Hollands, R. (1990) *The Long Transition: Class, Culture and Youth Training*, London, Macmillan.

Hollands, R. (1997) 'Shifting Youth Transitions and Identities', in J. Wheelock and A. Manussen (eds) *Households, Work and Economic Change: The Comparative Institutional Perspective*, London: Klewer.

Hollway, W. (1981) ' "I Just Wanted to Kill a Woman": Why? The Ripper and Male Sexuality', *Feminist Review*, 9: 33.

Hollway, W. (1989) *Subjectivity and Method in Psychology: Gender, Meaning and Science*, London. Sage.

Hollway, W. and Jefferson, T. (1994) 'Date Rape', paper presented to the 1994 American Society of Criminology Conference, Miami, November.

Home Office (1993) *Information on the Criminal Justice System in England and Wales*, London: HMSO.

Howe, A. (1994) *Punish and Critique: Towards a Feminist Analysis of Penality*, London: Routledge.

Hume, M. (1996) 'What's Wrong With Masculinity?', *Living Marxism*, May 1996: 4–5.

Hutton, W. (1995) *The State We're In*, London: Jonathan Cape.

Jackson, D. (1990) *Unmasking Masculinity: A Critical Autobiography*, London: Routledge.

Jackson, D. (1992) 'Riding for Joy', *Achilles' Heel*, Summer: 18.

Jackson, D. (1995) *Destroying the Baby in Themselves: Why Did the Two Boys Kill James Bulger?*, Nottingham: Mushroom Publications.

Jackson, D. and Salisbury, J. (1996) 'Why Should Secondary Schools Take Working With Boys Seriously?', *Gender and Education*, 8 (1): 103–15.

James, A. (1993) *Childhood Identities, Self and Social Relations in the Experience of the Child*, Edinburgh: Edinburgh University Press.

James, A. and Prout, A. (eds) (1990) *Constructing and Reconstructing Childhood*, London: Falmer Press.

Jardine, A. and Smith, P. (eds) (1987) *Men in Feminism*, London: Methuen.

Jefferson, T. (1992) 'Wheelin' and Stealin'', *Achilles' Heel*, Summer: 10–12.

Jefferson, T. (1994a) 'Theorizing masculine subjectivity', in T. Newburn and E.A. Stanko (eds) *Just Boys Doing Business? Men, Masculinities and Crime*, London: Routledge.

Jefferson, T (1994b) 'Crime, Criminology, Masculinity and Young Men', in A. Coote (ed.) *Families, Children and Crime*, London: IPPR Publishers.

Jefferson, T. (1996) 'From "Little Fairy Boy", to "The Compleat Destroyer": Subjectivity and Transformation in the Biography of Mike Tyson', in M. Mac an Ghaill (ed.) *Understanding Masculinities*, Buckingham: Open University Press.

Jefferson, T. (1997) 'Masculinities and Crime', in M. Maguire, R. Morgan, and R. Reiner (eds) *The Oxford Handbook of Criminology: Second Edition*, Oxford: Clarendon Press.

Jenkins, R. (1992) *Pierre Bourdieu*, London: Routledge.

Jenks, C, (1982) *The Sociology of Childhood*, Aldershot: Gregg.

Jenks, C. (1996) *Childhood*, London: Routledge.

Jordan, E. (1995) 'Fighting Boys and Fantasy Play: The Construction of Masculinity in the Early Years of School', *Gender and Education*, 7: 69–86.

Justice (1996) *Children and Homicide: Justice Report*, London: Justice.

Katz, J. (1988) *Seductions of Crime: Moral and Sensual Attractions in Doing Evil*, New York: Basic Books.

Katz, M. (ed.) (1993) *The 'Underclass' Debate: Views from History*, Princeton: Princeton University Press.

Kehily, M. and Nayak, A. (1997) ' "Lads and Laughter": Humour and the Production of Heterosexual Hierarchies', *Gender and Education*, 9 (1): 69–87.

Kelly, L. (1988) *Surviving Sexual Violence*. Oxford: Polity Press.

Kershaw, A. and Macbeth, D. (1993) 'Crimes of the Tyne', *Gentlemen's Quarterly*, April: 91–9.

Kersten, J. (1996) 'Culture, Masculinities and Violence Against Women', *British Journal of Criminology*, 36 (3): 381–95.

Kimmell, M. (1987) 'The Contemporary "Crisis" of Masculinity', in H. Brod (ed.) *The Making of Masculinities*, New York: Allen and Unwin.

Kimmell, M. and Kaufman, M. (1994) 'Weekend Warriors: The New Men's Movement', in M. Kimmell and M. Kaufman (eds) *Theorizing Masculinities*, London: Sage.

King, M. (1995) 'The James Bulger Murder Trial: Moral Dilemmas, and Social Solutions', *The International Journal of Children's Rights*, 3: 167–87.

Knight, C. (1997) 'Managing Gender Differences in Co-Workers Confronting Domestic Violence from Men', paper presented to the British Criminology Conference, Belfast, 15–18 July.

Labour Research (1987) 'Who Are the Judges?', *Labour Research*, 76 (1): 9–11.

Lacey, N. (ed.) (1994) *A Reader on Criminal Justice*, Oxford: Oxford University Press.

Lea, J. and Young, J. (1984) *What Is To Be Done About Law and Order?*, Harmondsworth: Penguin.

Lea, J. and Young, J. (1993) *What Is To Be Done About Law and Order?* (2nd edition), London: Pluto.

Lees, S. (1986) *Losing Out*, London, Hutchinson.

Leng, K.W. (1995) 'New Australian Feminism: Towards a Discursive Politics of Australian Feminist Thought', *Antithesis*, 7 (1): 47–63.

Leonard, E. (1982) *Women, Crime and Society: A Critique of Criminological Theory*, London: Longman.

Lever, S. (ed.) (1996) *The Oxford Book of Australian Women's Verse*, Oxford: Oxford University Press.

Levi, M. (1994) 'Masculinities and white-collar crime', in T. Newburn and E.A. Stanko (eds) *Just Boys Doing Business? Men, Masculinities and Crime*, London: Routledge.

Lewis, C. (1986) *Becoming a Father*, Milton Keynes: Open University Press.

Lewis, C. and O'Brien, M. (1987) *Reassessing Fatherhood: New Observations on Fathers and the Modern Family*, London: Sage.

Liddle, M (1996) 'State, Masculinity and Law: Some Comments on English Gender and English State Formation', *British Journal of Criminology*, 36 (3): 361–79.

Lilly, J.R., Cullen, F.T. and Ball, R.A. (1995) *Criminological Theory: Context and Consequences* (2nd edition), London: Sage.

Longbenton Youth Project (1994) *Annual Report*, Newcastle upon Tyne: Longbenton Youth Project.

Lyndon, N. (1992) *No More Sex War*, London: Sinclair Stephenson.

Lyotard, J-F. (1986) *The Postmodern Condition: A Report on Knowledge*, Manchester: Manchester University Press.

Mac an Ghaill, M. (1994) *The Making of Men*, Buckingham: Open University Press.

Mac an Ghaill, M (1996) ' "What about the Boys?": Schooling Class and Crisis Masculinity', *The Sociological Review*, 381–97.

McDowell, L. (1995) 'Body Work: Heterosexual Gender Performances in City Workplaces', in D. Bell and G. Valentine (eds) *Mapping Desire*, London: Routledge.

McEvoy, K. (1996) 'Newspapers and Crime: Narrative and the Construction of Identity', in J. Morison and C. Bell (eds) *Tall Stories? Reading Law and Literature*, Aldershot: Dartmouth.

McGlynn, C. (1996) 'Sex Discrimination at the Margins', *New Law Journal*, 15 March: 379–81.

McGlynn, C. and Graham, C (1995) *Soliciting Equality: Equality and Opportunity in the Solicitors' Profession*, London: Young Women Lawyers.

McIntosh, M. (1993) 'Queer Theory and the War of the Sexes', in J. Bristow and A. Wilson (eds) *Activating Theory: Lesbian, Gay, Bisexual Politics*, London: Lawrence and Wishart.

McKee, L. and O'Brien, M. (eds) (1982) *The Father Figure*, London: Tavistock.

MacKinnon, C. (1987) *Feminism Unmodified: Discourses on Life and Law*, Boston, MA: Harvard University Press.

MacKinnon, C. (1989) *Toward a Feminist Theory of the State*, Cambridge, MA: Harvard University Press.

McLaughlin, E. and Muncie, J. (eds) (1996) *Controlling Crime*, Buckingham: Open University Press.

McMahon, A (1993) 'Male Readings of Feminist Theory: The Psychologisation of Sexual Politics in the Masculinity Literature', *Theory and Society*, 22 (5): 675–96.

Macnicol, J. (1987) 'In Pursuit of the Underclass', *Journal of Social Policy*, 16 (3): 293–318.

McRobbie, A. (1980) 'Settling Accounts with Subcultures: A Feminist Critique', *Screen Education*, 34: 37–49.

McRobbie, A. (1991) *Feminism and Youth Culture: From Jackie to Just Seventeen*, London: Macmillan.

McRobbie, A. (1993) 'Shut-up and Dance: Youth Culture and Changing Modes of Femininity', *Cultural Studies*, 7 (3): 406–26.

McRobbie, A. (1994) *Postmodernism and Popular Culture*, London: Routledge.

McRobbie, A. and Garber, G. (1976) 'Girls and Subcultures', in S. Hall and T. Jefferson (eds) *Resistance Through Rituals: Youth Subcultures in Post-War Britain*, London, Hutchinson.

Maguire, M., Morgan, R. and Reiner, R. (eds) (1994) *The Oxford Handbook of Criminology*, Oxford: Clarendon Press.

Maguire, M., Morgan, R. and Reiner, R. (eds) (1997) *The Oxford Handbook of Criminology: Second Edition*, Oxford: Clarendon Press.

Mangan, J. and Walvin, J. (eds) (1987) *Manliness and Morality: Middle-Class Masculinity in Britain and America 1800–1940*, Manchester: Manchester University Press.

Marshall, P. (1997) *The Prevalence of Convictions for Sexual Offending*, Home Office Research and Statistics Directorate, No. 55, May.

Martin, S.E. and Jurik, N. (1996) *Doing Justice, Doing Gender: Women in Law and Criminal Justice Occupations*, London: Sage.

Masculinity and Crime: Issues of Theory and Practice (1993) Conference Report, Brunel University, Centre for Criminal Justice Research.

Massey, D. (1994) *Space, Place and Gender*, Cambridge, Polity Press.

Matza, D. (1964) *Delinquency and Drift*, New York: John Wiley and Sons.

Matza, D. (1969) *Becoming Deviant*. Englewood Cliffs, NJ: Prentice Hall.

Maudsen, M. (1993) 'What is Hegemonic Masculinity?', *Theory and Society*, 22: 643–57.

Maynard, M. and Purvis, J. (1995) *(Hetero)Sexual Politics*, London: Taylor and Francis.

Menkel-Meadow, C. (1986) 'Feminisation of the Legal Profession: The Comparative Sociology of Women Lawyers', *Osgoode Hall Law Journal*, 124: 897.

Merton, R. (1957) *Social Theory and Social Structure*, New York: Free Press (revised edition 1963).

Messerschmidt, J.W. (1986) *Capitalism, Patriarchy and Crime: Towards a Socialist Feminist Criminology*, Totowa, NJ: Rowman and Littlefield.

Messerschmidt, J.W. (1993) *Masculinities and Crime: Critique, and Reconceptualization of Theory*, Lanham, MD: Rowman and Littlefield.

Messerschmidt, J.W. (1994) 'Schooling, Masculinities, and Youth Crime by White Boys', in T. Newburn and E.A. Stanko (eds) *Just Boys Doing Business? Men, Masculinities and Crime*, London: Routledge.

Messerschmidt, J.W. (1997) *Crime as Structured Action: Gender, Race, Class and Crime*, Thousand Oaks, CA: Sage.

Messner, M. (1997) *The Politics of Masculinities: Men in Movements*, London: Sage.

Metcalf, A. and Humphries, M. (eds) (1985) *The Sexuality of Men*, London: Pluto.

Middleton, P. (1992) *The Inward Gaze: Masculinity and Subjectivity in Modern Culture*, London: Routledge.

Miller, W.B. (1958) 'Lower Class Culture as a Generating Milieu of Gang Delinquency', *Journal of Social Issues*, 14 (3): 5–19.

Millett, K. (1971) *Sexual Politics*, London: Abacus.

Moore, S. (1996) *Head Over Heels*, London: Viking.

Moran, L. (1996) *The Homosexual(ity) of Law*, London: Routledge.

Morgan, D. (1992) *Discovering Men*, London: Routledge.

Morgan, D. (1994) 'The "Family Man": A Contradiction in Terms?', Fifth Jacqueline Burgoyne Memorial Lecture, Sheffield Hallam University, February.

Morris, A. (1987) *Women, Crime and Criminal Justice*, Oxford: Basil Blackwell.

Morris, L. (1994) *Dangerous Classes: The Underclass and Social Citizenship*, London: Routledge.

Morris, M. (1988) 'The Pirates' Fiancées: Feminists and Philosophers or Maybe Tonight It'll Happen', in I. Diamond and L. Quinby (eds) *Feminism and Foucault*, Boston: Northeastern University Press.

Morrison, B. (1997) *As If*, London: Granta Books.

Mort, F. (1996) *Cultures of Consumption: Masculinities and Social Space in Late Twentieth Century Britain*, London: Routledge.

Mossman, M.J. (1994) 'Lawyers and Family Life: New Directions for the 1990s', *Feminist Legal Studies*, 2 (1): 61–82.

Mouffe, C. (1992) 'Feminism, Citizenship and Radical Democratic Politics', in J. Butler and J.W. Scott (eds) *Feminists Theorize the Political*, New York: Routledge.

Muncie, J., McLaughlin, E. and Langan, M. (eds) (1996) *Criminological Perspectives: A Reader*, London: Sage.

Murphy, K. and Joels, J. (1993) 'Inner London Probation Service: Group Work on Men and Offending', in *Masculinity and Crime: Issues of Theory and Practice*,

Conference Report, Brunel University, Centre for Criminal Justice Research: 99–103.

Murphy, T. (1996) 'Bursting Binary Bubbles: Law, Literature and the Sexed Body', in J. Morison and C. Bell (eds) *Tall Stories? Reading Law and Literature*, Aldershot: Dartmouth.

Murray, C. (1984) *Losing Ground*, New York: Basic Books.

Murray, C. (1990) *The Emerging British Underclass* (with responses by Frank Field, Joan C. Brown, Nicholas Deakin and Alan Walker), London: IEA Health and Welfare Unit.

Naffine, N. (1985) 'The Masculinity–Femininity Hypothesis', *British Journal of Sociology*, 25 (4): 365–81.

Naffine, N. (1987) *Female Crime: The Construction of Women in Criminology*, Sydney: Allen and Unwin.

Naffine, N. (1990) *Law and the Sexes: Explorations in Feminist Jurisprudence*, Sydney: Allen and Unwin.

Naffine, N. (1994) 'Possession: Erotic Love in the Law of Rape', *Modern Law Review*, 57: 10–37.

Naffine, N. (ed.) (1995) *Gender, Crime and Feminism*, Aldershot: Dartmouth.

Naffine, N. (1997) *Feminism and Criminology*, Cambridge: Polity Press.

Naffine, N. and Gale, F. (1989) 'Testing the Nexus: Crime, Gender and Unemployment', *British Journal of Criminology*, 26 (2): 144–57.

National Association for the Care and Resettlement of Offenders (NACRO) (1996) 'Ten Key Messages About Crime', London: NACRO.

Nayak, A. and Kehily, M.J. (1996) 'Playing it Straight: Masculinity, Homophobia and Schools', *Journal of Gender Studies*, 5 (2): 211–30.

Nelken, D. (1994) 'White-Collar Crime', in M. Maguire, R. Morgan and R. Reiner (eds.) *The Oxford Handbook of Criminology*, Oxford: Clarendon Press.

Newburn, T. and Stanko, E.A. (eds) (1994a) *Just Boys Doing Business? Men, Masculinities and Crime*, London: Routledge.

Newburn, T. and Stanko, E.A. (1994b) 'Introduction', in T. Newburn and E.A. Stanko (eds) *Just Boys Doing Business? Men, Masculinities and Crime*, London: Routledge.

Newburn, T. and Stanko, E.A. (1994c) 'When Men are Victims: The Failure of Victimology', in T. Newburn and E.A. Stanko (eds) *Just Boys Doing Business? Men, Masculinities and Crime*, London: Routledge.

Newton, C. (1994) 'Gender Theory and Prison Sociology: Using Theories of Masculinities to Interpret the Sociology of Prisons for Men', *Howard Journal of Criminal Justice*, 33 (3): 193–204.

Nicholson, L. (ed.) (1990) *Feminism/Post-Modernism*, Routledge, London.

Nixon, S. (1996) *Hard Looks: Masculinities, Spectatorship and Contemporary Consumption*, London: University College London Press.

Northumbria Probation Service (1992) *The Dog That Finally Barked: The Tyneside Disturbances of September 1991*, A Northumbria Probation Perspective.

Oakley, A. (1972) *Sex, Gender and Society*, London: Temple-Smith.

O'Donovan, K. (1993) *Family Law Matters*, London: Pluto.

Orbach, S. and Schwartz, J. (1997) 'Playing the Gender Game', *The Guardian*, 14 June.

O'Sullivan, J. (1996) 'We're Still in the Dark Over West's Madness', *The Independent*, 12 September.

Osborne, P. (1995) *The Politics of Time*, London: Verso.

Park, R.E. (1952) *Human Communities*, Glencoe, IL: Free Press.

Parsloe, P. (1978) *Juvenile Justice in Britain and the United States*, London: Routledge and Kegan Paul.

Parsons, T. (1954) *Essays in Sociological Theory*, Glencoe, IL: Free Press.

Pavarini, M. (1994) 'Is Criminology Worth Saving?', in D. Nelken (ed.) *The Futures of Criminology*, London: Sage.

Pearce, J. (1993) 'Juvenile Justice: A Masculinist Project – The Gendered Self in Practice with Young People', in *Masculinity and Crime: Issues of Theory and Practice*, Conference Report, Brunel University, Centre for Criminal Justice Research: 104–9.

Pearson, G. (1983) *Hooligan: A History of Respectable Fears*, London: Macmillan.

Pearson, G. (1994) 'Youth, Crime and Society', in M. Maguire, R. Morgan and R. Reiner (eds) *The Oxford Handbook of Criminology*, Oxford, Clarendon Press.

Pembridge, E. (1996) 'My Daft Learned Friend: Shut Up!', *The Independent*, 22 April.

Person, E.S. (1980) 'Sexuality as the Mainstay of Identity', *Signs*, 5 (4): 605.

Phillips, A. (1993) *The Trouble With Boys: Parenting the Men of the Future*, London: Pandora.

Phillips, M. (1995) 'Unhappy Families on the Merry-Go-Round', *The Observer*, 29 October.

Phoenix, A. (1991) *Young Mothers*, Cambridge: Polity Press.

Pile, S. and Thrift, N. (1995) 'Mapping the Subject', in S. Pile and N. Thrift (eds) *Mapping the Subject: Geographies of Cultural Transformation*, London: Routledge.

Pitts, J. (1996) 'The Politics and Practice of Youth Justice', in E. McLaughlin and J. Muncie (eds) *Controlling Crime*, Buckingham: Open University Press.

Podmore, D. and Spencer, A. (1982) 'Law as a Sexed Typed Profession', *Journal of Law and Society*, 9 (1): 21–36.

Polk, K. (1994a) 'Masculinity, Honour and Confrontational Homicide', in T. Newburn and E.A. Stanko (eds) *Just Boys Doing Business? Men, Masculinities and Crime*, London: Routledge.

Polk, K. (1994b) *When Men Kill*, Cambridge: Cambridge University Press.

Power, M.J., Alderson, M.R., Phillipson, C.M., Shoenberg, E and Morris, J.N. (1967) 'Delinquent Schools', *New Society*, 10: 542–3.

Pringle, K. (1995) *Men, Masculinities and Social Welfare*, London: University College London Press.

Probyn, E. (1993) *Sexing the Self: Gender Positions in Cultural Studies*, London, Routledge.

Probyn, E. (1996) *Outside Belongings*, New York: Routledge.

Quinney, R. (1974) *Critique of Legal Order: Crime Control in Capitalist Society*, Boston: Little, Brown.

Radzinowicz, Sir Lyon (1994) 'Reflections of the State of Criminology', *British Journal of Criminology*, 34 (2): 99–104.

Rappaport, R. (1988) 'The Serial and Mass Murder: Patterns, Differentiation, Pathology', *American Journal of Forensic Psychiatry*, 9: 38–48.

Redhead, S. (1995) *Unpopular Cultures: The Birth of Law and Popular Culture*, Manchester: Manchester University Press.

Reynaud, E. (1983) *Holy Virility*, London: Pluto.

Richardson, D. (ed.) (1996) *Theorising Heterosexuality: Telling it Straight*, Buckingham: Open University Press.

Roberts, H. (1981) *Doing Feminist Research*, London, Routledge and Kegan Paul.

Roberts, Y. (1992) *Mad About Women*, London: Virago.

Robinson, D. (1994) *No Less a Man: Masculinist Art in a Feminist Age*, Bowling Green, OH: Bowling Green State University Press.

Robinson, V. (1996) 'Heterosexuality and Masculinity: Theorising Male Power or the Wounded Male Psyche?', in D. Richardson (ed.) *Theorising Heterosexuality*, Buckingham: Open University Press.

Rock, P. (1988) 'The Present State of Criminology in Britain', *British Journal of Criminology*, 28: 188–99.

Rock, P. (1994) 'The Social Organistion of British Criminology', in M. Maguire, R. Morgan and R. Reiner (eds) *The Oxford Handbook of Criminology*, Oxford: Clarendon Press.

Roper, M. and Tosh, J. (eds) (1991) *Manful Assertions: Masculinities in Britain Since 1800*, London: Routledge.

Rose, G. (1993) *Feminism and Geography: The Limits of Geographical Knowledge*, Cambridge: Polity Press.

Rose, N. (1987) 'Transcending the Public/Private', *Journal of Law and Society*, 14 (1): 61–75.

Rose, N. (1989) *Governing the Soul*, London: Routledge.

Rotundo, E.A. (1993) *American Manhood*, New York: Basic Books.

Rowen, J. (1987) *The Horned God: Feminism and Men as Wounding and Healing*, London: Routledge and Kegan Paul.

Rowlands, M. (1990) 'Multiple Murder: A Review of the International Literature', *Journal of the College of Prison Medicine*, 1: 3–7.

Rutter, M., Maughan, B., Mortimore, P. and Ouston, J (1979) *Fifteen Thousand Hours*, London: Open Books.

Ryder, R. (1991) 'The Cult of Machismo', *Criminal Justice*, 9 (1): 12–13.

Sachs, A. and Wilson, J. (1978) *Sexism and the Law: A Study of Male Beliefs and Judicial Bias*, Oxford: Martin Robertson.

Saco, D. (1992) 'Masculinity as Signs: Poststructuralist Feminist Approaches to the Study of Gender', in S. Craig (ed.) *Men, Masculinity and the Media*, London: Sage.

Sandland, R. (1995) 'Between "Truth" and "Difference": Poststructuralism, Law and the Power of Feminism', *Feminist Legal Studies*, 3 (1): 3–47.

Schwendinger, H. and Schwendinger, J. (1985) *Adolescent Subcultures and Delinquency*, New York: Praeger.

Scraton, P. (ed.) (1987) *Law, Order and the Authoritarian State: Readings in Critical Criminology*, Milton Keynes: Open University Press.

Scraton, P. (1990) 'Scientific Knowledge or Masculine Discourses? Challenging Patriarchy in Criminology', in L. Gelsthorpe and A. Morris (eds) *Feminist Perspectives in Criminology*, Milton Keynes: Open University Press.

Sedgwick, E. (1985) *Between Men: English Literature and Male Homosocial Desire*, New York: Columbia University Press.

Sedgwick, E. (1994) *Epistemology of the Closet*, London: Penguin Books.

Segal, L. (1990) *Slow Motion: Changing Masculinities, Changing Men*, London: Virago.

Segal, L. (1994) *Straight Sex: The Politics of Pleasure*, London: Virago.

Seidler, V. (1989) *Rediscovering Masculinity: Reason, Language and Sexuality*, London: Routledge.

Seidler, V. (1992) *Men, Sex and Relationships: Readings from Achilles' Heel*, London: Routledge.

Seidler, V. (1995) 'Men, Heterosexualities and Emotional Life', in S. Pile and N. Thrift (eds) *Mapping the Subject: Geographies of Cultural Transfomation*, London: Routledge.

Seron, C. and Ferris, K. (1995) 'Negotiating Professionalism', *Work and Occupations*, 22 (1): 22–48.

Shaw, C.R. and McKay, H.D. (1942) *Juvenile Delinquency in Urban Areas*, Chicago, University of Chicago Press.

Sheptycki, J. (1997) 'Open Letter to the British Society of Criminology', *Newsletter*, 28, June: 11–12.

Sheptycki, J. and Westmarland, L. (1993) 'Metaphors, Masculinity and the Reproduction of Manliness in Policing Discourse', in *Masculinity and Crime: Issues of*

Theory and Practice, Conference Report, Brunel University, Centre for Criminal Justice Research: 114–28.

Showalter, E. (1992) *Sexual Anarchy*, London: Virago.

Sim, J. (1994) 'Tougher Than the Rest?: Men in Prison', in T. Newburn and E.A. Stanko (eds) *Just Boys Doing Business? Men, Masculinities and Crime*, London: Routledge.

Simpson, B., Vorlyon, J., McArthy, P. and Walker, J. (1995) *Post-Divorce Fatherhood*, Family and Community Dispute Research Centre, Newcastle: University of Newcastle upon Tyne.

Skeggs, B. (1991) 'Challenging Masculinity and Using Sexuality', *British Journal of the Sociology of Education*, 12: 127–37.

Skelton, C. (1994) 'Sex, Male Teachers and Young Children', *Gender and Education*, 6 (1): 87–93.

Smart, C. (1977) *Women, Crime and Criminology*, London: Routledge and Kegan Paul.

Smart, C. (1987a) 'Review of "Capitalism, Patriarchy and Crime"', *Contemporary Crises*, 11 (3): 327–9.

Smart, C. (1987b) ' "There Is Of Course a Distinction Dictated by Nature": Law and the Problem of Paternity', in M. Stanworth (ed.) *Reproductive Technologies*, Cambridge: Polity Press.

Smart, C. (1989) *Feminism and the Power of Law*, London: Routledge.

Smart, C. (1990) 'Feminist Approaches to Criminology or Postmodern Woman Meets Atavistic Man', in L. Gelsthorpe and A. Morris (eds) *Feminist Perspectives in Criminology*, Buckingham: Open University Press.

Smart, C. (ed.) (1992) *Regulating Womanhood: Historical Essays on Marriage, Motherhood and Sexuality*, London: Routledge.

Smart, C. (1995) *Law, Crime and Sexuality: Essays in Feminism*, London: Sage.

Smart, C. (1996a) 'Collusion, Collaboration and Confession: On Moving Beyond the Heterosexuality Debate', in D. Richardson (ed.) *Theorising Heterosexuality: Telling it Straight*, Buckingham: Open University Press.

Smart, C. (1996b) 'Desperately Seeking Post-Heterosexual Woman', in J. Holland and L. Adkins (eds) *Sex, Sensibility and the Gendered Body*, London: Macmillan.

Snow, J. (1996) 'Scandal of the True Abusers', *The Guardian*, 6 June.

Somerlad, H. (1994) 'The Myth of Feminisation: Women and Cultural Change in the Legal Profession', *International Journal of the Legal Profession*, 1 (1): 31–53.

Soper, K. (1995) 'Heterosexual Utopianism', *Radical Philosophy*, 69: 5–15.

Sparks, R. (1996) 'Masculinity and Heroism in the Hollywood "Blockbuster"', *British Journal of Criminology*, 36 (3): 348–59.

Spelman, E.V. (1990) *Inessential Woman: Problems of Exclusion in Feminist Thought*, London: The Women's Press.

Spivak, G.C. (1987) *In Other Worlds: Essays in Cultural Politics*, London: Methuen.

Stanko, E.A. (1985) *Intimate Intrusions*, London: Unwin Hyman.

Stanko, E.A. (1988) 'Hidden Violence Against Women', in J. Pointing and M. Maguire (eds) *Victims of Crime: A New Deal?* Milton Keynes, Open University Press.

Stanko, E.A. (1990) *Everyday Violence: How Women and Men Experience Sexual and Physical Danger*, London: Pandora.

Stanko, E.A. (1994) 'Challenging the Problem of Men's Individual Violence', in T. Newburn and E.A. Stanko (eds) *Just Boys Doing Business? Men, Masculinities and Crime*, London: Routledge.

Stanko, E.A. (1995) 'Gender and Crime', *Criminal Justice Matters*, 19: 3–4.

Stanko, E.A. and Hobdell, K. (1993) 'Assault on Men: Masculinity and Male Victimisation', *British Journal of Criminology*, 33 (3): 400–15.

Stanley, L. and Wise, S. (1983) *Breaking Out: Feminist Conscience and Feminist Research*, London, Routledge and Kegan Paul.

Stanworth, M. (ed.) (1987) *Reproductive Technologies*, Cambridge: Polity Press.

Stedman-Jones, G. (1976) *Outcast London: A Study in the Relationship Between Classes in Victorian Society*, Harmondsworth: Penguin.

Stein, A. and Plummer, K. (1996) ' "I Can't Even Think Straight": "Queer" Theory and the Missing Sexual Revolution in Sociology', in S. Seidman (ed.) *Queer Theory/Sociology*, Oxford: Basil Blackwell.

Stoller, R. (1968) *Sex and Gender*, London: Hogarth Press.

Stratton, J. (1996) 'Serial Killing and the Transformation of the Social', *Theory, Culture and Society*, 13 (1): 77–98.

Stychin, C. (1996) *Law's Desire*, London: Routledge.

Sugarman, D. (1994) 'Blurred Boundaries: The Overlapping Worlds of Law, Business and Politics', in M. Cain and C. Harrington (eds) *Lawyers in a Postmodern World*, Milton Keynes: Open University Press.

Sumner, C. (1990) 'Foucault, Gender and the Censure of Deviance', in L. Gelsthorpe and A. Morris (eds) *Feminist Perspectives in Criminology*, Buckingham: Open University Press.

Sunley, R. (1996) *Criminal Justice and the 'Crisis of Masculinity'*, Scarman Centre for the Study of Public Order, Leicester: University of Leicester.

Taylor, I. (1994) 'The Political Economy of Crime', in M. Maguire, R. Morgan and R. Reiner (eds) *The Oxford Handbook of Criminology*, Oxford: Clarendon Press.

Taylor, I., Walton, P. and Young, J. (1973) *The New Criminology*, London: Routledge and Kegan Paul.

Taylor, I., Walton, P. and Young, J. (1975) *Critical Criminology*, London: Routledge and Kegan Paul.

Thomas, D. (1993) *Not Guilty*, London: Weidenfeld and Nicolson.

Thornton, M. (1989) 'Hegemonic Masculinity and the Academy', *International Journal of the Sociology of Law*, 17: 115–33.

Thornton, M. (1994) 'Discord in the Legal Academy: The Case of the Feminist Legal Scholar', *The Australian Feminist Law Journal*, 3: 53–71.

Thornton, M. (1996a) *Dissonance and Distrust: Women in the Legal Profession*, Oxford: Oxford University Press.

Thornton, M. (1996b) 'Authority and Corporeality: The Conundrum for Women in Law', paper presented to the Joint International Conference of the American Law and Society Association and the Research Committee on the Sociology of Law of the International Sociological Association, University of Strathclyde, Glasgow, 10–13 July.

Thrasher, F. (1936) *The Gang* (2nd edition), Chicago: University of Chicago Press.

Thurston, R. (1996) 'Are You Sitting Comfortably? Men's Storytellings, Masculinities, Prison Culture and Violence', in M. Mac an Ghaill (ed.) *Understanding Masculinities*, Buckingham: Open University Press.

Tolson, A. (1977) *The Limits of Masculinity*, New York: Harper and Row.

Tredre, R. (1997) 'Scared of Strangers, Bullied in Class', *The Observer*, 9 March.

Vennard, J., Hedderman, C. and Sugg, D. (1997) *Changing Offenders' Attitudes and Behaviour: What Works?*, Home Office Research and Statistics Directorate, No. 61, London: HMSO.

Virilio, P. (1986) *Speed and Politics*, New York: Semiotext(e).

Waldby, C. (1995) 'Destruction: Boundary Erotics and Refigurations of the Heterosexual Male Body', in E. Grosz and E. Probyn (eds) *Sexy Bodies: The Strange Carnalities of Feminism*, London: Routledge.

Walkerdine, V. (1995) 'Subject to Change Without Notice: Psychology, Postmodernity and the Popular', in S. Pile and N. Thrift (eds) *Mapping the Subject: Geographies of Cultural Transformation*, London: Routledge.

Walklate, S. (1995) *Gender and Crime: An Introduction*, Hemel Hempstead: Prentice Hall/Harvester Wheatsheaf.

Warner, M. (ed.) (1993) *Fear of a Queer Planet*, Minneapolis: University of Minnesota Press.

Weedon, C. (1987) *Feminist Practice and Poststructuralist Theory*, Oxford: Basil Blackwell.

Weiner, G. (ed.) (1985) *Just a Bunch of Girls*, Milton Keynes: Open University Press.

West, C. and Zimmerman, D. (1987) 'Doing Gender', *Gender and Society*, 1: 125–51.

Westmarland, L. (1997) 'Uniformed Bodies of Men', paper presented at SLSA Conference 'Crossing Boundaries', University of Cardiff, April.

Westwood, S. (1996) ' "Feckless Fathers": Masculinities and the British State', in M. Mac an Ghaill (ed.) *Understanding Masculinities*, Buckingham: Open University Press.

White, N.R. (1994) 'About Fathers: Masculinity and the Social Construction of Fatherhood', *Australian and New Zealand Journal of Sociology*, 30 (2): 119–31.

Whyte, W.F. (1943) *Street Corner Society: The Social Structure of an Italian Slum*, Chicago: University of Chicago Press.

Wilkinson, S. and Kitzinger, C. (eds) (1993) *Heterosexuality: A Feminism and Psychology Reader*, London: Sage.

Williams, K. (1991) *Textbook on Criminology* (1st edition), London: Blackstone.

Willis, P. (1976) 'The Class Significance of School Counter-Culture', in M. Hammersley and P. Woods (eds) *The Process of Schooling*, London, Routledge.

Willis, P. (1977) *Learning to Labour: How Working-Class Kids Get Working-Class Jobs*, Farnborough: Saxon House.

Wills, J. (1996) 'Laboring For Love? A Comment on Academics and their Hours of Work', *Antipode*, 28 (3): 292–303.

Wittig, M. (1992) *The Straight Mind*, Boston: Beacon Press.

Wolf-Light, P. (1996) 'The Everyman Centre', in A. Coote (ed.) *Families, Children and Crime*, London: IPPR Publishers.

Women and Geography Study Group (1997) *Feminist Geographies: Explorations in Diversity and Difference*, Harlow: Longman.

Woodhull, W. (1988) 'Sexuality, Power and the Question of Rape', in I. Diamond and L. Quinby (eds) *Feminism and Foucault*, Boston: Northeastern University Press.

Worrall, A. (1990) *Offending Women: Female Lawbreakers and the Criminal Justice System*, London: Routledge.

Young, A. (1993) 'The Authority of the Name', in S. Wilkinson and C. Kitzinger (eds) *Heterosexuality: A Feminism and Psychology Reader*, London: Sage.

Young, A. (1996) *Imagining Crime*, London: Sage.

Young, A. and Rush, P. (1994) 'The Law of Victimage in Urban Realism', in D. Nelken (ed.) *The Futures of Criminology*, London: Sage.

Young, J. (1986) 'The Failure of Criminology: The Need for Radical Realism', in R. Matthews and J. Young (eds) *Confronting Crime*, London: Sage.

Young, J. (1988) 'Radical Criminology in Britain: The Emergence of a Competing Paradigm', *British Journal of Criminology*, 28 (2): 159–83.

Young, J. (1994) 'Recent Paradigms in British Criminology', in M. Maguire, R. Morgan, and R. Reiner (eds) *The Oxford Handbook of Criminology*, Oxford: Clarendon Press.

Young, J. and Matthews, R. (1992) *Rethinking Criminology: The Realist Debate*, London: Sage.

Younge, G. (1996) 'He Just Shot Everyone Coming In', *The Guardian*, 29 April.

Index

Printed in the United Kingdom
by Lightning Source UK Ltd.
122757UK00001B/694-702/A